Notices

Responsibility. Knowledge and best practice in the field of engineering and software development are constantly changing. Practitioners and researchers must always rely on their own experience and knowledge in evaluating and using any information, methods, compounds, or experiments described herein. In using such information or methods, they should be mindful of their own safety and the safety of others, including parties for whom they have a professional responsibility.

To the fullest extent of the law, neither the author nor contributors, or editors, assume any liability for any injury and/or damage to persons or property as a matter of products liability, negligence or otherwise, or from any use or operations of any methods, products, instructions, or ideas contained in the material herein.

Trademarks. Designations used by companies to distinguish their products are often claimed as trademarks or registered trademarks. Intel, Intel Core, Intel Xeon, Intel Pentium, Intel Vtune, and Intel Advisor are trademarks of Intel Corporation in the U.S. and/or other countries. AMD is a trademark of Advanced Micro Devices Corporation in the U.S. and/or other countries. ARM is a trademark of Arm Limited (or its subsidiaries) in the U.S. and/or elsewhere. Readers, however, should contact the appropriate companies for complete information regarding trademarks and registration.

Affiliation. At the time of writing, the book's primary author (Denis Bakhvalov) is an employee of Intel Corporation. All information presented in the book is not an official position of the aforementioned company, but rather is an individual knowledge and opinions of the author. The primary author did not receive any financial sponsorship from Intel Corporation for writing this book.

Advertisement. This book does not advertise any software, hardware, or any other product.

Copyright

Copyright © 2020 by Denis Bakhvalov under Creative Commons license (CC BY 4.0).

Preface

About The Author

Denis Bakhvalov is a senior developer at Intel, where he works on C++ compiler projects that aim at generating optimal code for a variety of different architectures. Performance engineering and compilers were always among the primary interests for him. Denis has started his career as a software developer in 2008 and has since worked in multiple areas, including developing desktop applications, embedded, performance analysis, and compiler development. In 2016 Denis started his easyperf.net blog, where he writes about performance analysis and tuning, C/C++ compilers, and CPU microarchitecture. Denis is a big proponent of an active lifestyle, which he practices in his free time. You can find him playing soccer, tennis, running, and playing chess. Besides that, Denis is a father of 2 beautiful daughters.

Contacts:

- Email: dendibakh@gmail.com
- Twitter: @dendibakh
- LinkedIn: @dendibakh

From The Author

I started this book with a simple goal: educate software developers to better understand their applications' performance on modern hardware. I know how confusing this topic might be for a beginner or even for an experienced developer. This confusion mostly happens to developers that don't have prior occasions of working on performance-related tasks. And that's fine since every expert was once a beginner.

I remember the days when I was starting with performance analysis. I was staring at unfamiliar metrics trying to match the data that didn't match. And I was baffled. It took me years until it finally "clicked", and all pieces of the puzzle came together. At the time, the only good sources of information were software developer manuals, which are not what mainstream developers like to read. So I decided to write this book, which will hopefully make it easier for developers to learn performance analysis concepts.

Developers who consider themselves beginners in performance analysis can start from the beginning of the book and read sequentially, chapter by chapter. Chapters 2-4 give developers a minimal set of knowledge required by later chapters. Readers already familiar with these concepts may choose to skip those. Additionally, this book can be used as a reference or a checklist for optimizing SW applications. Developers can use chapters 7-11 as a source of ideas for tuning their code.

Target Audience

This book will be primarily useful for software developers who work with performance-critical applications and do low-level optimizations. To name just a few areas: High-Performance Computing (HPC), Game Development, data-center applications (like Facebook, Google, etc.), High-Frequency Trading. But the scope of the book is not limited to the mentioned industries. This book will be useful for any developer who wants to understand the performance of their application better and know how it can be diagnosed and improved. The author hopes that the material presented in this book will help readers develop new skills that can be applied in their daily work.

Readers are expected to have a minimal background in C/C++ programming languages to understand the book's examples. The ability to read basic x86 assembly is desired but is not a strict requirement. The author also expects familiarity with basic concepts of computer architecture and operating systems like central processor, memory, process, thread, virtual and physical memory, context switch, etc. If any of the mentioned terms are new to you, I suggest studying this material first.

Acknowledgments

Huge thanks to Mark E. Dawson, Jr. for his help writing several sections of this book: "Optimizing For DTLB" (section 8.1.3), "Optimizing for ITLB" (section 7.8), "Cache Warming" (section 10.3), System Tuning (section 10.5), section 11.1 about performance scaling and overhead of multithreaded applications, section 11.5 about using COZ profiler, section 11.6 about eBPF, "Detecting Coherence Issues" (section 11.7). Mark is a recognized expert in the High-Frequency Trading industry. Mark was kind enough to share his expertise and feedback at different stages of this book's writing.

Next, I want to thank Sridhar Lakshmanamurthy, who authored the major part of section 3 about CPU microarchitecture. Sridhar has spent decades working at Intel, and he is a veteran of the semiconductor industry.

Big thanks to Nadav Rotem, the original author of the vectorization framework in the LLVM compiler, who helped me write the section 8.2.3 about vectorization.

Clément Grégoire authored a section 8.2.3.7 about ISPC compiler. Clément has an extensive background in the game development industry. His comments and feedback helped address in the book some of the challenges in the game development industry.

This book wouldn't have come out of the draft without its reviewers: Dick Sites, Wojciech Muła, Thomas Dullien, Matt Fleming, Daniel Lemire, Ahmad Yasin, Michele Adduci, Clément Grégoire, Arun S. Kumar, Surya Narayanan, Alex Blewitt, Nadav Rotem, Alexander Yermolovich, Suchakrapani Datt Sharma, Renat Idrisov, Sean Heelan, Jumana Mundichipparakkal, Todd Lipcon, Rajiv Chauhan, Shay Morag, and others.

Also, I would like to thank the whole performance community for countless blog articles and papers. I was able to learn a lot from reading blogs by Travis Downs, Daniel Lemire, Andi Kleen, Agner Fog, Bruce Dawson, Brendan Gregg, and many others. I stand on the shoulders of giants, and the success of this book should not be attributed only to myself. This book is my way to thank and give back to the whole community.

Last but not least, thanks to my family, who were patient enough to tolerate me missing weekend trips and evening walks. Without their support, I wouldn't have finished this book.

Table Of Contents

Table Of Contents — 5

1 **Introduction** — 10
  1.1 Why Do We Still Need Performance Tuning? — 11
  1.2 Who Needs Performance Tuning? — 15
  1.3 What Is Performance Analysis? — 17
  1.4 What is discussed in this book? — 19
  1.5 What is not in this book? — 20
  1.6 Chapter Summary — 21

Part1. Performance analysis on a modern CPU — 22

2 **Measuring Performance** — 22
  2.1 Noise In Modern Systems — 23
  2.2 Measuring Performance In Production — 26
  2.3 Automated Detection of Performance Regressions — 27
  2.4 Manual Performance Testing — 30
  2.5 Software and Hardware Timers — 35
  2.6 Microbenchmarks — 37
  2.7 Chapter Summary — 38

3 **CPU Microarchitecture** — 40
  3.1 Instruction Set Architecture — 40
  3.2 Pipelining — 41
  3.3 Exploiting Instruction Level Parallelism (ILP) — 44
    3.3.1 OOO Execution — 44
    3.3.2 Superscalar Engines and VLIW — 45
    3.3.3 Speculative Execution — 46
  3.4 Exploiting Thread Level Parallelism — 48
    3.4.1 Simultaneous Multithreading — 48
  3.5 Memory Hierarchy — 48
    3.5.1 Cache Hierarchy — 49
      3.5.1.1 Placement of data within the cache. — 49

		3.5.1.2	Finding data in the cache.	50
		3.5.1.3	Managing misses.	51
		3.5.1.4	Managing writes.	51
		3.5.1.5	Other cache optimization techniques.	52
	3.5.2	Main Memory		53
3.6	Virtual Memory			54
3.7	SIMD Multiprocessors			55
3.8	Modern CPU design			57
	3.8.1	CPU Front-End.		57
	3.8.2	CPU Back-End		59
3.9	Performance Monitoring Unit			59
	3.9.1	Performance Monitoring Counters		60

4 Terminology and metrics in performance analysis — 63
- 4.1 Retired vs. Executed Instruction — 63
- 4.2 CPU Utilization — 64
- 4.3 CPI & IPC — 64
- 4.4 UOPs (micro-ops) — 65
- 4.5 Pipeline Slot — 66
- 4.6 Core vs. Reference Cycles — 67
- 4.7 Cache miss — 68
- 4.8 Mispredicted branch — 70

5 Performance Analysis Approaches — 71
- 5.1 Code Instrumentation — 72
- 5.2 Tracing — 74
- 5.3 Workload Characterization — 76
  - 5.3.1 Counting Performance Events — 76
  - 5.3.2 Manual performance counters collection — 78
  - 5.3.3 Multiplexing and scaling events — 79
- 5.4 Sampling — 81
  - 5.4.1 User-Mode And Hardware Event-based Sampling — 82
  - 5.4.2 Finding Hotspots — 82
  - 5.4.3 Collecting Call Stacks — 85
  - 5.4.4 Flame Graphs — 87
- 5.5 Roofline Performance Model — 88
- 5.6 Static Performance Analysis — 93
  - 5.6.1 Static vs. Dynamic Analyzers — 94
- 5.7 Compiler Optimization Reports — 95
- 5.8 Chapter Summary — 98

6 CPU Features For Performance Analysis — 100

- 6.1 Top-Down Microarchitecture Analysis 102
  - 6.1.1 TMA in Intel® VTune™ Profiler 105
  - 6.1.2 TMA in Linux Perf 106
  - 6.1.3 Step1: Identify the bottleneck 107
  - 6.1.4 Step2: Locate the place in the code 109
  - 6.1.5 Step3: Fix the issue 111
  - 6.1.6 Summary 112
- 6.2 Last Branch Record 113
  - 6.2.1 Collecting LBR stacks 116
  - 6.2.2 Capture call graph 117
  - 6.2.3 Identify hot branches 118
  - 6.2.4 Analyze branch misprediction rate 118
  - 6.2.5 Precise timing of machine code 119
  - 6.2.6 Estimating branch outcome probability 122
  - 6.2.7 Other use cases 122
- 6.3 Processor Event-Based Sampling 123
  - 6.3.1 Precise events 124
  - 6.3.2 Lower sampling overhead 126
  - 6.3.3 Analyzing memory accesses 126
- 6.4 Intel Processor Traces 127
  - 6.4.1 Workflow 128
  - 6.4.2 Timing Packets 129
  - 6.4.3 Collecting and Decoding Traces 130
  - 6.4.4 Usages 131
  - 6.4.5 Disk Space and Decoding Time 132
- 6.5 Chapter Summary 133

Part2. Source Code Tuning For CPU   **135**

7 CPU Front-End Optimizations   **139**
- 7.1 Machine code layout 139
- 7.2 Basic Block 140
- 7.3 Basic block placement 141
- 7.4 Basic block alignment 143
- 7.5 Function splitting 145
- 7.6 Function grouping 147
- 7.7 Profile Guided Optimizations 149
- 7.8 Optimizing for ITLB 150
- 7.9 Chapter Summary 151

8 CPU Back-End Optimizations   **153**
- 8.1 Memory Bound 153

        8.1.1   Cache-Friendly Data Structures 154
- 8.1.1.1 Access data sequentially. 154
- 8.1.1.2 Use appropriate containers. 155
- 8.1.1.3 Packing the data. 156
- 8.1.1.4 Aligning and padding. 157
- 8.1.1.5 Dynamic memory allocation. 159
- 8.1.1.6 Tune the code for memory hierarchy. 160
- 8.1.2 Explicit Memory Prefetching 160
- 8.1.3 Optimizing For DTLB 162
  - 8.1.3.1 Explicit Hugepages. 163
  - 8.1.3.2 Transparent Hugepages. 164
  - 8.1.3.3 Explicit vs. Transparent Hugepages. . 165
- 8.2 Core Bound 165
  - 8.2.1 Inlining Functions 166
  - 8.2.2 Loop Optimizations 168
    - 8.2.2.1 Low-level optimizations. 169
    - 8.2.2.2 High-level optimizations. 171
    - 8.2.2.3 Discovering loop optimization opportunities. 174
    - 8.2.2.4 Use Loop Optimization Frameworks . 175
  - 8.2.3 Vectorization 176
    - 8.2.3.1 Compiler Autovectorization. 178
    - 8.2.3.2 Discovering vectorization opportunities. 179
    - 8.2.3.3 Vectorization is illegal. 180
    - 8.2.3.4 Vectorization is not beneficial. 183
    - 8.2.3.5 Loop vectorized but scalar version used. 184
    - 8.2.3.6 Loop vectorized in a suboptimal way. 185
    - 8.2.3.7 Use languages with explicit vectorization. 185
- 8.3 Chapter Summary 188

9 Optimizing Bad Speculation   189
- 9.1 Replace branches with lookup 190
- 9.2 Replace branches with predication 191
- 9.3 Chapter Summary 194

10 Other Tuning Areas   195
- 10.1 Compile-Time Computations 195
- 10.2 Compiler Intrinsics 196
- 10.3 Cache Warming 198
- 10.4 Detecting Slow FP Arithmetic 198

10.5 System Tuning 199

11 Optimizing Multithreaded Applications   **202**
   11.1 Performance Scaling And Overhead 202
   11.2 Parallel Efficiency Metrics 205
       11.2.1 Effective CPU Utilization 205
       11.2.2 Thread Count 206
       11.2.3 Wait Time 206
       11.2.4 Spin Time 207
   11.3 Analysis With Intel VTune Profiler 207
       11.3.1 Find Expensive Locks 207
       11.3.2 Platform View 209
   11.4 Analysis with Linux Perf 210
       11.4.1 Find Expensive Locks 211
   11.5 Analysis with Coz 213
   11.6 Analysis with eBPF and GAPP 214
   11.7 Detecting Coherence Issues 214
       11.7.1 Cache Coherency Protocols 214
       11.7.2 True Sharing 216
       11.7.3 False Sharing 217
   11.8 Chapter Summary 219

Epilog   **220**

Glossary   **222**

References   **223**

Appendix A. Reducing Measurement Noise   **228**

Appendix B. The LLVM Vectorizer   **233**

1 Introduction

They say, "performance is king". It was true a decade ago, and it certainly is now. According to [Dom, 2017], in 2017, the world has been creating 2.5 quintillions[1] bytes of data every day, and as predicted in [Sta, 2018], this number is growing 25% per year. In our increasingly data-centric world, the growth of information exchange fuels the need for both faster software (SW) and faster hardware (HW). Fair to say, the data growth puts demand not only on computing power but also on storage and network systems.

In the PC era[2], developers usually were programming directly on top of the operating system, with possibly a few libraries in between. As the world moved to the cloud era, the SW stack got deeper and more complex. The top layer of the stack on which most developers are working has moved further away from the HW. Those additional layers abstract away the actual HW, which allows using new types of accelerators for emerging workloads. However, the negative side of such evolution is that developers of modern applications have less affinity to the actual HW on which their SW is running.

Software programmers have had an "easy ride" for decades, thanks to Moore's law. It used to be the case that some SW vendors preferred to wait for a new generation of HW to speed up their application and did not spend human resources on making improvements in their code. By looking at Figure 1, we can see that single-threaded performance[3] growth is slowing down.

When it's no longer the case that each HW generation provides a significant performance boost [Leiserson et al., 2020], we must start paying more attention to how fast our code runs. When seeking ways to improve performance, developers should not rely on HW. Instead, they should start optimizing the code of their applications.

> "Software today is massively inefficient; it's become prime time again for software programmers to get really good at

---

[1] Quintillion is a thousand raised to the power of six (10^{18}).
[2] From the late 1990s to the late 2000s where personal computers where dominating the market of computing devices.
[3] Single-threaded performance is a performance of a single HW thread inside the CPU core.

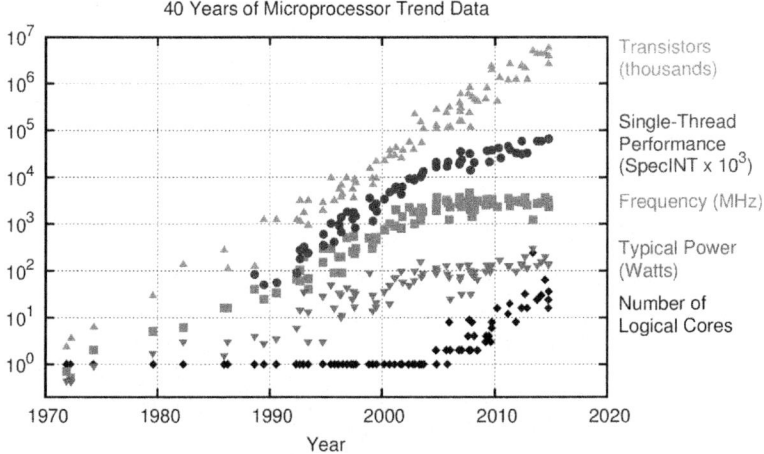

Figure 1: 40 Years of Microprocessor Trend Data. © *Image by K. Rupp via karlrupp.net*

optimization." - Marc Andreessen, the US entrepreneur and investor (a16z Podcast, 2020)

Personal Experience: While working at Intel, I hear the same story from time to time: when Intel clients experience slowness in their application, they immediately and unconsciously start blaming Intel for having slow CPUs. But when Intel sends one of our performance ninjas to work with them and help them improve their application, it is not unusual that they help speed it up by a factor of 5x, sometimes even 10x.

Reaching high-level performance is challenging and usually requires substantial efforts, but hopefully, this book will give you the tools to help you achieve it.

1.1 Why Do We Still Need Performance Tuning?

Modern CPUs are getting more and more cores each year. As of the end of 2019, you can buy a high-end server processor which will have more than 100 logical cores. This is very impressive, but that doesn't mean we don't have to care about performance anymore. Very often, application performance might not get better with more CPU cores. The performance of a typical general-purpose multithread application doesn't always scale linearly with the number of CPU cores we assign to the task. Understanding why that happens and possible ways to fix it is critical for the future growth of a product. Not being able to do proper performance analysis and tuning leaves lots of performance and money on the table and can kill the product.

According to [Leiserson et al., 2020], at least in the near term, a large portion of performance gains for most applications will originate from the SW stack. Sadly, applications do not get optimal performance by default. Article [Leiserson et al., 2020] also provides an excellent example that illustrates the potential for performance improvements that could be done on a source code level. Speedups from performance engineering a program that multiplies two 4096-by-4096 matrices are summarized in Table 1. The end result of applying multiple optimizations is a program that runs over 60,000 times faster. The reason for providing this example is not to pick on Python or Java (which are great languages), but rather to break beliefs that software has "good enough" performance by default.

Table 1: Speedups from performance engineering a program that multiplies two 4096-by-4096 matrices running on a dual-socket Intel Xeon E5-2666 v3 system with a total of 60 GB of memory. From [Leiserson et al., 2020].

Version	Implementation	Absolute speedup	Relative speedup
1	Python	1	—
2	Java	11	10.8
3	C	47	4.4
4	Parallel loops	366	7.8
5	Parallel divide and conquer	6,727	18.4
6	plus vectorization	23,224	3.5
7	plus AVX intrinsics	62,806	2.7

Here are some of the most important factors that prevent systems

1.1 Why Do We Still Need Performance Tuning?

from achieving optimal performance by default:

1. **CPU limitations.** It's so tempting to ask: "*Why doesn't HW solve all our problems?*" Modern CPUs execute instructions at incredible speed and are getting better with every generation. But still, they cannot do much if instructions that are used to perform the job are not optimal or even redundant. Processors cannot magically transform suboptimal code into something that performs better. For example, if we implement a sorting routine using BubbleSort[4] algorithm, a CPU will not make any attempts to recognize it and use the better alternatives, for example, QuickSort[5]. It will blindly execute whatever it was told to do.
2. **Compilers limitations.** "*But isn't it what compilers are supposed to do? Why don't compilers solve all our problems?*" Indeed, compilers are amazingly smart nowadays, but can still generate suboptimal code. Compilers are great at eliminating redundant work, but when it comes to making more complex decisions like function inlining, loop unrolling, etc. they may not generate the best possible code. For example, there is no binary "yes" or "no" answer to the question of whether a compiler should always inline a function into the place where it's called. It usually depends on many factors which a compiler should take into account. Often, compilers rely on complex cost models and heuristics, which may not work for every possible scenario. Additionally, compilers cannot perform optimizations unless they are certain it is safe to do so, and it does not affect the correctness of the resulting machine code. It may be very difficult for compiler developers to ensure that a particular optimization will generate correct code under all possible circumstances, so they often have to be conservative and refrain from doing some optimizations[6]. Finally, compilers generally do not transform data structures used by the program, which are also crucial in terms of performance.
3. **Algorithmic complexity analysis limitations.** Developers are frequently overly obsessed with complexity analysis of the algorithms, which leads them to choose the popular algorithm with the optimal algorithmic complexity, even though it may not be the most efficient for a given problem. Considering

---

[4] BubbleSort algorithm - https://en.wikipedia.org/wiki/Bubble_sort
[5] QuickSort algorithm - https://en.wikipedia.org/wiki/Quicksort
[6] This is certainly the case with the order of floating-point operations.

1.1 Why Do We Still Need Performance Tuning?

two sorting algorithms InsertionSort[7] and QuickSort, the latter clearly wins in terms of Big O notation for the average case: InsertionSort is $O(N^2)$ while QuickSort is only $O(N \log N)$. Yet for relatively small sizes[8] of N, InsertionSort outperforms QuickSort. Complexity analysis cannot account for all the branch prediction and caching effects of various algorithms, so they just encapsulate them in an implicit constant `c`, which sometimes can make drastic impact on performance. Blindly trusting Big O notation without testing on the target workload could lead developers down an incorrect path. So, the best-known algorithm for a certain problem is not necessarily the most performant in practice for every possible input.

Limitations described above leave the room for tuning the performance of our SW to reach its full potential. Broadly speaking, the SW stack includes many layers, e.g., firmware, BIOS, OS, libraries, and the source code of an application. But since most of the lower SW layers are not under our direct control, a major focus will be made on the source code. Another important piece of SW that we will touch on a lot is a compiler. It's possible to obtain attractive speedups by making the compiler generate the desired machine code through various hints. You will find many such examples throughout the book.

> **Personal Experience:** To successfully implement the needed improvements in your application, you don't have to be a compiler expert. Based on my experience, at least 90% of all transformations can be done at a source code level without the need to dig down into compiler sources. Although, understanding how the compiler works and how you can make it do what you want is always advantageous in performance-related work.

Also, nowadays, it's essential to enable applications to scale up by distributing them across many cores since single-threaded performance tends to reach a plateau. Such enabling calls for efficient communication between the threads of application, eliminating unnecessary consumption of resources and other issues typical for multi-threaded programs.

---

[7] InsertionSort algorithm - https://en.wikipedia.org/wiki/Insertion_sort
[8] Typically between 7 and 50 elements

It is important to mention that performance gains will not only come from tuning SW. According to [Leiserson et al., 2020], two other major sources of potential speedups in the future are algorithms (especially for new problem domains like machine learning) and streamlined hardware design. Algorithms obviously play a big role in the performance of an application, but we will not cover this topic in this book. We will not be discussing the topic of new hardware designs either, since most of the time, SW developers have to deal with existing HW. However, understanding modern CPU design is important for optimizing applications.

> "During the post-Moore era, it will become ever more important to make code run fast and, in particular, to tailor it to the hardware on which it runs." [Leiserson et al., 2020]

The methodologies in this book focus on squeezing out the last bit of performance from your application. Such transformations can be attributed along rows 6 and 7 in Table 1. The types of improvements that will be discussed are usually not big and often do not exceed 10%. However, do not underestimate the importance of a 10% speedup. It is especially relevant for large distributed applications running in cloud configurations. According to [Hennessy, 2018], in the year 2018, Google spends roughly the same amount of money on actual computing servers that run the cloud as it spends on power and cooling infrastructure. Energy efficiency is a very important problem, which can be improved by optimizing SW.

> "At such scale, understanding performance characteristics becomes critical – even small improvements in performance or utilization can translate into immense cost savings." [Kanev et al., 2015]

1.2 Who Needs Performance Tuning?

Performance engineering does not need to be justified much in industries like High-Performance Computing (HPC), Cloud Services, High-Frequency Trading (HFT), Game Development, and other performance-critical areas. For instance, Google reported that a 2% slower search caused 2% fewer searches[9] per user. For Yahoo!

---

[9] Slides by Marissa Mayer - https://assets.en.oreilly.com/1/event/29/Keynote Presentation 2.pdf

400 milliseconds faster page load caused 5-9% more traffic[10]. In the game of big numbers, small improvements can make a significant impact. Such examples prove that the slower the service works, the fewer people will use it.

Interestingly, performance engineering is not only needed in the aforementioned areas. Nowadays, it is also required in the field of general-purpose applications and services. Many tools that we use every day simply would not exist if they failed to meet their performance requirements. For example, Visual C++ IntelliSense[11] features that are integrated into Microsoft Visual Studio IDE have very tight performance constraints. For IntelliSense autocomplete feature to work, they have to parse the entire source codebase in the order of milliseconds[12]. Nobody will use source code editors if it takes them several seconds to suggest autocomplete options. Such a feature has to be very responsive and provide valid continuations as the user types new code. The success of similar applications can only be achieved by designing SW with performance in mind and thoughtful performance engineering.

Sometimes fast tools find use in the areas they were not initially designed for. For example, nowadays, game engines like Unreal[13] and Unity[14] are used in architecture, 3d visualization, film making, and other areas. Because they are so performant, they are a natural choice for applications that require 2d and 3d rendering, physics engine, collision detection, sound, animation, etc.

> "Fast tools don't just allow users to accomplish tasks faster; they allow users to accomplish entirely new types of tasks, in entirely new ways." - Nelson Elhage wrote in article[15] on his blog (2020).

---

[10] Slides by Stoyan Stefanov - https://www.slideshare.net/stoyan/dont-make-me-wait-or-building-highperformance-web-applications

[11] Visual C++ IntelliSense - https://docs.microsoft.com/en-us/visualstudio/ide/visual-cpp-intellisense

[12] In fact, it's not possible to parse the entire codebase in the order of milliseconds. Instead, IntelliSense only reconstructs the portions of AST that has been changed. Watch more details on how the Microsoft team achieves this in the video: https://channel9.msdn.com/Blogs/Seth-Juarez/Anders-Hejlsberg-on-Modern-Compiler-Construction.

[13] Unreal Engine - https://www.unrealengine.com.

[14] Unity Engine - https://unity.com/.

[15] Reflections on software performance by N. Elhage - https://blog.nelhage.com/post/reflections-on-performance/

I hope it goes without saying that people hate using slow software. Performance characteristics of an application can be a single factor for your customer to switch to a competitor's product. By putting emphasis on performance, you can give your product a competitive advantage.

Performance engineering is important and rewarding work, but it may be very time-consuming. In fact, performance optimization is a never-ending game. There will always be something to optimize. Inevitably, the developer will reach the point of diminishing returns at which further improvement will come at a very high engineering cost and likely will not be worth the efforts. From that perspective, knowing when to stop optimizing is a critical aspect of performance work[16]. Some organizations achieve it by integrating this information into the code review process: source code lines are annotated with the corresponding "cost" metric. Using that data, developers can decide whether improving the performance of a particular piece of code is worth it.

Before starting performance tuning, make sure you have a strong reason to do so. Optimization just for optimization's sake is useless if it doesn't add value to your product. Mindful performance engineering starts with clearly defined performance goals, stating what you are trying to achieve and why you are doing it. Also, you should pick the metrics you will use to measure if you reach the goal. You can read more on the topic of setting performance goals in [Gregg, 2013] and [Akinshin, 2019].

Nevertheless, it is always great to practice and master the skill of performance analysis and tuning. If you picked up the book for that reason, you are more than welcome to keep on reading.

1.3 What Is Performance Analysis?

Ever found yourself debating with a coworker about the performance of a certain piece of code? Then you probably know how hard it is to predict which code is going to work the best. With so many moving parts inside modern processors, even a small tweak to the code can trigger significant performance change. That's why the first advice in this book is: *Always Measure*.

---

[16] Roofline model (section 5.5) and Top-Down Microarchitecture Analysis (section 6.1) may help to assess performance against HW theoretical maximums.

Personal Experience: I see many people rely on intuition when they try to optimize their application. And usually, it ends up with random fixes here and there without making any real impact on the performance of the application.

Inexperienced developers often make changes in the source code and hope it will improve the performance of the program. One such example is replacing `i++` with `++i` all over the code base, assuming that the previous value of `i` is not used. In the general case, this change will make no difference to the generated code because every decent optimizing compiler will recognize that the previous value of `i` is not used and will eliminate redundant copies anyway.

Many micro-optimization tricks that circulate around the world were valid in the past, but current compilers have already learned them. Additionally, some people tend to overuse legacy bit-twiddling tricks. One of such examples is using XOR-based swap idiom[17], while in reality, simple `std::swap` produces faster code. Such accidental changes likely won't improve the performance of the application. Finding the right place to fix should be a result of careful performance analysis, not intuition and guesses.

There are many performance analysis methodologies[18] that may or may not lead you to a discovery. The CPU-specific approaches to performance analysis presented in this book have one thing in common: they are based on collecting certain information about how the program executes. Any change that ends up being made in the source code of the program is driven by analyzing and interpreting collected data.

Locating a performance bottleneck is only half of the engineer's job. The second half is to fix it properly. Sometimes changing one line in the program source code can yield a drastic performance boost. Performance analysis and tuning are all about how to find and fix this line. Missing such opportunities can be a big waste.

---

[17] XOR-based swap idiom - https://en.wikipedia.org/wiki/XOR_swap_algorithm

[18] Performance Analysis Methodology by B. Gregg - http://www.brendangregg.com/methodology.html

1.4 What is discussed in this book?

This book is written to help developers better understand the performance of their application, learn to find inefficiencies, and eliminate them. *Why my hand-written archiver performs two times slower than the conventional one? Why did my change in the function cause two times performance drop? Customers are complaining about the slowness of my application, and I don't know where to start? Have I optimized the program to its full potential? What do I do with all that cache misses and branch mispredictions?* Hopefully, by the end of this book, you will have the answers to those questions.

Here is the outline of what this book contains:

- Chapter 2 discusses how to conduct fair performance experiments and analyze their results. It introduces the best practices of performance testing and comparing results.
- Chapters 3 and 4 provide basics of CPU microarchitecture and terminology in performance analysis; feel free to skip if you know this already.
- Chapter 5 explores several most popular approaches for doing performance analysis. It explains how profiling techniques work and what data can be collected.
- Chapter 6 gives information about features provided by the modern CPU to support and enhance performance analysis. It shows how they work and what problems they are capable of solving.
- Chapters 7-9 contain recipes for typical performance problems. It is organized in the most convenient way to be used with Top-Down Microarchitecture Analysis (see section 6.1), which is one of the most important concepts of the book.
- Chapter 10 contains optimization topics not specifically related to any of the categories covered in the previous three chapters, still important enough to find their place in this book.
- Chapter 11 discusses techniques for analyzing multithreaded applications. It outlines some of the most important challenges of optimizing the performance of multithreaded applications and the tools that can be used to analyze it. The topic itself is quite big, so the chapter only focuses on HW-specific issues, like "False Sharing".

Examples provided in this book are primarily based on open-source software: Linux as the operating system, LLVM-based Clang compiler for C and C++ languages, and Linux `perf` as the profiling tool. The reason for such a choice is not only the popularity of mentioned technologies but also the fact that their source code is open, which allows us to better understand the underlying mechanism of how they work. This is especially useful for learning the concepts presented in this book. We will also sometimes showcase proprietary tools that are "big players" in their areas, for example, Intel® VTune™ Profiler.

1.5 What is not in this book?

System performance depends on different components: CPU, OS, memory, I/O devices, etc. Applications could benefit from tuning various components of the system. In general, engineers should analyze the performance of the whole system. However, the biggest factor in systems performance is its heart, the CPU. This is why this book primarily focuses on performance analysis from a CPU perspective, occasionally touching on OS and memory subsystems.

The scope of the book does not go beyond a single CPU socket, so we will not discuss optimization techniques for distributed, NUMA, and heterogeneous systems. Offloading computations to accelerators (GPU, FPGA, etc.) using solutions like OpenCL and openMP is not discussed in this book.

This book centers around Intel x86 CPU architecture and does not provide specific tuning recipes for AMD, ARM, or RISC-V chips. Nonetheless, many of the principles discussed in further chapters apply well to those processors. Also, Linux is the OS of choice for this book, but again, for most of the examples in this book, it doesn't matter since the same techniques benefit applications that run on Windows and Mac operating systems.

All the code snippets in this book are written in C, C++, or x86 assembly languages, but to a large degree, ideas from this book can be applied to other languages that are compiled to native code like Rust, Go, and even Fortran. Since this book targets user-mode applications that run close to the hardware, we will not discuss managed environments, e.g., Java.

Finally, the author assumes that readers have full control over the software that they develop, including the choice of libraries and compiler they use. Hence, this book is not about tuning purchased commercial packages, e.g., tuning SQL database queries.

1.6 Chapter Summary

- HW is not getting that much performance boosts in single-threaded performance as it used to in the past years. That's why performance tuning is becoming more important than it has been for the last 40 years. The computing industry is changing now much more heavily than at any time since the 90s.
- According to [Leiserson et al., 2020], SW tuning will be one of the key drivers for performance gains in the near future. The importance of performance tuning should not be underestimated. For large distributed applications, every small performance improvement results in immense cost savings.
- Software doesn't have an optimal performance by default. Certain limitations exist that prevent applications to reach their full performance potential. Both HW and SW environments have such limitations. CPUs cannot magically speed up slow algorithms. Compilers are far from generating optimal code for every program. Due to HW specifics, the best-known algorithm for a certain problem is not always the most performant. All this leaves the room for tuning the performance of our applications.
- For some types of applications, performance is not just a feature. It enables users to solve new kinds of problems in a new way.
- SW optimizations should be backed by strong business needs. Developers should set quantifiable goals and metrics which must be used to measure progress.
- Predicting the performance of a certain piece of code is nearly impossible since there are so many factors that affect the performance of modern platforms. When implementing SW optimizations, developers should not rely on intuition but use careful performance analysis instead.

Part1. Performance analysis on a modern CPU

2 Measuring Performance

The first step on the path to understanding an application's performance is knowing how to measure it. Some people attribute performance as one of the features of the application[19]. But unlike other features, performance is not a boolean property: applications always have some level of performance. This is why it's impossible to answer "yes" or "no" to the question of whether an application has the performance.

Performance problems are usually harder to track down and reproduce than most functional issues[20]. Every run of the benchmark is different from each other. For example, when unpacking a zip-file, we get the same result over and over again, which means this operation is reproducible[21]. However, it's impossible to reproduce exactly the same performance profile of this operation.

Anyone ever concerned with performance evaluations likely knows how hard it is to conduct fair performance measurements and draw accurate conclusions from it. Performance measurements sometimes can be very much unexpected. Changing a seemingly unrelated part of the source code can surprise us with a significant impact on program performance. This phenomenon is called measurement bias. Because of the presence of error in measurements, performance analysis requires statistical methods to process them. This topic deserves a whole book just by itself. There are many corner cases and a huge amount of research done in this field. We will not go all the way down this rabbit hole. Instead, we will just focus on high-level ideas and directions to follow.

---

[19] Blog post by Nelson Elhage "Reflections on software performance": https://blog.nelhage.com/post/reflections-on-performance/.

[20] Sometimes, we have to deal with non-deterministic and hard to reproduce bugs, but it's not that often.

[21] Assuming no data races.

Conducting fair performance experiments is an essential step towards getting accurate and meaningful results. Designing performance tests and configuring the environment are both important components in the process of evaluating performance. This chapter will give a brief introduction to why modern systems yield noisy performance measurements and what you can do about it. We will touch on the importance of measuring performance in real production deployments.

Not a single long-living product exists without ever having performance regressions. This is especially important for large projects with lots of contributors where changes are coming at a very fast pace. This chapter devotes a few pages discussing the automated process of tracking performance changes in Continuous Integration and Continuous Delivery (CI/CD) systems. We also present general guidance on how to properly collect and analyze performance measurements when developers implement changes in their source codebase.

The end of the chapter describes SW and HW timers that can be used by developers in time-based measurements and common pitfalls when designing and writing a good microbenchmark.

2.1 Noise In Modern Systems

There are many features in HW and SW that are intended to increase performance. But not all of them have deterministic behavior. Let's consider Dynamic Frequency Scaling[22] (DFS): this is a feature that allows a CPU to increase its frequency for a short time interval, making it run significantly faster. However, the CPU can't stay in "overclocked" mode for a long time, so later, it decreases its frequency back to the base value. DFS usually depends a lot on a core temperature, which makes it hard to predict the impact on our experiments.

If we start two runs of the benchmark, one right after another on a "cold" processor[23], the first run could possibly work for some time in "overclocked" mode and then decrease its frequency back to the base level. However, it's possible that the second run might not have this advantage and will operate at the base frequency without entering "turbo mode". Even though we run the exact same version

---

[22] Dynamic Frequency Scaling - https://en.wikipedia.org/wiki/Dynamic_frequency_scaling.
[23] By cold processor, I mean the CPU that stayed in an idle mode for a while, allowing it to cool down.

2.1 Noise In Modern Systems

of the program two times, the environment in which they run is not the same. Figure 2 shows a situation where dynamic frequency scaling can cause variance in measurements. Such a scenario can frequently happen when benchmarking on laptops since usually they have limited heat dissipation.

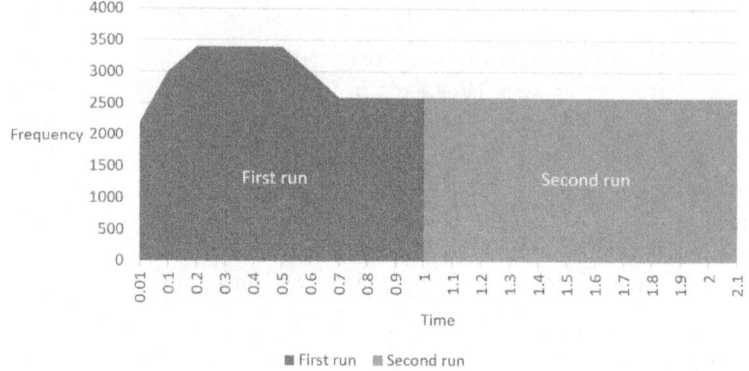

Figure 2: Variance in measurements caused by frequency scaling.

Frequency Scaling is an HW feature, but variations in measurements might also come from SW features. Let's consider the example of a filesystem cache. If we benchmark an application that does lots of file manipulation, the filesystem can play a big role in performance. When the first iteration of the benchmark runs, the required entries in the filesystem cache could be missing. However, the filesystem cache will be warmed-up when running the same benchmark a second time, making it significantly faster than the first run.

Unfortunately, measurement bias does not only come from environment configuration. [Mytkowicz et al., 2009] paper demonstrates that UNIX environment size (i.e., the total number of bytes required to store the environment variables) and link order (the order of object files that are given to the linker) can affect performance in unpredictable ways. Moreover, there are numerous other ways of affecting memory layout and potentially affecting performance measurements. One approach to enable statistically sound performance analysis of software on modern architectures was presented in [Curtsinger and Berger, 2013]. This work shows that it's possible to eliminate measurement bias that comes from memory layout by efficiently and repeatedly randomizing the placement of code, stack, and heap objects at runtime. Sadly, these ideas didn't go much further, and right now, this project is almost abandoned.

Personal Experience: Remember that even running a task manager tool, like Linux top, can affect measurements since some CPU core will be activated and assigned to it. This might affect the frequency of the core that is running the actual benchmark.

Having consistent measurements requires running all iterations of the benchmark with the same conditions. However, it is not possible to replicate the exact same environment and eliminate bias completely: there could be different temperature conditions, power delivery spikes, neighbor processes running, etc. Chasing all potential sources of noise and variation in the system can be a never-ending story. Sometimes it cannot be achieved, for example, when benchmarking large distributed cloud service.

So, eliminating non-determinism in a system is helpful for well-defined, stable performance tests, e.g., microbenchmarks. For instance, when you implement some code change and want to know the relative speedup ratio by benchmarking two different versions of the same program. This is a scenario where you can control most of the variables in the benchmark, including its input, environment configuration, etc. In this situation, eliminating non-determinism in a system helps to get a more consistent and accurate comparison. After finishing with local testing, remember to make sure projected performance improvements were mirrored in real-world measurements. Readers can find some examples of features that can bring noise into performance measurements and how to disable them in Appendix A. Also, there are tools that can set up the environment to ensure benchmarking results with a low variance; one of them is temci[24].

It is not recommended to eliminate system non-deterministic behavior when estimating real-world performance improvements. Engineers should try to replicate the target system configuration, which they are optimizing for. Introducing any artificial tuning to the system under test will diverge results from what users of your service will see in practice. Also, any performance analysis work, including profiling (see section 5.4), should be done on a system that is configured similar to what will be used in a real deployment.

---

[24] Temci - https://github.com/parttimenerd/temci.

Finally, it's important to keep in mind that even if a particular HW or SW feature has non-deterministic behavior, that doesn't mean it is considered harmful. It could give an inconsistent result, but it is designed to improve the overall performance of the system. Disabling such a feature might reduce the noise in microbenchmarks but make the whole suite run longer. This might be especially important for CI/CD performance testing when there are time limits for how long it should take to run the whole benchmark suite.

2.2 Measuring Performance In Production

When an application runs on shared infrastructure (typical in a public cloud), there usually will be other workloads from other customers running on the same servers. With technologies like virtualization and containers becoming more popular, public cloud providers try to fully utilize the capacity of their servers. Unfortunately, it creates additional obstacles for measuring performance in such an environment. Sharing resources with neighbor processes can influence performance measurements in unpredictable ways.

Analyzing production workloads by recreating them in a lab can be tricky. Sometimes it's not possible to synthesize exact behavior for "in-house" performance testing. This is why more and more often, cloud providers and hyperscalers choose to profile and monitor performance directly on production systems [Ren et al., 2010]. Measuring performance when there are "no other players" may not reflect real-world scenarios. It would be a waste of time to implement code optimizations that perform well in a lab environment but not in a production environment. Having said that, it doesn't eliminate the need for continuous "in-house" testing to catch performance problems early. Not all performance regressions can be caught in a lab, but engineers should design performance benchmarks representative of real-world scenarios.

It's becoming a trend for large service providers to implement telemetry systems that monitor performance on user devices. One such example is the Netflix Icarus[25] telemetry service, which runs on thousands of different devices spread all around the world. Such a telemetry system helps Netflix understand how real users perceive Netflix's app performance. It allows engineers to analyze data col-

---

[25] Presented at CMG 2019, https://www.youtube.com/watch?v=4RG2DUK03_0.

lected from many devices and to find issues that would be impossible to find otherwise. This kind of data allows making better-informed decisions on where to focus the optimization efforts.

One important caveat of monitoring production deployments is measurement overhead. Because any kind of monitoring affects the performance of a running service, it's recommended to use only lightweight profiling methods. According to [Ren et al., 2010]: "To conduct continuous profiling on datacenter machines serving real traffic, extremely low overhead is paramount". Usually, acceptable aggregated overhead is considered below 1%. Performance monitoring overhead can be reduced by limiting the set of profiled machines as well as using smaller time intervals.

Measuring performance in such production environments means that we must accept its noisy nature and use statistical methods to analyze results. A good example of how large companies like LinkedIn use statistical methods to measure and compare quantile-based metrics (e.g., 90th percentile Page Load Times) in their A/B testing in the production environment can be found in [Liu et al., 2019].

2.3 Automated Detection of Performance Regressions

It is becoming a trend that SW vendors try to increase the frequency of deployments. Companies constantly seek ways to accelerate the rate of delivering their products to the market. Unfortunately, this doesn't automatically imply that SW products become better with each new release. In particular, software performance defects tend to leak into production software at an alarming rate [Jin et al., 2012]. A large number of changes in software impose a challenge to analyze all of those results and historical data to detect performance regressions.

Software performance regressions are defects that are erroneously introduced into software as it evolves from one version to the next. Catching performance bugs and improvements means detecting which commits change the performance of the software (as measured by performance tests) in the presence of the noise from the testing infrastructure. From database systems to search engines to compilers, performance regressions are commonly experienced by almost all large-scale software systems during their continuous evolution and deployment life cycle. It may be impossible to entirely avoid performance regressions during software development, but with proper

2.3 Automated Detection of Performance Regressions

testing and diagnostic tools, the likelihood for such defects to silently leak into production code could be minimized.

The first option that comes to mind is: having humans to look at the graphs and compare results. It shouldn't be surprising that we want to move away from that option very quickly. People tend to lose focus quickly and can miss regressions, especially on a noisy chart, like the one shown in figure 3. Humans will likely catch performance regression that happened around August 5th, but it's not obvious that humans will detect later regressions. In addition to being error-prone, having humans in the loop is also a time consuming and boring job that must be performed daily.

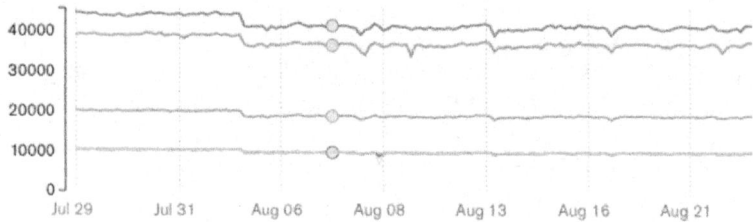

Figure 3: Performance trend graph for four tests with a small drop in performance on August 5th (the higher value, the better). © *Image from [Daly et al., 2020]*

The second option is to have a simple threshold. It is somewhat better than the first option but still has its own drawbacks. Fluctuations in performance tests are inevitable: sometimes, even a harmless code change[26] can trigger performance variation in a benchmark. Choosing the right value for the threshold is extremely hard and does not guarantee a low rate of false-positive as well as false-negative alarms. Setting the threshold too low might lead to analyzing a bunch of small regressions that were not caused by the change in source code but due to some random noise. Setting the threshold too high might lead to filtering out real performance regressions. Small changes can pile up slowly into a bigger regression, which can be left unnoticed[27]. By looking at the figure 3, we can make an observation

---

[26] The following article shows that changing the order of the functions or removing dead functions can cause variations in performance: https://easyperf.net/blog/2018/01/18/Code_alignment_issues.

[27] E.g., suppose you have a threshold of 2%. If you have two consecutive 1.5% regressions, they both will be filtered out. But throughout two days, performance regression will sum up to 3%, which is bigger than the threshold.

2.3 Automated Detection of Performance Regressions

that the threshold requires per test adjustment. The threshold that might work for the green (upper line) test will not necessarily work equally well for the purple (lower line) test since they have a different level of noise. An example of a CI system where each test requires setting explicit threshold values for alerting a regression is LUCI[28], which is a part of the Chromium project.

One of the recent approaches to identify performance regressions was taken in [Daly et al., 2020]. MongoDB developers implemented change point analysis for identifying performance changes in the evolving code base of their database products. According to [Matteson and James, 2014], change point analysis is the process of detecting distributional changes within time-ordered observations. MongoDB developers utilized an "E-Divisive means" algorithm that works by hierarchically selecting distributional change points that divide the time series into clusters. Their open-sourced CI system called Evergreen[29] incorporates this algorithm to display change points on the chart and opens Jira tickets. More details about this automated performance testing system can be found in [Ingo and Daly, 2020].

Another interesting approach is presented in [Alam et al., 2019]. The authors of this paper presented `AutoPerf`, which uses hardware performance counters (PMC, see section 3.9.1) to diagnose performance regressions in a modified program. First, it learns the distribution of the performance of a modified function based on its PMC profile data collected from the original program. Then, it detects deviations of performance as anomalies based on the PMC profile data collected from the modified program. `AutoPerf` showed that this design could effectively diagnose some of the most complex software performance bugs, like those hidden in parallel programs.

Regardless of the underlying algorithm of detecting performance regressions, a typical CI system should automate the following actions:

1. Setup a system under test.
2. Run a workload.
3. Report the results.
4. Decide if performance has changed.
5. Visualize the results.

CI system should support both automated and manual benchmarking,

---

[28] LUCI - https://chromium.googlesource.com/chromium/src.git/+/master/docs/tour_of_luci_ui.md

[29] Evergreen - https://github.com/evergreen-ci/evergreen.

yield repeatable results, and open tickets for performance regressions that were found. It is very important to detect regressions promptly. First, because fewer changes were merged since a regression happened. This allows us to have a person responsible for regression to look into the problem before they move to another task. Also, it is a lot easier for a developer to approach the regression since all the details are still fresh in their head as opposed to several weeks after that.

2.4 Manual Performance Testing

It is great when engineers can leverage existing performance testing infrastructure during development. In the previous section, we discussed that one of the nice-to-have features of the CI system is the possibility to submit performance evaluation jobs to it. If this is supported, then the system would return the results of testing a patch that the developer wants to commit to the codebase. It may not always be possible due to various reasons, like hardware unavailability, setup is too complicated for testing infrastructure, a need to collect additional metrics. In this section, we provide basic advice for local performance evaluations.

When making performance improvements in our code, we need a way to prove that we actually made it better. Also, when we commit a regular code change, we want to make sure performance did not regress. Typically, we do this by 1) measuring the baseline performance, 2) measuring the performance of the modified program, and 3) comparing them with each other. The goal in such a scenario is to compare the performance of two different versions of the same functional program. For example, we have a program that recursively calculates Fibonacci numbers, and we decided to rewrite it in an iterative fashion. Both are functionally correct and yield the same numbers. Now we need to compare the performance of two programs.

It is highly recommended to get not just a single measurement but to run the benchmark multiple times. So, we have N measurements for the baseline and N measurements for the modified version of the program. Now we need a way to compare those two sets of measurements to decide which one is faster. This task is intractable by itself, and there are many ways to be fooled by the measurements and potentially derive wrong conclusions from them. If you ask any data scientist, they will tell you that you should not rely on a single metric (min/mean/median, etc.).

2.4 Manual Performance Testing

Consider two distributions of performance measurements collected for two versions of a program in Figure 4. This chart displays the probability we get a particular timing for a given version of a program. For example, there is a ~32% chance the version A will finish in ~102 seconds. It's tempting to say that A is faster than B. However, it is true only with some probability P. This is because there are some measurements of B that are faster than A. Even in the situation when all the measurements of B are slower than every measurement of A probability P is not equal to 100%. This is because we can always produce one additional sample for B, which may be faster than some samples of A.

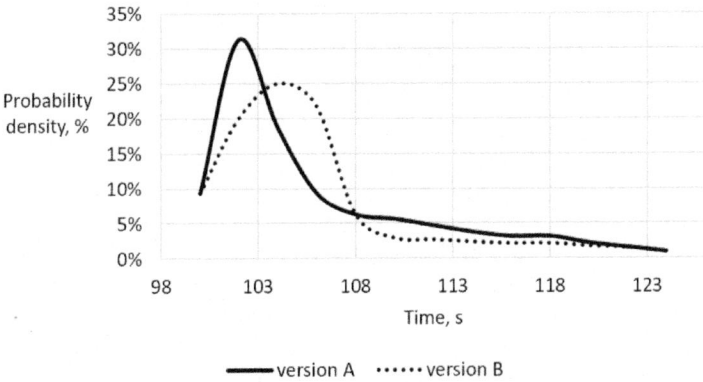

Figure 4: Comparing 2 performance measurement distributions.

An interesting advantage of using distribution plots is that it allows you to spot unwanted behavior of the benchmark[30]. If the distribution is bimodal, the benchmark likely experiences two different types of behavior. A common cause of bimodally distributed measurements is code that has both a fast and a slow path, such as accessing a cache (cache hit vs. cache miss) and acquiring a lock (contended lock vs. uncontended lock). To "fix" this, different functional patterns should be isolated and benchmarked separately.

Data scientists often present measurements by plotting the distributions and avoid calculating speedup ratios. This eliminates biased conclusions and allows readers to interpret the data themselves. One

---

[30] Another way to check this is to run the normality test: https://en.wikipedia.org/wiki/Normality_test.

of the popular ways to plot distributions is by using box plots (see Figure 5), which allow comparisons of multiple distributions on the same chart.

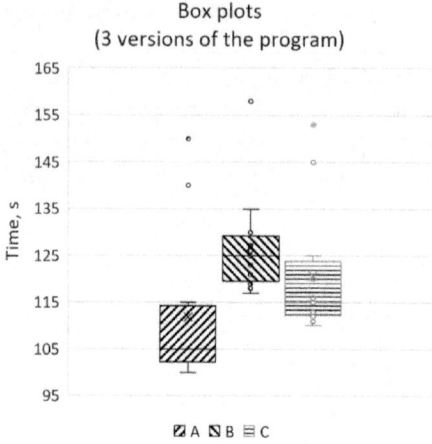

Figure 5: Box plots.

While visualizing performance distributions may help you discover certain anomalies, developers shouldn't use them for calculating speedups. In general, it's hard to estimate the speedup by looking at performance measurement distributions. Also, as discussed in the previous section, it doesn't work for automated benchmarking systems. Usually, we want to get a scalar value that will represent a speedup ratio between performance distributions of 2 versions of a program, for example, "version A is faster than version B by X%".

The statistical relationship between the two distributions is identified using Hypothesis Testing methods. A comparison is deemed *statistically significant* if the relationship between the data-sets would reject the null hypothesis[31] according to a threshold probability (the significance level). If the distributions[32] are Gaussian (normal[33]), then using a parametric hypothesis test (e.g., Student's T-test[34]) to

---

[31] Null hypothesis - https://en.wikipedia.org/wiki/Null_hypothesis.

[32] It is worth to mention that Gaussian distributions are very rarely seen in performance data. So, be cautious using formulas from statistics textbooks assuming Gaussian distributions.

[33] Normal distribution - https://en.wikipedia.org/wiki/Normal_distribution.

[34] Student's t-test - https://en.wikipedia.org/wiki/Student's_t-test.

2.4 Manual Performance Testing

compare the distributions will suffice. If the distributions being compared are not Gaussian (e.g., heavily skewed or multimodal), then it's possible to use non-parametric tests (e.g., Mann-Whitney[35], Kruskal Wallis[36], etc.). Hypothesis Testing methods are great for determining whether a speedup (or slowdown) is random or not[37]. A good reference specifically about statistics for performance engineering is a book[38] by Dror G. Feitelson, "Workload Modeling for Computer Systems Performance Evaluation", that has more information on modal distributions, skewness, and other related topics.

Once it's determined that the difference is statistically significant via the hypothesis test, then the speedup can be calculated as a ratio between the means or geometric means, but there are caveats. On a small collection of samples, the mean and geometric mean can be affected by outliers. Unless distributions have low variance, do not consider averages alone. If the variance in the measurements is on the same order of magnitude as the mean, the average is not a representative metric. Figure 6 shows an example of 2 versions of the program. By looking only at averages (6a), it's tempting to say that version A is a 20% speedup over version B. However, taking into account the variance of the measurements (6b), we can see that it is not always the case. If we take the worse score for version A and the best score for version B, we can say that version B is a 20% speedup over version A. For normal distributions, a combination of mean, standard deviation, and standard error can be used to gauge a speedup between two versions of a program. Otherwise, for skewed or multimodal samples, one would have to use percentiles that are more appropriate for the benchmark, e.g., min, median, 90th, 95th, 99th, max, or some combination of these.

One of the most important factors in calculating accurate speedup ratios is collecting a rich collection of samples, i.e., run the benchmark a large number of times. This may sound obvious, but it is not always achievable. For example, some of the SPEC benchmarks[39] run for

---

[35] Mann-Whitney U test - https://en.wikipedia.org/wiki/Mann-Whitney_U_test.

[36] Kruskal-Wallis analysis of variance - https://en.wikipedia.org/wiki/Kruskal-Wallis_one-way_analysis_of_variance.

[37] Therefore, it is best used in Automated Testing Frameworks to verify that the commit didn't introduce any performance regressions.

[38] Book "Workload Modeling for Computer Systems Performance Evaluation" - https://www.cs.huji.ac.il/~feit/wlmod/.

[39] SPEC CPU 2017 benchmarks - http://spec.org/cpu2017/Docs/overview.html#benchmarks

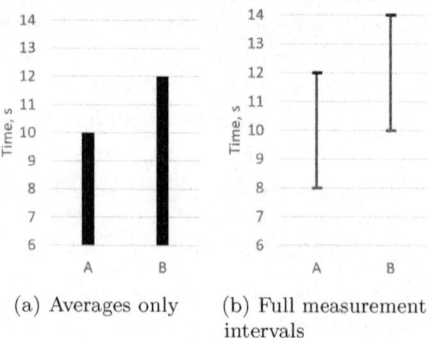

(a) Averages only (b) Full measurement intervals

Figure 6: Two histograms showing how averages could be misleading.

more than 10 minutes on a modern machine. That means it would take 1 hour to produce just three samples: 30 minutes for each version of the program. Imagine that you have not just a single benchmark in your suite, but hundreds. It would become very expensive to collect statistically sufficient data even if you distribute the work across multiple machines.

How do you know how many samples are required to reach statistically sufficient distribution? The answer to this question again depends on how much accuracy you want your comparison to have. The lower the variance between the samples in the distribution, the lower number of samples you need. Standard deviation[40] is the metric that tells you how consistent the measurements in the distribution are. One can implement an adaptive strategy by dynamically limiting the number of benchmark iterations based on standard deviation, i.e., you collect samples until you get a standard deviation that lies in a certain range[41]. Once you have a standard deviation lower than some threshold, you could stop collecting measurements. This strategy is explained in more detail in [Akinshin, 2019, Chapter 4].

Another important thing to watch out for is the presence of outliers. It is OK to discard some samples (for example, cold runs) as outliers by using confidence intervals, but do not deliberately discard unwanted

---

[40] Standard deviation - https://en.wikipedia.org/wiki/Standard_deviation
[41] This approach requires the number of measurements to be more than 1. Otherwise, the algorithm will stop after the first sample because a single run of a benchmark has std.dev. equals to zero.

samples from the measurement set. For some types of benchmarks, outliers can be one of the most important metrics. For example, when benchmarking SW that has real-time constraints, 99-percentile could be very interesting. There is a series of talks about measuring latency by Gil Tene on YouTube that covers this topic well.

2.5 Software and Hardware Timers

To benchmark execution time, engineers usually use two different timers, which all the modern platforms provide:

- **System-wide high-resolution timer.** This is a system timer that is typically implemented as a simple count of the number of ticks that have transpired since some arbitrary starting date, called the epoch[42]. This clock is monotonic; i.e., it always goes up. System timer has a nano-seconds resolution[43] and is consistent between all the CPUs. It is suitable for measuring events with a duration of more than a microsecond. System time can be retrieved from the OS with a system call[44]. The system-wide timer is independent of CPU frequency. Accessing the system timer on Linux systems is possible via the clock_gettime system call[45]. The de facto standard for accessing system timer in C++ is using std::chrono as shown in Listing 1.

- **Time Stamp Counter (TSC).** This is an HW timer which is implemented as an HW register. TSC is monotonic and has a constant rate, i.e., it doesn't account for frequency changes. Every CPU has its own TSC, which is simply the number of reference cycles (see section 4.6) elapsed. It is suitable for measuring short events with a duration from nanoseconds and up to a minute. The value of TSC can be retrieved by using compiler built-in function __rdtsc as shown in Listing 2, which uses RDTSC assembly instruction under the hood. More low-level details on benchmarking the code using RDTSC assembly instruction can be accessed in a white paper [Paoloni, 2010].

---

[42] Unix epoch starts at 1 January 1970 00:00:00 UT: https://en.wikipedia.org/wiki/Unix_epoch.

[43] Even though the system timer can return timestamps with nano-seconds accuracy, it is not suitable for measuring short running events because it takes a long time to obtain the timestamp via the clock_gettime system call.

[44] Retrieving system time - https://en.wikipedia.org/wiki/System_time#Retrieving_system_time

[45] On Linux, one can query CPU time for each thread using the

2.5 Software and Hardware Timers

Listing 1 Using C++ std::chrono to access system timer

```
#include <cstdint>
#include <chrono>

// returns elapsed time in nanoseconds
uint64_t timeWithChrono() {
  using namespace std::chrono;
  uint64_t start = duration_cast<nanoseconds>
      (steady_clock::now().time_since_epoch()).count();
  // run something
  uint64_t end = duration_cast<nanoseconds>
      (steady_clock::now().time_since_epoch()).count();
  uint64_t delta = end - start;
  return delta;
}
```

Listing 2 Using __rdtsc compiler builtins to access TSC

```
#include <x86intrin.h>
#include <cstdint>

// returns the number of elapsed reference clocks
uint64_t timeWithTSC() {
    uint64_t start = __rdtsc();
    // run something
    return __rdtsc() - start;
}
```

Choosing which timer to use is very simple and depends on how long the thing is that you want to measure. If you measure something over a very small time period, TSC will give you better accuracy. Conversely, it's pointless to use the TSC to measure a program that runs for hours. Unless you really need cycle accuracy, the system timer should be enough for a large proportion of cases. It's important to keep in mind that accessing system timer usually has higher latency than accessing TSC. Making a `clock_gettime` system call can be easily ten times slower than executing RDTSC instruction, which takes 20+ CPU cycles. This may become important for minimizing measurement overhead, especially in the production environment. Performance comparison of different APIs for accessing timers on various platforms is available on wiki page[46] of CppPerformanceBenchmarks repository.

pthread_getcpuclockid system call.

[46] CppPerformanceBenchmarks wiki - https://gitlab.com/chriscox/CppPerfo

36

2.6 Microbenchmarks

It's possible to write a self-contained microbenchmark for quickly testing some hypotheses. Usually, microbenchmarks are used to track progress while optimizing some particular functionality. Nearly all modern languages have benchmarking frameworks, for C++ use the Google benchmark[47] library, C# has BenchmarkDotNet[48] library, Julia has the BenchmarkTools[49] package, Java has JMH[50] (Java Microbenchmark Harness), etc.

When writing microbenchmarks, it's very important to ensure that the scenario you want to test is actually executed by your microbenchmark at runtime. Optimizing compilers can eliminate important code that could make the experiment useless, or even worse, drive you to the wrong conclusion. In the example below, modern compilers are likely to eliminate the whole loop:

```
// foo DOES NOT benchmark string creation
void foo() {
  for (int i = 0; i < 1000; i++)
    std::string s("hi");
}
```

A simple way to test this is to check the profile of the benchmark and see if the intended code stands out as the hotspot. Sometimes abnormal timings can be spotted instantly, so use common sense while analyzing and comparing benchmark runs. One of the popular ways to keep the compiler from optimizing away important code is to use `DoNotOptimize`-like[51] helper functions, which do the necessary inline assembly magic under the hood:

```
// foo benchmarks string creation
void foo() {
  for (int i = 0; i < 1000; i++) {
    std::string s("hi");
    DoNotOptimize(s);
  }
}
```

---

rmanceBenchmarks/-/wikis/ClockTimeAnalysis
 [47] Google benchmark library - https://github.com/google/benchmark
 [48] BenchmarkDotNet - https://github.com/dotnet/BenchmarkDotNet
 [49] Julia BenchmarkTools - https://github.com/JuliaCI/BenchmarkTools.jl
 [50] Java Microbenchmark Harness - http://openjdk.java.net/projects/code-tools/jmh/etc
 [51] For JMH, this is known as the `Blackhole.consume()`.

If written well, microbenchmarks can be a good source of performance data. They are often used for comparing the performance of different implementations of a critical function. What defines a good benchmark is whether it tests performance in realistic conditions in which functionality will be used. If a benchmark uses synthetic input that is different from what will be given in practice, then the benchmark will likely mislead you and will drive you to the wrong conclusions. Besides that, when a benchmark runs on a system free from other demanding processes, it has all resources available to it, including DRAM and cache space. Such a benchmark will likely champion the faster version of the function even if it consumes more memory than the other version. However, the outcome can be the opposite if there are neighbor processes that consume a significant part of DRAM, which causes memory regions that belong to the benchmark process to be swapped to the disk.

For the same reason, be careful when concluding results obtained from unit-testing a function. Modern unit-testing frameworks[52] provide the duration of each test. However, this information cannot substitute a carefully written benchmark that tests the function in practical conditions using realistic input (see more in [Fog, 2004, chapter 16.2]). It is not always possible to replicate the exact input and environment as it will be in practice, but it is something developers should take into account when writing a good benchmark.

2.7 Chapter Summary

- Debugging performance issues is usually harder than debugging functional bugs due to measurement instability.
- You can never stop optimizing unless you set a particular goal. To know if you reached the desired goal, you need to come up with meaningful definitions and metrics for how you will measure that. Depending on what you care about, it could be throughput, latency, operations per second (roofline performance), etc.
- Modern systems have non-deterministic performance. Eliminating non-determinism in a system is helpful for well-defined, stable performance tests, e.g., microbenchmarks. Measuring performance in production deployment requires dealing with a noisy environment by using statistical methods for analyzing

---

[52] For instance, GoogleTest (https://github.com/google/googletest).

results.
- More and more often, vendors of large distributed SW choose to profile and monitor performance directly on production systems, which requires using only light-weight profiling techniques.
- It is very beneficial to employ an automated performance tracking system for preventing performance regressions from leaking into production software. Such CI systems are supposed to run automated performance tests, visualize results, and flag potential defects.
- Visualizing performance distributions may help to discover performance anomalies. It is also a safe way of presenting performance results to a wide audience.
- Statistical relationship between performance distributions is identified using Hypothesis Testing methods, e.g., Student's T-test. Once it's determined that the difference is statistically significant, then the speedup can be calculated as a ratio between the means or geometric means.
- It's OK to discard cold runs in order to ensure that everything is running hot, but do not deliberately discard unwanted data. If you choose to discard some samples, do it uniformly for all distributions.
- To benchmark execution time, engineers can use two different timers, which all the modern platforms provide. The system-wide high-resolution timer is suitable for measuring events whose duration is more than a microsecond. For measuring short events with high accuracy, use Time Stamp Counter.
- Microbenchmarks are good for proving something quickly, but you should always verify your ideas on a real application in practical conditions. Make sure that you are benchmarking the meaningful code by checking performance profiles.

3 CPU Microarchitecture

This chapter provides a brief summary of the critical CPU architecture and microarchitecture features that impact performance. The goal of this chapter is not to cover the details and trade-offs of CPU architectures, covered extensively in the literature [Hennessy and Patterson, 2011]. We will provide a quick recap of the CPU hardware features that have a direct impact on software performance.

3.1 Instruction Set Architecture

The instruction set is the vocabulary used by software to communicate with the hardware. The instruction set architecture (ISA) defines the contract between the software and the hardware. Intel x86, ARM v8, RISC-V are examples of current-day ISA that are most widely deployed. All of these are 64-bit architectures, i.e., all address computation uses 64-bit. ISA developers and CPU architects typically ensure that software or firmware that conforms to the specification will execute on any processor built using the specification. Widely deployed ISA franchises also typically ensure backward compatibility such that code written for the GenX version of a processor will continue to execute on GenX+i.

Most modern architectures can be classified as general purpose register-based, load-store architectures where the operands are explicitly specified, and memory is accessed only using load and store instructions. In addition to providing the basic functions in the ISA such as load, store, control, scalar arithmetic operations using integers and floating-point, the widely deployed architectures continue to enhance their ISA to support new computing paradigms. These include enhanced vector processing instructions (e.g., Intel AVX2, AVX512, ARM SVE) and matrix/tensor instructions (Intel AMX). Software mapped to use these advanced instructions typically provide orders of magnitude improvement in performance.

Modern CPUs support 32b and 64b precision for arithmetic operations. With the fast-evolving field of deep learning, the industry has a renewed interest in alternate numeric formats for variables to drive significant performance improvements. Research has shown that deep learning models perform just as good, using fewer bits to represent the variables, saving on both compute and memory bandwidth. As a result, several CPU franchises have recently added support for lower precision data types such as 8bit integers (int8, e.g., Intel VNNI), 16b floating-point (fp16, bf16) in the ISA, in addition to the traditional 32-bit and 64-bit formats for arithmetic operations.

3.2 Pipelining

Overlapping of instructions during execution

Pipelining is the foundational technique used to make CPUs fast wherein multiple instructions are overlapped during their execution. Pipelining in CPUs drew inspiration from the automotive assembly lines. The processing of instructions is divided into stages. The stages operate in parallel, working on different parts of different instructions. DLX is an example of a simple 5-stage pipeline defined by [Hennessy and Patterson, 2011] and consists of:

1. Instruction fetch (IF)
2. Instruction decode (ID)
3. Execute (EXE)
4. Memory access (MEM)
5. Write back (WB) ⇒ *this needs to be in order*

Instruction	Clock cycle								
	1	2	3	4	5	6	7	8	9
Instruction x	IF	ID	EXE	MEM	WB				
Instruction x+1		IF	ID	EXE	MEM	WB			
Instruction x+2			IF	ID	EXE	MEM	WB		
Instruction x+3				IF	ID	EXE	MEM	WB	
Instruction x+4					IF	ID	EXE	MEM	WB

Figure 7: Simple 5-stage pipeline diagram.

Figure 7 shows an ideal pipeline view of the 5-stage pipeline CPU. In cycle 1, instruction x enters the IF stage of the pipeline. In the next cycle, as instruction x moves to the ID stage, the next instruction in the program enters the IF stage, and so on. Once the pipeline is full, as in cycle 5 above, all pipeline stages of the CPU are busy working on different instructions. Without pipelining, instruction x+1 couldn't start its execution until instruction x finishes its work.

Most modern CPUs are deeply pipelined, aka super pipelined. The throughput of a pipelined CPU is defined as the number of instructions that complete and exit the pipeline per unit of time. The latency for any given instruction is the total time through all the stages of the pipeline. Since all the stages of the pipeline are linked together, each stage must be ready to move to the next instruction in lockstep. The time required to move an instruction from one stage to the other defines the basic machine cycle or clock for the CPU. The value chosen for the clock for a given pipeline is defined by the slowest stage of the pipeline. CPU hardware designers strive to balance the amount of work that can be done in a stage as this directly defines the frequency of operation of the CPU. Increasing the frequency improves performance and typically involves balancing and re-pipelining to eliminate bottlenecks caused by the slowest pipeline stages.

In an ideal pipeline that is perfectly balanced and doesn't incur any stalls, the time per instruction in the pipelined machine is given by

$$\text{Time per instruction (pipelined)} = \frac{\text{Time per instruction (nonpipelined)}}{\text{Number of pipe stages}}$$

In real implementations, pipelining introduces several constraints that limit the ideal model shown above. Pipeline hazards prevent the ideal pipeline behavior resulting in stalls. The three classes of hazards are structural hazards, data hazards, and control hazards. Luckily for the programmer, in modern CPUs, all classes of hazards are handled by the hardware.

- **Structural hazards** are caused by resource conflicts. To a large extent, they could be eliminated by replicating the hardware resources, such as using multi-ported registers or memories. However, eliminating all such hazards could potentially become quite expensive in terms of silicon area and power.

- **Data hazards** are caused by data dependencies in the program and are classified into three types:

    Read-after-write (RAW) hazard requires dependent read to execute after write. It occurs when an instruction x+1 reads a source before a previous instruction x writes to the source, resulting in the wrong value being read. CPUs implement data forwarding from a later stage of the pipeline to an earlier stage (called "*bypassing*") to mitigate the penalty associated with the RAW hazard. The idea is that results from instruction x can be forwarded to instruction x+1 before instruction x is fully completed. If we take a look at the example:

3.2 Pipelining

```
R1 = R0 ADD 1
R2 = R1 ADD 2
```
(handwritten: forwarding the result / bypassing)

There is a RAW dependency for register R1. If we take the value directly after addition R0 ADD 1 is done (from the EXE pipeline stage), we don't need to wait until the WB stage finishes, and the value will be written to the register file. Bypassing helps to save a few cycles. The longer the pipeline, the more effective bypassing becomes.

Write-after-read (WAR) hazard requires dependent write to execute after read. It occurs when an instruction x+1 writes a source before a previous instruction x reads the source, resulting in the wrong new value being read. WAR hazard is not a true dependency and is eliminated by a technique called register renaming[53]. It is a technique that abstracts logical registers from physical registers. CPUs support register renaming by keeping a large number of physical registers. Logical (architectural) registers, the ones that are defined by the ISA, are just aliases over a wider register file. With such decoupling of architectural state[54], solving WAR hazards is simple; we just need to use a different physical register for the write operation. For example:

```
R1 = R0 ADD 1
R0 = R2 ADD 2
```
(handwritten: rename R0 register from here)

There is a WAR dependency for register R0. Since we have a large pool of physical registers, we can simply rename all the occurrences of R0 register starting from the write operation and below. Once we eliminated WAR hazard by renaming register R0, we can safely execute the two operations in any order.

Write-after-write (WAW) hazard requires dependent write to execute after write. It occurs when instruction x+1 writes a source before instruction x writes to the source, resulting in the wrong order of writes. WAW hazards are also eliminated by register renaming, allowing both writes to execute in any order while preserving the correct final result.

- **Control hazards** are caused due to changes in the program flow. They arise from pipelining branches and other instructions that change the program flow. The branch condition that

---

[53] Register renaming - https://en.wikipedia.org/wiki/Register_renaming.
[54] Architectural state - https://en.wikipedia.org/wiki/Architectural_state.

determines the direction of the branch (taken vs. not-taken) is resolved in the execute pipeline stage. As a result, the fetch of the next instruction cannot be pipelined unless the control hazard is eliminated. Techniques such as dynamic branch prediction and speculative execution described in the next section are used to overcome control hazards.

3.3 Exploiting Instruction Level Parallelism (ILP)

Most instructions in a program lend themselves to be pipelined and executed in parallel, as they are independent. Modern CPUs implement a large menu of additional hardware features to exploit such instruction-level parallelism (ILP). Working in concert with advanced compiler techniques, these hardware features provide significant performance improvements.

3.3.1 OOO Execution

The pipeline example in Figure 7 shows all instructions moving through the different stages of the pipeline in-order, i.e., in the same order as they appear in the program. Most modern CPUs support out-of-order (OOO) execution, i.e., sequential instructions can enter the execution pipeline stage in any arbitrary order only limited by their dependencies. OOO execution CPUs must still give the same result as if all instructions were executed in the program order. An instruction is called *retired* when it is finally executed, and its results are correct and visible in the architectural state. To ensure correctness, CPUs must retire all instructions in the program order. OOO is primarily used to avoid underutilization of CPU resources due to stalls caused by dependencies, especially in superscalar engines described in the next section.

Dynamic scheduling of these instructions is enabled by sophisticated hardware structures such as scoreboards and techniques such as register renaming to reduce data hazards. Tomasulo algorithm[55] implemented in the IBM360 and Scoreboading[56] implemented in the CDC6600 in the 1960s are pioneering efforts to support dynamic scheduling and out-of-order execution that have influenced all modern CPU architectures. The scoreboard hardware is used to schedule the

---
[55] Tomasulo algorithm - https://en.wikipedia.org/wiki/Tomasulo_algorithm.
[56] Scoreboarding - https://en.wikipedia.org/wiki/Scoreboarding.

in-order retirement and all machine state updates. It keeps track of data dependencies of every instruction and where in the pipe the data is available. Most implementations strive to balance the hardware cost with the potential return. Typically, the size of the scoreboard determines how far ahead the hardware can look for scheduling such independent instructions.

Instruction	Clock cycle									
	1	2	3	4	5	6	7	8	9	10
Instruction x	IF	ID	EXE	MEM	WB					
Instruction x+1		IF	ID			EXE	MEM	WB		
Instruction x+2			IF	ID	EXE	MEM			WB	
Instruction x+3				IF	ID			EXE	MEM	WB

Figure 8: The concept of Out-Of-Order execution.

Figure 8 details the concept underlying out-of-order execution with an example. Assume instruction x+1 cannot execute in cycles 4 and 5 due to some conflict. An in-order CPU would stall all subsequent instructions from entering the EXE pipeline stage. In an OOO CPU, subsequent instructions that do not have any conflicts (e.g., instruction x+2) can enter and complete its execution. All instructions still retire in order, i.e., the instructions complete the WB stage in the program order.

3.3.2 Superscalar Engines and VLIW

Most modern CPUs are superscalar i.e., they can issue more than one instruction in a given cycle. Issue-width is the maximum number of instructions that can be issued during the same cycle. Typical issue-width of current generation CPUs ranges from 2-6. To ensure the right balance, such superscalar engines also support more than one execution unit and/or pipelined execution units. CPUs also combine superscalar capability with deep pipelines and out-of-order execution to extract the maximum ILP for a given piece of software.

Figure 9 shows an example CPU that supports 2-wide issue width, i.e., in each cycle, two instructions are processed in each stage of the pipeline. Superscalar CPUs typically support multiple, independent execution units to keep the instructions in the pipeline flowing through without conflicts. Replicated execution units increase the throughput

3.3 Exploiting Instruction Level Parallelism (ILP)

Instruction	Clock cycle					
	1	2	3	4	5	6
Instruction x	IF	ID	EXE	MEM	WB	
Instruction x+1	IF	ID	EXE	MEM	WB	
Instruction x+2		IF	ID	EXE	MEM	WB
Instruction x+3		IF	ID	EXE	MEM	WB

Figure 9: The pipeline diagram for a simple 2-way superscalar CPU.

of the machine in contrast with simple pipelined processors shown in figure 7.

Architectures such as the Intel Itanium moved the burden of scheduling a superscalar, multi-execution unit machine from the hardware to the compiler using a technique known as VLIW - Very Long Instruction Word. The rationale is to simplify the hardware by requiring the compiler to choose the right mix of instructions to keep the machine fully utilized. Compilers can use techniques such as software pipelining, loop unrolling, etc. to look further ahead than can be reasonably supported by hardware structures to find the right ILP.

3.3.3 Speculative Execution   *to cope with control hazard*

As noted in the previous section, control hazards can cause significant performance loss in a pipeline if instructions are stalled until the branch condition is resolved. One technique to avoid this performance loss is hardware branch prediction logic to predict the likely direction of branches and allow executing instructions from the predicted path (speculative execution).

Let's consider a short code example in Listing 3. For a processor to understand which function it should execute next, it should know whether the condition a < b is false or true. Without knowing that, the CPU waits until the result of the branch instruction will be determined, as shown in figure 10a.

With speculative execution, the CPU takes a guess on an outcome of the branch and initiates processing instructions from the chosen path. Suppose a processor predicted that condition a < b will be evaluated as true. It proceeded without waiting for the branch outcome and speculatively called function foo (see figure 10b, speculative work is marked with *). State changes to the machine cannot be committed

Listing 3 Speculative execution

```
if (a < b)
  foo();
else
  bar();
```

Instruction	Clock cycle							
	1	2	3	4	5	6	7	8
BRANCH (a < b)	IF	ID	EXE	MEM	WB			
CALL foo				IF	ID	EXE	MEM	WB
// INSTR from foo					IF	ID	EXE	MEM

(a) No speculation

Instruction	Clock cycle						
	1	2	3	4	5	6	7
BRANCH (a < b)	IF	ID	EXE	MEM	WB		
CALL foo		IF*	ID*	EXE	MEM	WB	
// INSTR from foo			IF*	ID	EXE	MEM	WB

(b) Speculative execution

Figure 10: The concept of speculative execution.

until the condition is resolved to ensure that the architecture state of the machine is never impacted by speculatively executing instructions. In the example above, the branch instruction compares two scalar values, which is fast. But in reality, a branch instruction can be dependent on a value loaded from memory, which can take hundreds of cycles. If the prediction turns out to be correct, it saves a lot of cycles. However, sometimes the prediction is incorrect, and the function `bar` should be called instead. In such a case, the results from the speculative execution must be squashed and thrown away. This is called the branch misprediction penalty, which we discuss in section 4.8.

To track the progress of speculation, the CPU supports a structure called the reorder buffer (ROB). The ROB maintains the status of all instruction execution and retires instructions in-order. Results from speculative execution are written to the ROB and are committed to the architecture registers, in the same order as the program flow and only if the speculation is correct. CPUs can also combine speculative

Results from speculative execution are written in ReOrder Buffer and committed to architecture registers execution with out-of-order execution and use the ROB to track both speculation and out-of-order execution.

3.4 Exploiting Thread Level Parallelism

Techniques described previously rely on the available parallelism in a program to speed up execution. In addition, CPUs support techniques to exploit parallelism across processes and/or threads executing on the CPU. A hardware multi-threaded CPU supports dedicated hardware resources to track the state (aka context) of each thread independently in the CPU instead of tracking the state for only a single executing thread or process. The main motivation for such a multi-threaded CPU is to switch from one context to another with the smallest latency (without incurring the cost of saving and restoring thread context) when a thread is blocked due to a long latency activity such as memory references.

3.4.1 Simultaneous Multithreading

Modern CPUs combine ILP techniques and multi-threading by supporting simultaneous multi-threading to eke out the most efficiency from the available hardware resources. Instructions from multiple threads execute concurrently in the same cycle. Dispatching instructions simultaneously from multiple threads increases the probability of utilizing the available superscalar resources, improving the overall performance of the CPU. In order to support SMT, the CPU must replicate hardware to store the thread state (program counter, registers). Resources to track OOO and speculative execution can either be replicated or partitioned across threads. Typically cache resources are dynamically shared amongst the hardware threads. Modern multi-threaded CPUs support either two threads (SMT2) or four threads (SMT4).

3.5 Memory Hierarchy

In order to effectively utilize all the hardware resources provisioned in the CPU, the machine needs to be fed with the right data at the right time. Understanding the memory hierarchy is critically important to deliver on the performance capabilities of a CPU. Most programs exhibit the property of locality; they don't access all code or data uniformly. A CPU memory hierarchy is built on two fundamental properties:

48

3.5 Memory Hierarchy

- **Temporal locality**: when a given memory location was accessed, it is likely that the same location is accessed again in the near future. Ideally, we want this information to be in the cache next time we need it.
- **Spatial locality**: when a given memory location was accessed, it is likely that nearby locations are accessed in the near future. This refers to placing related data close to each other. When the program reads a single byte from memory, typically, a larger chunk of memory (cache line) is fetched because very often, the program will require that data soon.

This section provides a summary of the key attributes of memory hierarchy systems supported on modern CPUs.

3.5.1 Cache Hierarchy

Cache reserved for 1. code, 2. data
i-cache / d-cache, a unified

A cache is the first level of the memory hierarchy for any request (for code or data) issued from the CPU pipeline. Ideally, the pipeline performs best with an infinite cache with the smallest access latency. In reality, the access time for any cache increases as a function of the size. Therefore, the cache is organized as a hierarchy of small, fast storage blocks closest to the execution units, backed up by larger, slower blocks. A particular level of the cache hierarchy can be used exclusively for code (instruction cache, i-cache) or for data (data cache, d-cache), or shared between code and data (unified cache). Furthermore, some levels of the hierarchy can be private to a particular CPU, while other levels can be shared among CPUs.

Caches are organized as blocks with a defined block size (**cache line**). The typical cache line size in modern CPUs is 64 bytes. Caches closest to the execution pipeline typically range in size from 8KiB to 32KiB. Caches further out in the hierarchy can be 64KiB to 16MiB in modern CPUs. The architecture for any level of a cache is defined by the following four attributes.

3.5.1.1 Placement of data within the cache.
The address for a request is used to access the cache. In direct-mapped caches, a given block address can appear only in one location in the cache and is defined by a mapping function shown below.

$$\text{Number of Blocks in the Cache} = \frac{\text{Cache Size}}{\text{Cache Block Size}}$$

Number of cache lines

CACHE LINE: 64 bytes

8K - 32K → L1 1000 uint-64 → 4000
64K - 16MB → 8000 uint → 2,000,000

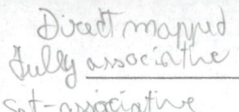

3.5 Memory Hierarchy

Direct mapped location =(block address) mod
(Number of Blocks in the Cache)

In a fully associative cache, a given block can be placed in any location in the cache.

An intermediate option between the direct mapping and fully associative mapping is a set-associative mapping. In such a cache, the blocks are organized as sets, typically each set containing 2,4 or 8 blocks. A given address is first mapped to a set. Within a set, the address can be placed anywhere, among the blocks in that set. A cache with m blocks per set is described as an m-way set-associative cache. The formulas for a set-associative cache are:

$$\text{Number of Sets in the Cache} = \frac{\text{Number of Blocks in the Cache}}{\text{Number of Blocks per Set (associativity)}}$$

Set (m-way) associative location =(block address) mod
(Number of Sets in the Cache)

3.5.1.2 Finding data in the cache.

Every block in the m-way set-associative cache has an address tag associated with it. In addition, the tag also contains state bits such as valid bits to indicate whether the data is valid. Tags can also contain additional bits to indicate access information, sharing information, etc. that will be described in later sections.

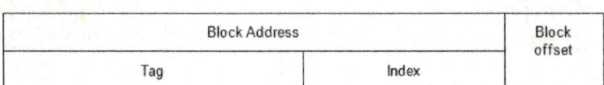

Figure 11: Address organization for cache lookup.

The figure 11 shows how the address generated from the pipeline is used to check the caches. The lowest order address bits define the offset within a given block; the block offset bits (5 bits for 32-byte cache lines, 6 bits for 64-byte cache lines). The set is selected using the index bits based on the formulas described above. Once the set is selected, the tag bits are used to compare against all the tags in that set. If one of the tags matches the tag of the incoming request and the valid bit is set, a cache hit results. The data associated with that block entry (read out of the data array of the cache in parallel to the tag lookup) is provided to the execution pipeline. A cache miss occurs in cases where the tag is not a match.

3.5.1.3 Managing misses.

When a cache miss occurs, the controller must select a block in the cache to be replaced to allocate the address that incurred the miss. For a direct-mapped cache, since the new address can be allocated only in a single location, the previous entry mapping to that location is deallocated, and the new entry is installed in its place. In a set-associative cache, since the new cache block can be placed in any of the blocks of the set, a replacement algorithm is required. The typical replacement algorithm used is the LRU (least recently used) policy, where the block that was least recently accessed is evicted to make room for the miss address. Another alternative is to randomly select one of the blocks as the victim block. Most CPUs define these capabilities in hardware, making it easier for executing software.

3.5.1.4 Managing writes.

Read accesses to caches are the most common case as programs typically read instructions, and data reads are larger than data writes. Handling writes in caches is harder, and CPU implementations use various techniques to handle this complexity. Software developers should pay special attention to the various write caching flows supported by the hardware to ensure the best performance of their code.

CPU designs use two basic mechanisms to handle writes that hit in the cache:

- In a write-through cache, hit data is written to both the block in the cache and to the next lower level of the hierarchy.
- In a write-back cache, hit data is only written to the cache. Subsequently, lower levels of the hierarchy contain stale data. The state of the modified line is tracked through a dirty bit in the tag. When a modified cache line is eventually evicted from the cache, a write-back operation forces the data to be written back to the next lower level.

Cache misses on write operations can be handled in two ways:

- In a *write-allocate or fetch on write miss* cache, the data for the missed location is loaded into the cache from the lower level of the hierarchy, and the write operation is subsequently handled like a write hit.
- If the cache uses a *no-write-allocate policy*, the cache miss transaction is sent directly to the lower levels of the hierarchy, and the block is not loaded into the cache.

3.5 Memory Hierarchy

Out of these options, most designs typically choose to implement a write-back cache with a write-allocate policy as both of these techniques try to convert subsequent write transactions into cache-hits, without additional traffic to the lower levels of the hierarchy. Write through caches typically use the no-write-allocate policy.

3.5.1.5 Other cache optimization techniques. For a programmer, understanding the behavior of the cache hierarchy is critical to extract performance from any application. This is especially true when CPU clock frequencies increase while the memory technology speeds lag behind. From the perspective of the pipeline, the latency to access any request is given by the following formula that can be applied recursively to all the levels of the cache hierarchy up to the main memory:

Average Access Latency = Hit Time + Miss Rate × Miss Penalty

Hardware designers take on the challenge of reducing the hit time and miss penalty through many novel micro-architecture techniques. Fundamentally, cache misses stall the pipeline and hurt performance. The miss rate for any cache is highly dependent on the cache architecture (block size, associativity) and the software running on the machine. As a result, optimizing the miss rate becomes a hardware-software co-design effort. As described in the previous sections, CPUs provide optimal hardware organization for the caches. Additional techniques that can be implemented both in hardware and software to minimize cache miss rates are described below.

3.5.1.5.1 HW and SW Prefetching. One method to reduce a cache miss and the subsequent stall is to prefetch instructions as well as data into different levels of the cache hierarchy prior to when the pipeline demands. The assumption is the time to handle the miss penalty can be mostly hidden if the prefetch request is issued sufficiently ahead in the pipeline. Most CPUs support implicit hardware-based prefetching that is complemented by explicit software prefetching that programmers can control.

Hardware prefetchers observe the behavior of a running application and initiate prefetching on repetitive patterns of cache misses. Hardware prefetching can automatically adapt to the dynamic behavior of the application, such as varying data sets, and does not require support from an optimizing compiler or profiling support. Also, the hardware prefetching works without the overhead of additional address-generation and prefetch instructions. However, hardware prefetching is limited to learning and prefetching for a limited set of cache-miss patterns that are implemented in hardware.

Software memory prefetching complements the one done by the HW. Developers can specify which memory locations are needed ahead of time via dedicated HW instruction (see section 8.1.2). Compilers can also automatically add prefetch instructions into the code to request data before it is required. Prefetch techniques need to balance between demand and prefetch requests to guard against prefetch traffic slowing down demand traffic.

3.5.2 Main Memory

Main memory is the next level of the hierarchy, downstream from the caches. Main memory uses DRAM (dynamic RAM) technology that supports large capacities at reasonable cost points. The main memory is described by three main attributes - latency, bandwidth, and capacity. Latency is typically specified by two components. Memory access time is the time elapsed between the request to when the data word is available. Memory cycle time defines the minimum time required between two consecutive accesses to the memory.

DDR (double data rate) DRAM technology is the predominant DRAM technology supported by most CPUs. Historically, DRAM bandwidths have improved every generation while the DRAM latencies have stayed the same or even increased. The table 2 shows the top data rate and the corresponding latency for the last three generations of DDR technologies. The data rate is measured as a million transfers per sec (MT/s). The latencies shown in this table correspond to the latency in the DRAM device itself. Typically, the latencies as seen from the CPU pipeline (cache miss on a load to use) are higher (in the 70ns-150ns range) due to additional latencies and queuing delays incurred in the cache controllers, memory controllers, and on-die interconnects.

Table 2: The top data rate and the corresponding latency for the last three generations of DDR technologies.

DDR Generation	Highest Data Rate (MT/s)	Typical Read Latency (ns)
DDR3	2133	10.3
DDR4	3200	12.5
DDR5	6400	14

New DRAM technologies such as GDDR (Graphics DDR) and HBM (High Bandwidth Memory) are used by custom processors that require higher bandwidth, not supported by DDR interfaces.

Modern CPUs support multiple, independent channels of DDR DRAM memory. Typically, each channel of memory is either 32-bit or 64-bit wide.

3.6 Virtual Memory

Virtual memory is the mechanism to share the physical memory attached to a CPU with all the processes executing on the CPU. Virtual memory provides a protection mechanism, restricting access to the memory allocated to a given process from other processes. Virtual memory also provides relocation, the ability to load a program anywhere in physical memory without changing the addressing in the program.

In a CPU that supports virtual memory, programs use virtual addresses for their accesses. These virtual addresses are translated to a physical address by dedicated hardware tables that provide a mapping between virtual addresses and physical addresses. These tables are referred to as page tables. The address translation mechanism is shown below. The virtual address is split into two parts. The virtual page number is used to index into the page table (the page table can either be a single level or nested) to produce a mapping between the virtual page number and the corresponding physical page. The page offset from the virtual address is then used to access the physical memory location at the same offset in the mapped physical page. A page fault results if a requested page is not in the main memory. The operating system is responsible for providing hints to the hardware

PAGE TABLE IS to translate from virtual address to physical address

to handle page faults such that one of the least recently used pages can be swapped out to make space for the new page.

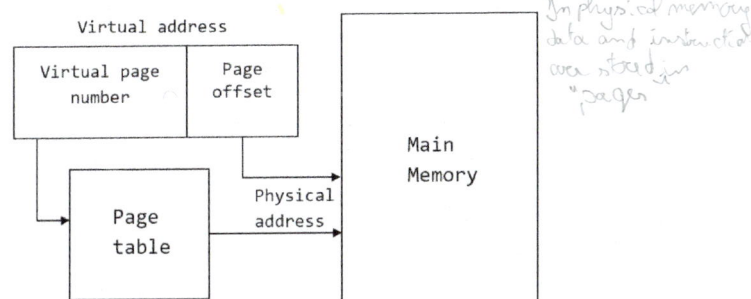

In physical memory data and instructions are stored in "pages"

Figure 12: Address organization for cache lookup.

CPUs typically use a hierarchical page table format to map virtual address bits efficiently to the available physical memory. A page miss in such a system would be expensive, requiring traversing through the hierarchy. To reduce the address translation time, CPUs support a hardware structure called translation lookaside buffer (TLB) to cache the most recently used translations.

TLB is a hardware cache of the most recent translations

3.7 SIMD Multiprocessors

Another variant of multiprocessing that is widely used for certain workloads is referred to as SIMD (Single Instruction, Multiple Data) multiprocessors, in contrast to the MIMD approach described in the previous section. As the name indicates, in SIMD processors, a single instruction typically operates on many data elements in a single cycle using many independent functional units. Scientific computations on vectors and matrices lend themselves well to SIMD architectures as every element of a vector or matrix needs to be processed using the same instruction. SIMD multiprocessors are used primarily for such special purpose tasks that are data-parallel and require only a limited set of functions and operations.

Figure 13 shows scalar and SIMD execution modes for the code listed in Listing 4. In a traditional SISD (Single Instruction, Single Data) mode, addition operation is separately applied to each element of array a and b. However, in SIMD mode, addition is applied to multiple elements at the same time. SIMD CPUs support execution units that

TLB: cache of translation from virtual addresses to physical addresses

2^{32} = 4GB
2^{16} = 65536
2^{12} = 4096 → 4K = $2^8 \cdot 2^4$ = 16

are capable of performing different operations on vector elements. The data elements themselves can be either integers or floating-point numbers. SIMD architecture allows more efficient processing of a large amount of data and works best for data-parallel applications that involve vector operations.

Listing 4 SIMD execution

```
double *a, *b, *c;
for (int i = 0; i < N; ++i) {
  c[i] = a[i] + b[i];
}
```

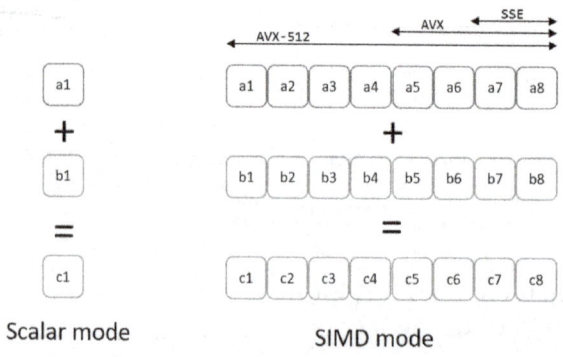

Figure 13: Example of scalar and SIMD operations.

Most of the popular CPU architectures feature vector instructions, including x86, PowerPC, ARM, and RISC-V. In 1996 Intel released a new instruction set, MMX, which was a SIMD instruction set that was designed for multimedia applications. Following MMX, Intel introduced new instruction sets with added capabilities and increased vector size: SSE, AVX, AVX2, AVX512. As soon as the new instruction sets became available, work began to make them usable to software engineers. At first, the new SIMD instructions were programmed in assembly. Later, special compiler intrinsics were introduced. Today all of the major compilers support vectorization for the popular processors.

3.8 Modern CPU design

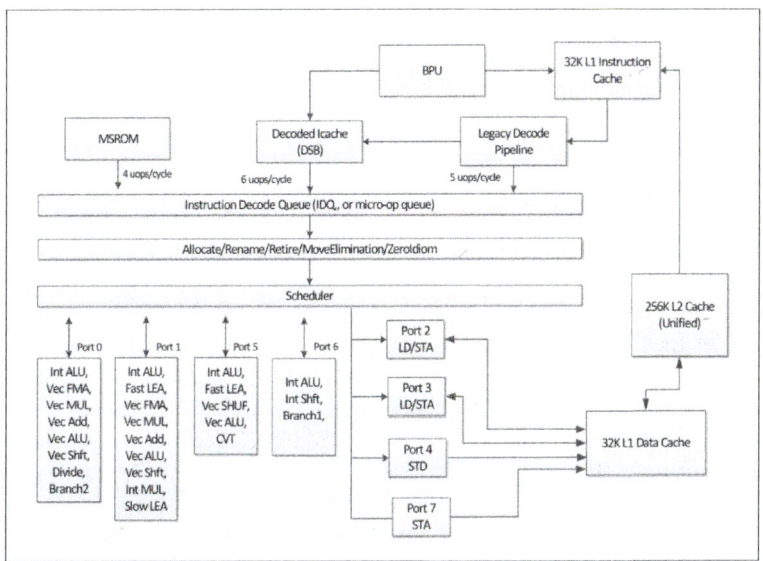

Figure 14: Block diagram of a CPU Core in the Intel Skylake Microarchitecture. © *Image from [Int, 2020]*.

3.8 Modern CPU design

The block diagram in figure 14 shows the details of Intel's 6th generation core, Skylake, that was announced in 2015 and is widely spread all over the world. The Skylake core is split into an in-order front-end that fetches and decodes x86 instructions into u-ops and an 8-way superscalar, out-of-order backend.

The core supports 2-way SMT. It has a 32KB, 8-way first-level instruction cache (L1 I-cache), and a 32KB, 8-way first-level data cache (L1 D-cache). The L1 caches are backed up by a unified 1MB second-level cache, the L2 cache. The L1 and L2 caches are private to each core.

3.8.1 CPU Front-End

The CPU Front-End consists of a number of data structures that serve the main goal to efficiently fetch and decode instructions from memory. Its main purpose is to feed prepared instructions to the CPU Back-End, which is responsible for the actual execution of instructions.

The CPU Front-End fetches 16 bytes per cycle of x86 instructions from the L1 I-cache. This is shared among the two threads, so each thread gets 16 bytes every other cycle. These are complex, variable-length x86 instructions. The pre-decode and decode stages of the pipeline convert these complex x86 instructions into micro Ops (UOPs, see section 4.4) that are queued into the Allocation Queue (IDQ).

First, the pre-decode determines and marks the boundaries of the variable instructions by inspecting the instruction. In x86, the instruction length can range from 1-byte to 15-bytes instructions. This stage also identifies branch instructions. The pre-decode stage moves up to 6 instructions (also referred to as Macro Instructions) to the instruction queue that is split between the two threads. The instruction queue also supports a macro-op fusion unit that detects that two macroinstructions can be fused into a single instruction (see section 4.4). This optimization saves bandwidth in the rest of the pipeline.

Up to five pre-decoded instructions are sent from the instruction queue to the decoder every cycle. The two threads share this interface and get access to every other cycle. The 5-way decoder converts the complex macro-Ops into fixed-length UOPs.

A major performance-boosting feature of the front-end is the Decoded Stream Buffer (DSB) or the UOP Cache. The motivation is to cache the macro-ops to UOPs conversion in a separate structure (DSB) that works in parallel with the L1 I-cache. During instruction fetch, the DSB is also checked to see if the UOPs translations are already available in the DSB. Frequently occurring macro-ops will hit in the DSB, and the pipeline will avoid repeating the expensive pre-decode and decode operations for the 16 bytes bundle. The DSB provides six UOPs that match the capacity of the front-end to back-end interface and helps to maintain the balance across the entire core. The DSB works in concert with the BPU, the branch prediction unit. The BPU predicts the direction of all branch instructions and steers the next instruction fetch based on this prediction.

Some very complicated instructions may require more UOPs than decoders can handle. UOPs for such instruction are served from Microcode Sequencer (MSROM). Examples of such instructions include HW operation support for string manipulation, encryption,

3.9 Performance Monitoring Unit

synchronization, and others. Also, MSROM keeps the microcode operations to handle exceptional situations like branch misprediction (which requires pipeline flush), floating-point assist (e.g., when an instruction operates with denormal floating-point value), and others.

The Instruction Decode Queue (IDQ) provides the interface between the in-order front-end and the out-of-order backend. IDQ queues up the UOPs in order. The IDQ has a total of 128 UOPs, 64 UOPs per hardware thread.

3.8.2 CPU Back-End

The CPU Back-End employs an Out-Of-Order engine that executes instructions and stores results.

The heart of the CPU backend is the 224 entry ReOrder buffer (ROB). This unit handles data dependencies. The ROB maps the architecture-visible registers to the physical registers used in the scheduler/reservation station unit. ROB also provides register renaming and tracks speculative execution. ROB entries are always retired in program order.

The Reservation Station/Scheduler (RS) is the structure that tracks the availability of all resources for a given UOP and dispatches the UOP to the assigned port once it is ready. The core is 8-way superscalar. Thus the RS can dispatch up to 8 UOPs per cycle. As shown in figure 14, each dispatch port supports different operations:

- Ports 0, 1, 5, and 6 provide all the integer, FP, and vector ALU. UOPs dispatched to those ports do not require memory operations.
- Ports 2 and 3 are used for address generation and for load operations.
- Port 4 is used for store operations.
- Port 7 is used for address generation.

3.9 Performance Monitoring Unit

Every modern CPU provides means to monitor performance, which are combined into the Performance Monitoring Unit (PMU). It incorporates features that help developers in analyzing the performance of their applications. An example of a PMU in a modern Intel CPU is provided in figure 15. Most modern PMUs have a set of Performance Monitoring Counters (PMC) that can be used to collect various performance events that happen during the execution of a program. Later in section 5.3, we will discuss how PMCs can be used in performance analysis. Also, there could be other features that enhance performance analysis, like LBR, PEBS, and PT, for which entire chapter 6 is devoted.

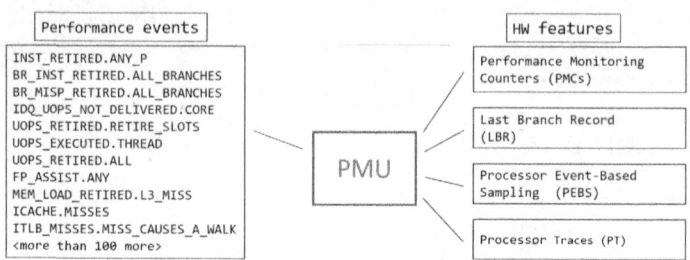

Figure 15: Performance Monitoring Unit of a modern Intel CPU.

As CPU design evolves with every new generation, so do their PMUs. It is possible to determine the version of the PMU in your CPU using the `cpuid` command, as shown on Listing 5.[57] Characteristics of each Intel PMU version, as well as changes to the previous version, can be found in [Int, 2020, Volume 3B, Chapter 18].

Listing 5 Querying your PMU

```
$ cpuid
...
Architecture Performance Monitoring Features (0xa/eax):
      version ID                            = 0x4 (4)
      number of counters per logical processor = 0x4 (4)
      bit width of counter                  = 0x30 (48)
...
Architecture Performance Monitoring Features (0xa/edx):
      number of fixed counters    = 0x3 (3)
      bit width of fixed counters = 0x30 (48)
...
```

3.9.1 Performance Monitoring Counters

If we imagine a simplified view of the processor, it may look something like what is shown in Figure 16. As we discussed earlier in this chapter,

---
[57] The same information can be extracted from the kernel message buffer by using the `dmesg` command.

3.9 Performance Monitoring Unit

a modern CPU has caches, branch predictor, execution pipeline, and other units. When connected to multiple units, a PMC can collect interesting statistics from them. For example, it can count how many clock cycles have passed, how many instructions executed, how many cache misses or branch mispredictions happened during that time, and other performance events.

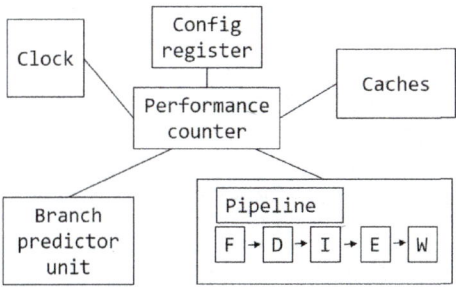

Figure 16: Simplified view of a CPU with a performance monitoring counter.

Typically, PMCs are 48 bit wide, which allows analysis tools to run longer without interrupting the program's execution[58]. Performance counters are HW registers implemented as Model Specific Registers (MSR). That means that the number of counters and their width can vary from model to model, and you can not rely on the same number of counters in your CPU. You should always query that first, using tools like cpuid, for example. PMCs are accessible via the RDMSR and WRMSR instructions, which can only be executed from kernel space.

It is so common that engineers want to count the number of executed instructions and elapsed cycles that the Intel PMU has dedicated PMCs for collecting such events. The Intel PMU has fixed and programmable PMCs. Fixed counters always measure the same thing inside the CPU core. With programmable counters, it's up to the user to choose what they want to measure. Often there are four fully programmable counters and three fixed-function counters per logical core. Fixed counters usually are set to count core clocks, reference clocks, and instructions retired (see section 4 for more details on these metrics).

---

[58] When the value of PMCs overflows, the execution of a program must be interrupted. SW then should save the fact of overflow.

It's not unusual for PMU to have a large number of performance events. Figure 15 shows just a small part of all the performance events available for monitoring on a modern Intel CPU. It's not hard to notice that the number of available PMCs is much smaller than the number of performance events. It's not possible to count all the events at the same time, but analysis tools solve this problem by multiplexing between groups of performance events during the execution of a program (see section 5.3.3).

The complete list of performance events for Intel CPUs can be found in [Int, 2020, Volume 3B, Chapter 19]. For ARM chips, it is not that strictly defined. Vendors implement cores following an ARM architecture, but performance events vary widely, both in what they mean and what events are supported.

4 Terminology and metrics in performance analysis

For a beginner, it can be a very hard time looking into a profile generated by an analysis tool like Linux `perf` and Intel VTune Profiler. Those profiles have lots of complex terms and metrics. This chapter is a gentle introduction to the basic terminology and metrics used in performance analysis.

4.1 Retired vs. Executed Instruction

Modern processors typically execute more instructions than the program flow requires. This happens because some of them are executed speculatively, as discussed in section 3.3.3. For usual instructions, the CPU commits results once they are available, and all preceding instructions are already retired. But for instructions executed speculatively, the CPU keeps their results without immediately committing their results. When the speculation turns out to be correct, the CPU unblocks such instructions and proceeds as normal. But when it comes out that the speculation happens to be wrong, the CPU throws away all the changes done by speculative instructions and does not retire them. So, an instruction processed by the CPU can be executed but not necessarily retired. Taking this into account, we can usually expect the number of executed instructions to be higher than the number of retired instructions.[59]

There is a fixed performance counter (PMC) that collects the number of retired instructions. It can be easily obtained with Linux `perf` by running:

```
$ perf stat -e instructions ./a.exe
  2173414    instructions    #    0.80  insn per cycle
# or just simply do:
$ perf stat ./a.exe
```

---

[59] Usually, a retired instruction has also gone through the execution stage, except those times when it does not require an execution unit. An example of it can be "MOV elimination" and "zero idiom". Read more on easyperf blog: https://easyperf.net/blog/2018/04/22/What-optimizations-you-can-expect-from-CPU. So, theoretically, there could be a case when the number of retired instructions is higher than the number of executed instructions.

4.2 CPU Utilization

CPU utilization is the percentage of time the CPU was busy during some time period. Technically, a CPU is considered utilized when it is not running the kernel `idle` thread.

$$CPU\ Utilization = \frac{CPU\_CLK\_UNHALTED.REF\_TSC}{TSC},$$

where `CPU_CLK_UNHALTED.REF_TSC` PMC counts the number of reference cycles when the core is not in a halt state, `TSC` stands for timestamp counter (discussed in section 2.5), which is always ticking.

If CPU utilization is low, it usually means the poor performance of the application since some portion of the time was wasted by the CPU. However, high CPU utilization is not always good either. It is a sign that the system is doing some work but does not exactly say what it is doing: the CPU might be highly utilized even though it is stalled waiting on memory accesses. In a multithreaded context, a thread can also spin while waiting for resources to proceed, so there is Effective CPU utilization that filters spinning time (see section 11.2).

Linux `perf` automatically calculates CPU utilization across all CPUs on the system:

```
$ perf stat -- a.exe
  0.634874   task-clock (msec)   #   0.773 CPUs utilized
```

4.3 CPI & IPC

Those are two very important metrics that stand for:

- Cycles Per Instruction (CPI) - how many cycles it took to retire one instruction on average.
- Instructions Per Cycle (IPC) - how many instructions were retired per one cycle on average.

$$IPC = \frac{INST\_RETIRED.ANY}{CPU\_CLK\_UNHALTED.THREAD}$$

$$CPI = \frac{1}{IPC},$$

where `INST_RETIRED.ANY` PMC counts the number of retired instructions, `CPU_CLK_UNHALTED.THREAD` counts the number of core cycles while the thread is not in a halt state.

There are many types of analysis that can be done based on those metrics. It is useful for both evaluating HW and SW efficiency. HW engineers use this metric to compare CPU generations and CPUs from different vendors. SW engineers look at IPC and CPI when they optimize their application. Universally, we want to have low CPI and high IPC. Linux `perf` users can get to know IPC for their workload by running:

```
$ perf stat -e cycles,instructions -- a.exe
  2369632    cycles
  1725916    instructions   #    0,73  insn per cycle
# or just simply do:
$ perf stat ./a.exe
```

4.4 UOPs (micro-ops)

Microprocessors with the x86 architecture translate complex CISC-like[60] instructions into simple RISC-like[61] microoperations - abbreviated μops or uops. The main advantage of this is that μops can be executed out of order [Fog, 2012, chapter 2.1]. A simple addition instruction such as `ADD EAX,EBX` generates only one μop, while more complex instruction like `ADD EAX,[MEM1]` may generate two: one for reading from memory into a temporary (un-named) register, and one for adding the contents of the temporary register to `EAX`. The instruction `ADD [MEM1],EAX` may generate three μops: one for reading from memory, one for adding, and one for writing the result back to memory. The relationship between instructions and the way they are split into microoperations can vary across CPU generations[62].

On the opposite of splitting complex CISC-like instructions into RISC-like microoperations (Uops), the latter can also be fused. There are two types of fusion in modern Intel CPUs:

- Microfusion[63] - fuse uops from the same machine instruction. Microfusion can only be applied to two types of combinations:

---

[60] CISC - https://en.wikipedia.org/wiki/Complex_instruction_set_computer.
[61] RISC - https://en.wikipedia.org/wiki/Reduced_instruction_set_computer.
[62] However, for the latest Intel CPUs, the vast majority of instructions operating on registers generate exactly one uop.
[63] UOP Microfusion - https://easyperf.net/blog/2018/02/15/MicroFusion-in-Intel-CPUs.

memory write operations and read-modify operations. For example:

```
# Read the memory location [ESI] and add it to EAX
# Two uops are fused into one at the decoding step.
add     eax, [esi]
```

- Macrofusion[64] - fuse uops from different machine instructions. The decoders can fuse arithmetic or logic instruction with a subsequent conditional jump instruction into a single compute-and-branch µop in certain cases. For example:

```
# Two uops from DEC and JNZ instructions are fused into one
.loop:
  dec rdi
  jnz .loop
```

Both Micro- and Macrofusion save bandwidth in all stages of the pipeline from decoding to retirement. The fused operations share a single entry in the reorder buffer (ROB). The capacity of the ROB is increased when a fused uop uses only one entry. This single ROB entry represents two operations that have to be done by two different execution units. The fused ROB entry is dispatched to two different execution ports but is retired again as a single unit. [Fog, 2012]

Linux `perf` users can collect the number of issued, executed, and retired uops for their workload by running[65]:

```
$ perf stat -e uops_issued.any,uops_executed.thread,uops_retired.all
    -- a.exe
2856278    uops_issued.any
2720241    uops_executed.thread
2557884    uops_retired.all
```

Latency, throughput, port usage, and the number of uops for instructions on recent x86 microarchitectures can be found at uops.info website.

4.5 Pipeline Slot

A pipeline slot represents hardware resources needed to process one uop. Figure 17 demonstrates the execution pipeline of a CPU that

---

[64] UOP Macrofusion - https://easyperf.net/blog/2018/02/23/MacroFusion-in-Intel-CPUs.

[65] `UOPS_RETIRED.ALL` event is not available since Skylake. Use `UOPS_RETIRED.RETIRE_SLOTS`.

can handle four uops every cycle. Nearly all modern x86 CPUs are made with a pipeline width of 4 (4-wide). During six consecutive cycles on the diagram, only half of the available slots were utilized. From a microarchitecture perspective, the efficiency of executing such code is only 50%.

Cycle	1	2	3	4	5	6
Slot1	x	x	x	x		x
Slot2	x	x	x			x
Slot3	x	x	x			
Slot4	x					

Figure 17: Pipeline diagram of a 4-wide CPU.

Pipeline slot is one of the core metrics in Top-Down Microarchitecture Analysis (see section 6.1). For example, Front-End Bound and Back-End Bound metrics are expressed as a percentage of unutilized Pipeline Slots due to various reasons.

4.6 Core vs. Reference Cycles

Most CPUs employ a clock signal to pace their sequential operations. The clock signal is produced by an external generator that provides a consistent number of pulses each second. The frequency of the clock pulses determines the rate at which a CPU executes instructions. Consequently, the faster the clock, the more instructions the CPU will execute each second.

$$Frequency = \frac{Clockticks}{Time}$$

The majority of modern CPUs, including Intel and AMD CPUs, don't have a fixed frequency at which they operate. Instead, they implement dynamic frequency scaling[66]. In Intel's CPUs this technology is called Turbo Boost[67], in AMD's processors it's called Turbo Core[68]. It allows the CPU to increase and decrease its frequency dynamically – scaling the frequency reduces power-consumption at the expense of

---

[66] Dynamic frequency scaling - https://en.wikipedia.org/wiki/Dynamic_frequency_scaling.
[67] Intel Turbo Boost - https://en.wikipedia.org/wiki/Intel_Turbo_Boost.
[68] AMD Turbo Core - https://en.wikipedia.org/wiki/AMD_Turbo_Core.

performance, and scaling the frequency up improves performance but sacrifices power savings.

The core clock cycles counter is counting clock cycles at the actual clock frequency that the CPU core is running at, rather than the external clock (reference cycles). Let's take a look at an experiment on Skylake i7-6000 processor, which has a base frequency of 3.4 GHz:

```
$ perf stat -e cycles,ref-cycles ./a.exe
  43340884632   cycles      # 3.97 GHz
  37028245322   ref-cycles  # 3.39 GHz
     10,899462364 seconds time elapsed
```

Metric `ref-cycles` counts cycles as if there were no frequency scaling. The external clock on the setup has a frequency of 100 MHz, and if we scale it by clock multiplier, we will get the base frequency of the processor. The clock multiplier for Skylake i7-6000 processor equals 34: it means that for every external pulse, the CPU executes 34 internal cycles when it's running on the base frequency.

Metric `"cycles"` counts real CPU cycles, i.e., taking into account frequency scaling. We can also calculate how well the dynamic frequency scaling feature was utilized as:

$$Turbo\ Utilization = \frac{Core\ Cycles}{Reference\ Cycles},$$

The core clock cycle counter is very useful when testing which version of a piece of code is fastest because you can avoid the problem that the clock frequency goes up and down.[Fog, 2004]

4.7 Cache miss

As discussed in section 3.5, any memory request missing in a particular level of cache must be serviced by higher-level caches or DRAM. This implies a significant increase in the latency of such memory access. The typical latency of memory subsystem components is shown in table 3.[69] Performance greatly suffers, especially when a memory request misses in Last Level Cache (LLC) and goes all the way down to the main memory (DRAM). Intel® Memory Latency Checker[70]

---

[69] There is also an interactive view that visualizes the cost of different operations in modern systems: https://colin-scott.github.io/personal_website/research/interactive_latency.html.

[70] Memory Latency Checker - https://www.intel.com/software/mlc.

4.7 Cache miss

(MLC) is a tool used to measure memory latencies and bandwidth and how they change with increasing load on the system. MLC is useful for establishing a baseline for the system under test and for performance analysis.

Table 3: Typical latency of a memory subsystem.

Memory Hierarchy Component	Latency (cycle/time)
L1 Cache	4 cycles (~1 ns)
L2 Cache	10-25 cycles (5-10 ns)
L3 Cache	~40 cycles (20 ns)
Main Memory	200+ cycles (100 ns)

A cache miss might happen both for instructions and data. According to Top-Down Microarchitecture Analysis (see section 6.1), an instruction (I-cache) cache miss is characterized as a Front-End stall, while a data cache (D-cache) miss is characterized as a Back-End stall. When an I-cache miss happens during instruction fetch, it is attributed as a Front-End issue. Consequently, when the data requested by this load is not found in the D-cache, this will be categorized as a Back-End issue.

Linux `perf` users can collect the number of L1-cache misses by running:

```
$ perf stat -e mem_load_retired.fb_hit,mem_load_retired.l1_miss,
  mem_load_retired.l1_hit,mem_inst_retired.all_loads -- a.exe
    29580    mem_load_retired.fb_hit
    19036    mem_load_retired.l1_miss
   497204    mem_load_retired.l1_hit
   546230    mem_inst_retired.all_loads
```

Above is the breakdown of all loads for the L1 data cache. We can see that only 3.5% of all loads miss in the L1 cache. We can further break down L1 data misses and analyze L2 cache behavior by running:

```
$ perf stat -e mem_load_retired.l1_miss,
  mem_load_retired.l2_hit,mem_load_retired.l2_miss -- a.exe
    19521    mem_load_retired.l1_miss
    12360    mem_load_retired.l2_hit
     7188    mem_load_retired.l2_miss
```

From this example, we can see that 37% of loads that missed in the L1 D-cache also missed in the L2 cache. In a similar way, a breakdown for the L3 cache can be made.

4.8 Mispredicted branch

Modern CPUs try to predict the outcome of a branch instruction (taken or not taken). For example, when the processor sees code like this:

```
dec eax
jz .zero
# eax is not 0
...
zero:
# eax is 0
```

Instruction `jz` is a branch instruction, and in order to increase performance, modern CPU architectures try to predict the result of such a branch. This is also called "Speculative Execution". The processor will speculate that, for example, the branch will not be taken and will execute the code that corresponds to the situation when `eax is not 0`. However, if the guess was wrong, this is called "branch misprediction", and the CPU is required to undo all the speculative work that it has done recently. This typically involves a penalty between 10 and 20 clock cycles.

Linux `perf` users can check the number of branch mispredictions by running:

```
$ perf stat -e branches,branch-misses -- a.exe
    358209    branches
     14026    branch-misses   #   3,92% of all branches
# or simply do:
$ perf stat -- a.exe
```

5 Performance Analysis Approaches

When doing high-level optimization, it is usually easy to tell whether the performance was improved or not. When you write a better version of an algorithm, you expect to see a visible difference in the running time of the program. But also, there are situations when you see a change in execution time, but you have no clue where it's coming from. Time alone does not provide any insight into why that happens. In this case, we need more information about how our program executes. That's the situation when we need to do performance analysis to understand the underlying nature of the slowdown or speedup that we observe.

Both HW and SW track performance data while our program is running. In this context, by HW, we mean CPU, which executes the program, and by SW, we mean OS and all the tools enabled for analysis. Typically, the SW stack provides high-level metrics like time, number of context switches, and page-faults, while CPU is capable of observing cache-misses, branch mispredictions, etc. Depending on the problem we are trying to solve, some metrics would be more useful than others. So, it doesn't mean that HW metrics will always give us a more precise overview of the program execution. Some metrics, like the number of context-switches, for instance, cannot be provided by CPU. Performance analysis tools, like Linux perf, can consume data both from OS and CPU.

We will use Linux perf extensively throughout the book as it is one of the most popular performance analysis tools. This tool is available on most Linux distributions, which makes it accessible for a wide range of users. Another reason why the author prefers showcasing Linux perf is that it is open-sourced, which allows us to see the mechanics of what is going on in a typical profiling tool. This is especially useful for learning concepts presented in this book because GUI-based tools, like Intel® VTune™ Profiler, tend to hide all the complexity. More information about Linux perf is available on its wiki page[71].

In this chapter, we will introduce some of the most popular perfor-

---

[71] Linux perf wiki - https://perf.wiki.kernel.org/index.php/Main_Page.

mance analysis techniques: Code Instrumentation, Tracing, Characterization, and Sampling. We also discuss static performance analysis techniques and compiler optimization reports which do not involve running the actual application.

5.1 Code Instrumentation

Probably the first approach for doing performance analysis ever invented is Code Instrumentation. It is a technique that inserts extra code into a program to collect runtime information. Listing 6 shows the simplest example of inserting `printf` statements at the beginning of the function to count the number of times this function was called. I think every programmer in the world did it at some point at least once. This method provides very detailed information when you need specific knowledge about the execution of the program. Code instrumentation allows us to track any information about every variable in the program.

Listing 6 Code Instrumentation

```
int foo(int x) {
  printf("foo is called");
  // function body...
}
```

Instrumentation based profiling methods are mostly used on a macro level, not on the micro(low) level. Using such a method often yields the best insight when optimizing big pieces of code because you can use a top-down approach (instrumenting the main function then drilling down to its callees) of locating performance issues. While code instrumentation is not very helpful in the case of small programs, it gives the most value and insight by letting developers observe the architecture and flow of an application. This technique is especially helpful for someone working with an unfamiliar codebase.

It's also worth mentioning that code instrumentation shines in complex systems with many different components that react differently based on inputs or over time. Sampling techniques (discussed in section 5.4) squash that valuable information, not allowing us to detect abnormal behaviors. For example, in games, usually, there is a renderer thread, physics thread, animations thread, etc. Instrumenting such big modules help to reasonably quickly to understand what

5.1 Code Instrumentation

module is the source of issues. As sometimes, optimizing is not only a matter of optimizing code but also data. For example, rendering is too slow because of uncompressed mesh, or physics are too slow because of too many objects in the scene.

The technique is heavily used in real-time scenarios, such as video games and embedded development. Many profilers[72] mix up instrumentation with other techniques discussed in this chapter (tracing, sampling).

While code instrumentation is powerful in many cases, it does not provide any information about how the code executes from the OS or CPU perspective. For example, it can't give you information about how often the process was scheduled in and out from the execution (known by the OS) or how much branch mispredictions occurred (known by the CPU). Instrumented code is a part of an application and has the same privileges as the application itself. It runs in userspace and doesn't have access to the kernel.

But more importantly, the downside of this technique is that every time something new needs to be instrumented, say another variable, recompilation is required. This can become a burden to an engineer and increase analysis time. It is not all downsides, unfortunately. Since usually, you care about hot paths in the application, you're instrumenting the things that reside in the performance-critical part of the code. Inserting instrumentation code in a hot piece of code might easily result in a 2x slowdown of the overall benchmark[73]. Finally, by instrumenting the code, you change the behavior of the program, so you might not see the same effects you saw earlier.

All of the above increases time between experiments and consumes more development time, which is why engineers don't manually instrument their code very often these days. However, automated code instrumentation is still widely used by compilers. Compilers are capable of automatically instrumenting the whole program and collect interesting statistics about the execution. The most widely known use cases are code coverage analysis and Profile Guided Optimizations (see section 7.7).

When talking about instrumentation, it's important to mention binary

---

[72] A few examples: optick (https://optick.dev), tracy (https://bitbucket.org/wolfpld/tracy), superluminal (https://superluminal.eu).

[73] Remember not to benchmark instrumented code, i.e., do not measure score and do analysis in the same run.

instrumentation techniques. The idea behind binary instrumentation is similar but done on an already built executable file as opposed to on a source code level. There are two types of binary instrumentation: static (done ahead of time) and dynamic (instrumentation code inserted on-demand as a program executes). The main advantage of dynamic binary instrumentation is that it does not require program recompilation and relinking. Also, with dynamic instrumentation, one can limit the amount of instrumentation to only interesting code regions, not the whole program.

Binary instrumentation is very useful in performance analysis and debugging. One of the most popular tools for binary instrumentation is Intel Pin[74] tool. Pin intercepts the execution of the program in the occurrence of an interesting event and generates new instrumented code starting at this point in the program. It allows collecting various runtime information, for example:

- instruction count and function call counts.
- intercepting function calls and execution of any instruction in an application.
- allows "record and replay" the program region by capturing the memory and HW registers state at the beginning of the region.

Like code instrumentation, binary instrumentation only allows instrumenting user-level code and can be very slow.

5.2 Tracing

Tracing is conceptually very similar to instrumentation yet slightly different. Code instrumentation assumes that the user can orchestrate the code of their application. On the other hand, tracing relies on the existing instrumentation of a program's external dependencies. For example, strace tool allows us to trace system calls and can be considered as the instrumentation of the Linux kernel. Intel Processor Traces (see section 6.4) allows to log instructions executed by the program and can be considered as the instrumentation of a CPU. Traces can be obtained from components that were appropriately instrumented in advance and are not subject to change. Tracing is often used as the black-box approach, where a user cannot modify the code of the application, yet they want insight on what the program is doing behind the scenes.

---

[74] PIN - https://software.intel.com/en-us/articles/pin-a-dynamic-binary-instrumentation-tool

5.2 Tracing

An example of tracing system calls with Linux `strace` tool is demonstrated in Listing 7. This listing shows the first several lines of output when running the `git status` command. By tracing system calls with `strace` it's possible to know the timestamp for each system call (the leftmost column), its exit status, and the duration of each system call (in the angle brackets).

Listing 7 Tracing system calls with strace.

```
$ strace -tt -T -- git status
17:46:16.798861 execve("/usr/bin/git", ["git", "status"],
    0x7ffe705dcd78
                 /* 75 vars */) = 0 <0.000300>
17:46:16.799493 brk(NULL)            = 0x55f81d929000 <0.000062>
17:46:16.799692 access("/etc/ld.so.nohwcap", F_OK) = -1 ENOENT
                (No such file or directory) <0.000063>
17:46:16.799863 access("/etc/ld.so.preload", R_OK) = -1 ENOENT
                (No such file or directory) <0.000074>
17:46:16.800032 openat(AT_FDCWD, "/etc/ld.so.cache",
    O_RDONLY|O_CLOEXEC) = 3
                <0.000072>
17:46:16.800255 fstat(3, {st_mode=S_IFREG|0644, st_size=144852,
    ...}) = 0
                <0.000058>
17:46:16.800408 mmap(NULL, 144852, PROT_READ, MAP_PRIVATE, 3, 0)
                = 0x7f6ea7e48000 <0.000066>
17:46:16.800619 close(3)             = 0 <0.000123>
...
```

The overhead of tracing very much depends on what exactly we try to trace. For example, if we trace the program that almost never does system calls, the overhead of running it under `strace` will be close to zero. On the opposite, if we trace the program that heavily relies on system calls, the overhead could be very large, like 100x [75]. Also, tracing can generate a massive amount of data since it doesn't skip any sample. To compensate this, tracing tools provide the means to filter collection only for specific time slice or piece of code.

Usually, tracing similar to instrumentation is used for exploring anomalies in the system. For example, you may want to find what was going on in the application during the 10s period of unresponsiveness. Profiling is not designed for this, but with tracing, you can see what lead to the program being unresponsive. For example, with Intel PT

---

[75] An article about `strace` by B. Gregg - http://www.brendangregg.com/blog/2014-05-11/strace-wow-much-syscall.html

(see section 6.4), we can reconstruct the control flow of the program and know exactly what instructions were executed.

Tracing is also very useful for debugging. Its underlying nature enables "record and replay" use cases based on recorded traces. One of such tools is Mozilla rr[76] debugger, which does record and replay of processes, allows for backwards single stepping and much more. Most of the tracing tools are capable of decorating events with timestamps (see example in Listing 7), which allows us to have a correlation with external events that were happening during that time. I.e. when we observe a glitch in a program, we can take a look at the traces of our application and correlate this glitch with what was happening in the whole system during that time.

5.3 Workload Characterization

Workload characterization is a process of describing a workload by means of quantitative parameters and functions. Its goal is to define the behavior of the workload and its most important features. On a high level, an application can belong to one or many of the following types: interactive, database, network-based, parallel, etc. Different workloads can be characterized using different metrics and parameters to address a particular application domain.

In section 6.1, we will closely look at Top-Down Microarchitecture Analysis (TMA) methodology, which attempts to characterize an application by putting it into one of 4 buckets: Front End Bound, Back End Bound, Retiring, and Bad Speculation. TMA uses Performance Monitoring Counters (PMC, see section 3.9.1) to collect the needed information and identify the inefficient use of CPU microarchitecture.

5.3.1 Counting Performance Events

PMCs are a very important instrument of low-level performance analysis. They can provide unique information about the execution of our program. PMCs are generally used in two modes: "Counting" and "Sampling". Counting mode is used for workload characterization, while Sampling mode is used for finding hotspots, which we will discuss in section 5.4. The idea behind Counting is very simple: we want to count the number of certain performance events during the

---
[76] Mozilla rr debugger - https://rr-project.org/.

time our program was running. Figure 18 illustrates the process of counting performance events in the time perspective.

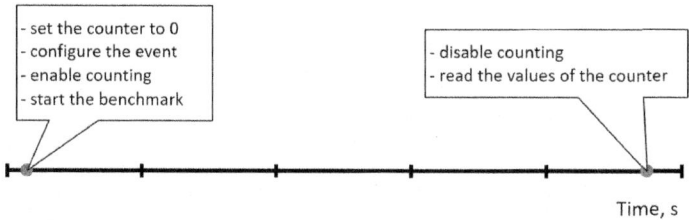

Figure 18: Counting performance events.

The steps outlined in figure 18 roughly represent what a typical analysis tool will do to count performance events. This process is implemented in the `perf stat` tool, which can be used to count various HW events, like the number of instructions, cycles, cache-misses, etc. Below is the example of output from `perf stat`:

```
$ perf stat -- ./a.exe
 10580290629   cycles          #    3,677 GHz
  8067576938   instructions    #    0,76  insn per cycle
  3005772086   branches        # 1044,472 M/sec
   239298395   branch-misses   #    7,96% of all branches
```

It is very informative to know this data. First of all, it allows us to quickly spot some anomalies like a high cache miss rate or poor IPC. But also, it might come in handy when you've just made code improvement and you want to validate performance gain. Looking at absolute numbers might help you justify or reject the code change.

> **Personal Experience:** I use 'perf stat' as a simple benchmark wrapper. Since the overhead of counting events is minimal, I run almost all benchmarks automatically under 'perf stat'. It serves me as a first step in performance investigation. Sometimes the anomalies can be spotted right away, which can save you some analysis time.

5.3.2 Manual performance counters collection

Modern CPUs have hundreds of countable performance events. It's very hard to remember all of them and their meanings. Understanding when to use a particular PMC is even harder. That is why generally, we don't recommend manually collecting specific PMCs unless you really know what you are doing. Instead, we recommend using tools like Intel Vtune Profiler that automate this process. Nevertheless, there are situations when you are interested in collecting specific PMC.

A complete list of performance events for all Intel CPU generations can be found in [Int, 2020, Volume 3B, Chapter 19].[77] Every event is encoded with `Event` and `Umask` hexadecimal values. Sometimes performance events can also be encoded with additional parameters, like `Cmask` and `Inv` and others. An example of encoding two performance events for the Intel Skylake microarchitecture is shown in the table 4.

Table 4: Example of encoding Skylake performance events.

Event Num.	Umask Value	Event Mask Mnemonic	Description
C0H	00H	INST_RETIRED.ANY_P	Number of instructions at retirement.
C4H	00H	BR_INST_RETIRED.ALL_BRANCHES	Number of branch instructions retired.

Linux `perf` provides mappings for commonly used performance counters. They can be accessed via pseudo names instead of specifying `Event` and `Umask` hexadecimal values. For example, `branches` is just a synonym for `BR_INST_RETIRED.ALL_BRANCHES` and will measure the same thing. List of available mapping names can be viewed with `perf list`:

```
$ perf list
    branches            [Hardware event]
    branch-misses       [Hardware event]
    bus-cycles          [Hardware event]
    cache-misses        [Hardware event]
    cycles              [Hardware event]
    instructions        [Hardware event]
    ref-cycles          [Hardware event]
```

---

[77] PMCs description is also available here: https://download.01.org/perfmon/index/.

However, Linux `perf` doesn't provide mappings for all performance counters for every CPU architecture. If the PMC you are looking for doesn't have a mapping, it can be collected with the following syntax:

```
$ perf stat -e
    cpu/event=0xc4,umask=0x0,name=BR_INST_RETIRED.ALL_BRANCHES/ --
    ./a.exe
```

Also there are wrappers around Linux `perf` that can do the mapping, for example, oprofile[78] and ocperf.py[79]. Below is an example of their usage:

```
$ ocperf -e uops_retired ./a.exe
$ ocperf.py stat -e uops_retired.retire_slots -- ./a.exe
```

Performance counters are not available in every environment since accessing PMCs requires root access, which applications running in a virtualized environment typically do not have. For programs executing in a public cloud, running a PMU-based profiler directly in a guest container does not result in useful output if a virtual machine (VM) manager does not expose the PMU programming interfaces properly to a guest. Thus profilers based on CPU performance counters do not work well in a virtualized and cloud environment [Du et al., 2010]. Although the situation is improving. VmWare® was one of the first VM managers to enable virtual CPU Performance Counters (vPMC). [80] AWS EC2 cloud enabled PMCs for dedicated hosts. [81]

5.3.3 Multiplexing and scaling events

There are situations when we want to count many different events at the same time. But with only one counter, it's possible to count only one thing at a time. That's why PMUs have multiple counters in it (typically 4 per HW thread). Even then, the number of fixed and programmable counter is not always sufficient. Top-Down Analysis Methodology (TMA) requires collecting up to 100 different performance events in a single execution of a program. Obviously, CPUs

---

[78] Oprofile - https://oprofile.sourceforge.io/about/
[79] PMU tools - https://github.com/andikleen/pmu-tools/blob/master/ocperf.py
[80] VMWare PMCs - https://www.vladan.fr/what-are-vmware-virtual-cpu-performance-monitoring-counters-vpmcs/
[81] Amazon EC2 PMCs - http://www.brendangregg.com/blog/2017-05-04/the-pmcs-of-ec2.html

don't have that many counters, and here is when multiplexing comes into play.

If there are more events than counters, the analysis tool uses time multiplexing to give each event a chance to access the monitoring hardware. Figure 19 shows an example of multiplexing between 8 performance events with only 4 PMCs available.

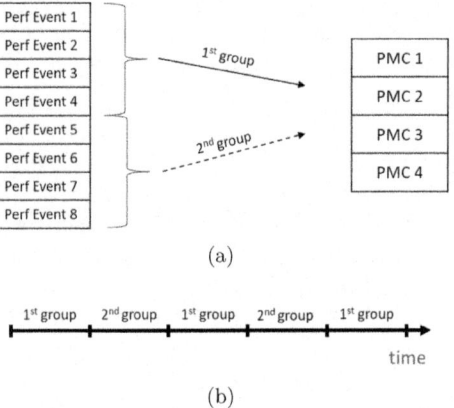

Figure 19: Multiplexing between 8 performance events with only 4 PMCs available.

With multiplexing, an event is not measured all the time, but rather only during some portion of it. At the end of the run, a profiling tool needs to scale the raw count based on total time enabled:

$$final\ count = raw\ count * (time\ running/time\ enabled)$$

For example, say during profiling, we were able to measure some counter during five time intervals. Each measurement interval lasted 100ms (`time enabled`). The program running time was 1s (`time running`). The total number of events for this counter was measured as 10000 (`raw count`). So, we need to scale the `final count` by 2, which will be equal to 20000:

$$final\ count = 10000 * (1000ms/500ms) = 20000$$

This provides an estimate of what the count would have been had the event been measured during the entire run. It is very important to understand that this is an estimate, not an actual count. Multiplexing and scaling can be used safely on steady workloads that execute the same code during long time intervals. On the opposite, if the program regularly jumps between different hotspots, there will be blind spots that can introduce errors during scaling. To avoid scaling, one can try to reduce the number of events to be not bigger than the number of physical PMCs available. However, this will require running the benchmark multiple times to measure all the counters one is interested in.

5.4 Sampling

Sampling is the most frequently used approach for doing performance analysis. People usually associate it with finding hotspots in the program. In general terms, sampling gives the answer to the question: which place in the code contributes to the greatest number of certain performance events. If we consider finding hotspots, the problem can be reformulated as which place in the code consumes the biggest amount of CPU cycles. People often use the term "Profiling" for what is technically called sampling. According to Wikipedia[82], profiling is a much broader term and includes a wide variety of techniques to collect data, including interrupts, code instrumentation, and PMC.

It may come as a surprise, but the simplest sampling profiler one can imagine is a debugger. In fact, you can identify hotspots by a) run the program under the debugger, b) pause the program every 10 seconds, and c) record the place where it stopped. If you repeat b) and c) many times, you will build a collection of samples. The line of code where you stopped the most will be the hottest place in the program. [83] Of course, this is an oversimplified description of how real profiling tools work. Modern profilers are capable of collecting thousands of samples per second, which gives a pretty accurate estimate about the hottest places in a benchmark.

As in the example with a debugger, the execution of the analyzed program is interrupted every time a new sample is captured. At the time of interrupt, the profiler collects the snapshot of the program state, which constitutes one sample. Information collected for every sample may include an instruction address that was executed at the time of interrupt, register state, call stack (see section 5.4.3), etc.

---

[82] Profiling(wikipedia) - https://en.wikipedia.org/wiki/Profiling_(computer_programming).
[83] This is an awkward way, though, and we don't recommend doing this. It's just to illustrate the concept.

Collected samples are stored in data collection files, which can be further used to display a call graph, the most time-consuming parts of the program, and control flow for statistically important code sections.

5.4.1 User-Mode And Hardware Event-based Sampling

Sampling can be performed in 2 different modes, using user-mode or HW event-based sampling (EBS). User-mode sampling is a pure SW approach that embeds an agent library into the profiled application. The agent sets up the OS timer for each thread in the application. Upon timer expiration, the application receives the SIGPROF signal that is handled by the collector. EBS uses hardware PMCs to trigger interrupts. In particular, the counter overflow feature of the PMU is used, which we will discuss in the next section.[Int, 2020]

User-mode sampling can only be used to identify hotspots, while EBS can be used for additional analysis types that involve PMCs, e.g., sampling on cache-misses, TMA (see section 6.1), etc.

User-mode sampling incurs more runtime overhead than EBS. The average overhead of the user-mode sampling is about 5% when sampling is using the default interval of 10ms. The average overhead of event-based sampling is about 2% on a 1ms sampling interval. Typically, EBS is more accurate since it allows collecting samples with higher frequency. However, user-mode sampling generates much fewer data to analyze, and it takes less time to process it.

5.4.2 Finding Hotspots

In this section, we will discuss the scenario of using PMCs with EBS. Figure 20 illustrates the counter overflow feature of the PMU, which is used to trigger performance monitoring interrupt (PMI).

In the beginning, we configure the event that we want to sample on. Identifying hotspots means knowing where the program spends most of the time. So sampling on cycles is very natural, and it is a default for many profiling tools. But it's not necessarily a strict rule; we can sample on any performance event we want. For example, if we would like to know the place where the program experiences the biggest number of L3-cache misses, we would sample on the corresponding event, i.e., MEM_LOAD_RETIRED.L3_MISS.

5.4 Sampling

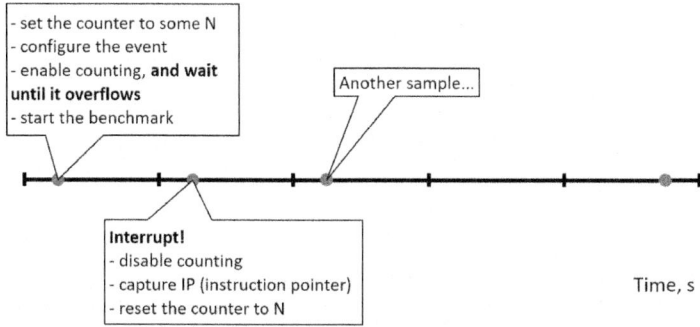

Figure 20: Using performance counter for sampling

After preparations are done, we enable counting and let the benchmark go. We configured PMC to count cycles, so it will be incremented every cycle. Eventually, it will overflow. At the time the counter overflows, HW will raise PMI. The profiling tool is configured to capture PMIs and has an Interrupt Service Routine (ISR) for handling them. Inside this routine, we do multiple steps: first of all, we disable counting; after that, we record the instruction which was executed by the CPU at the time the counter overflowed; then, we reset the counter to N and resume the benchmark.

Now, let us go back to the value N. Using this value, we can control how frequently we want to get a new interrupt. Say we want a finer granularity and have one sample every 1 million instructions. To achieve this, we can set the counter to -1 million so that it will overflow after every 1 million instructions. This value is usually referred to as the "sample after" value.

We repeat the process many times to build a sufficient collection of samples. If we later aggregate those samples, we could build a histogram of the hottest places in our program, like the one shown on the output from Linux `perf record/report` below. This gives us the breakdown of the overhead for functions of a program sorted in descending order (hotspots). Example of sampling x264[84] benchmark from Phoronix test suite[85] is shown below:

---
[84] x264 benchmark - https://openbenchmarking.org/test/pts/x264.
[85] Phoronix test suite - https://www.phoronix-test-suite.com/.

5.4 Sampling

```
$ perf record -- ./x264 -o /dev/null --slow --threads 8
    Bosphorus_1920x1080_120fps_420_8bit_YUV.y4m
$ perf report -n --stdio
# Samples: 364K of event 'cycles:ppp'
# Event count (approx.): 300110884245
# Overhead  Samples  Object  Symbol
# ........  .......  ......  ..........................................
#
    6.99%    25349    x264   [.] x264_8_me_search_ref
    6.70%    24294    x264   [.] get_ref_avx2
    6.50%    23397    x264   [.] refine_subpel
    5.20%    18590    x264   [.] x264_8_pixel_satd_8x8_internal_avx2
    4.69%    17272    x264   [.] x264_8_pixel_avg2_w16_sse2
    4.22%    15081    x264   [.] x264_8_pixel_avg2_w8_mmx2
    3.63%    13024    x264   [.] x264_8_mc_chroma_avx2
    3.21%    11827    x264   [.] x264_8_pixel_satd_16x8_internal_avx2
    2.25%     8192    x264   [.] rd_cost_mb
...
```

We would then naturally want to know the hot piece of code inside every function that appears in the hotspot list. To see the profiling data for functions that were inlined as well as assembly code generated for a particular source code region requires the application being built with debug information (-g compiler flag). Users can reduce[86] the amount of debugging information to just line numbers of the symbols as they appear in the source code by using the -gline-tables-only option. Tools like Linux perf that don't have rich graphic support, intermix source code with the generated assembly, as shown below:

```
# snippet of annotating source code of 'x264_8_me_search_ref'
    function
$ perf annotate x264_8_me_search_ref --stdio
Percent | Source code & Disassembly of x264 for cycles:ppp
-----------------------------------------------------------
   ...
        :             bmx += square1[bcost&15][0];  <== source code
   1.43 : 4eb10d: movsx  ecx,BYTE PTR [r8+rdx*2]   <== corresponding
                                                       machine code
        :             bmy += square1[bcost&15][1];
   0.36 : 4eb112: movsx  r12d,BYTE PTR [r8+rdx*2+0x1]
        :             bmx += square1[bcost&15][0];
   0.63 : 4eb118: add    DWORD PTR [rsp+0x38],ecx
        :             bmy += square1[bcost&15][1];
   ...
```

---

[86] If a user doesn't need full debug experience, having line numbers is enough for profiling the application. There were cases when LLVM transformation passes incorrectly, treated the presence of debugging intrinsics, and made wrong transformations in the presence of debug information.

5.4 Sampling

Most profilers with Graphical User Interface (GUI), like Intel VTune Profiler, can show source code and associated assembly side-by-side, as shown in figure 21.

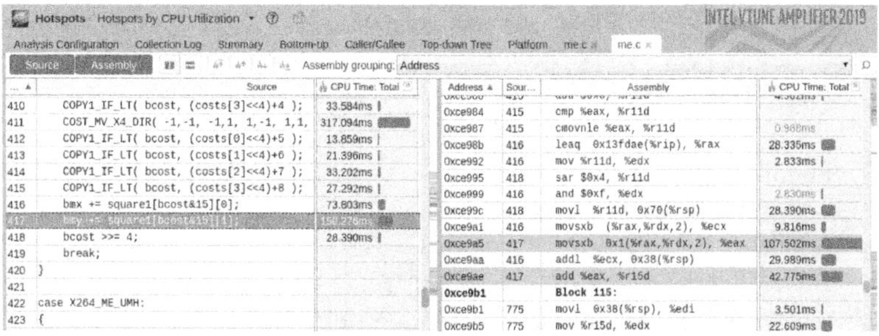

Figure 21: Intel® VTune™ Profiler source code and assembly view for x264 benchmark.

5.4.3 Collecting Call Stacks

Often when sampling, we might encounter a situation when the hottest function in a program gets called by multiple callers. An example of such a scenario is shown on figure 22. The output from the profiling tool might reveal that function `foo` is one of the hottest functions in the program, but if it has multiple callers, we would like to know which one of them call `foo` the most number of times. It is a typical situation for applications that have library functions like `memcpy` or `sqrt` appear in the hotspots. To understand why a particular function appeared as a hotspot, we need to know which path in the Control Flow Graph (CFG) of the program caused it.

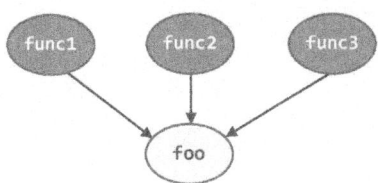

Figure 22: Control Flow Graph: hot function "foo" has multiple callers.

Analyzing the logic of all the callers of `foo` might be very time-consuming. We want to focus only on those callers that caused

85

foo to appear as a hotspot. In other words, we want to know the hottest path in the CFG of a program. Profiling tools achieve this by capturing the call stack of the process along with other information at the time of collecting performance samples. Then, all collected stacks are grouped, allowing us to see the hottest path that led to a particular function.

Collecting call stacks in Linux `perf` is possible with three methods:

1. Frame pointers (`perf record --call-graph fp`). Requires binary being built with `--fnoomit-frame-pointer`. Historically, frame pointer (RBP) was used for debugging since it allows us to get the call stack without popping all the arguments from the stack (stack unwinding). The frame pointer can tell the return address immediately. However, it consumes one register just for this purpose, so it was expensive. It is also used for profiling since it enables cheap stack unwinding.
2. DWARF debug info (`perf record --call-graph dwarf`). Requires binary being built with DWARF debug information `-g` (`-gline-tables-only`).
3. Intel Last Branch Record (LBR) Hardware feature `perf record --call-graph lbr`. Not as deep call graph as the first two methods. See more information about LBR in the section 6.2.

Below is the example of collecting call stacks in a program using Linux `perf`. By looking at the output, we know that 55% of the time `foo` was called from `func1`. We can clearly see the distribution of the overhead between callers of `foo` and can now focus our attention on the hottest edges in the CFG of the program.

```
$ perf record --call-graph lbr -- ./a.out
$ perf report -n --stdio --no-children
# Samples: 65K of event 'cycles:ppp'
# Event count (approx.): 61363317007
# Overhead       Samples  Command  Shared Object      Symbol
# ........       .......  .......  .............      ......
    99.96%         65217  a.out    a.out              [.] foo
              |
               --99.96%--foo
                         |
                         |--55.52%--func1
                         |          main
                         |          __libc_start_main
                         |          _start
                         |
                         |--33.32%--func2
                         |          main
```

```
        |         __libc_start_main
        |         _start
        |
        --11.12%--func3
                  main
                  __libc_start_main
                  _start
```

When using Intel Vtune Profiler, one can collect call stacks data by checking the corresponding "Collect stacks" box while configuring analysis[87]. When using command-line interface specify `-knob enable-stack-collection=true` option.

> **Personal Experience:** Mechanism of collecting call stacks is very important to understand. I've seen some developers that are not familiar with the concept try to obtain this information by using a debugger. They do this by interrupting the execution of a program and analyze the call stack (like 'backtrace' command in 'gdb' debugger). Developers should allow profiling tools to do the job, which is much faster and gives more accurate data.

5.4.4 Flame Graphs

A popular way of visualizing the profiling data and the most frequent code-paths in the program is by using flame graphs. It allows us to see which function calls take the biggest portion of execution time. Figure 23 shows the example of a flame graph for x264 benchmark. From the mentioned flame graph we can see that the path that takes the most amount of execution time is `x264 -> threadpool_thread_internal -> slices_write -> slice_write -> x264_8_macroblock_analyse`. The original output is interactive and allows us to zoom into a particular code path. The flame graph was generated with opensource scripts[88] developed by Brendan Gregg. There are other tools capable of emitting flame graphs, perhaps KDAB Hotspot[89] being the most popular alternative.

---

[87] See more details in Intel® VTune™ Profiler User Guide.

[88] Flame Graphs by Brendan Gregg: https://github.com/brendangregg/FlameGraph. See more details about all the features on Brendan's dedicated web page: http://www.brendangregg.com/flamegraphs.html.

[89] Hotspot profiler by KDAB - https://github.com/KDAB/hotspot.

5.5 Roofline Performance Model

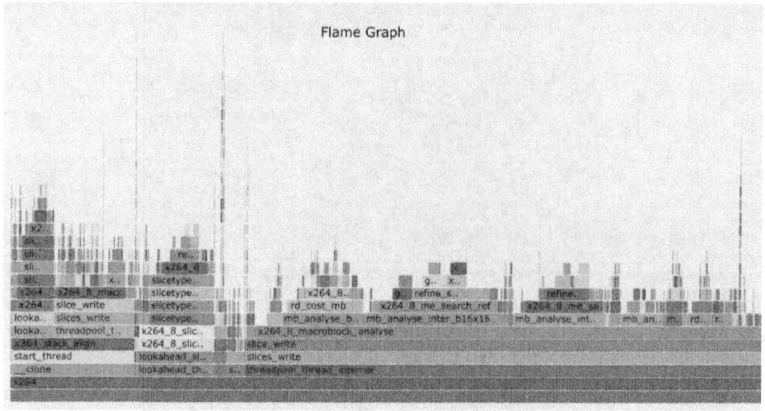

Figure 23: A Flame Graph for x264 benchmark.

5.5 Roofline Performance Model

Roofline Performance Model was developed at the University of California, Berkeley, in 2009. It is a throughput-oriented performance model that is heavily used in the HPC world. The "roofline" in this model expresses the fact that the performance of an application cannot exceed the machine's capabilities. Every function and every loop in a program is limited by either compute or memory capacity of a machine. This concept is represented in figure 24: the performance of an application will always be limited by a certain "roofline" function.

Hardware has two main limitations: how fast it can make calculations (peak compute performance, FLOPS) and how fast it can move the data (peak memory bandwidth, GB/s). The maximum performance of an application is limited by the minimum between peak FLOPS (horizontal line) and the platform bandwidth multiplied by arithmetic intensity (diagonal line). A roofline chart that is shown in figure 24 plots the performance of two applications A and B against hardware limitations. Different parts of a program could have different performance characteristics. Roofline model accounts for that and allows to display multiple functions and loops of an application on the same chart.

Arithmetic Intensity (AI) is a ratio between FLOPS and bytes and can be extracted for every loop in a program. Let's calculate the arithmetic intensity of code in Listing 8. In the innermost loop body,

5.5 Roofline Performance Model

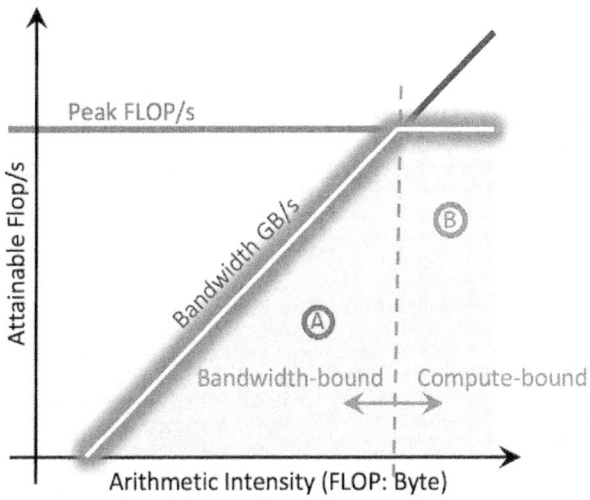

Figure 24: Roofline model. © *Image taken from NERSC Documentation.*

we have an addition and a multiplication; thus, we have 2 FLOPS. Also, we have three read operations and one write operation; thus, we transfer 4 ops * 4 bytes = 16 bytes. Arithmetic intensity of that code is 2 / 16 = 0.125. AI serves as the value on the X-axis of a given performance point.

Listing 8 Naive parallel matrix multiplication.

```
void matmul(int N, float a[][2048], float b[][2048], float
    c[][2048]) {
    #pragma omp parallel for
    for(int i = 0; i < N; i++) {
        for(int j = 0; j < N; j++) {
            for(int k = 0; k < N; k++) {
                c[i][j] = c[i][j] + a[i][k] * b[k][j];
            }
        }
    }
}
```

Traditional ways to speed up an application's performance is to fully utilize the SIMD and multicore capabilities of a machine. Often times, we need to optimize for many aspects: vectorization, memory, threading. Roofline methodology can assist in assessing these characteristics of your application. On a roofline chart, we can plot theoretical maximums for scalar single-core, SIMD single-core, and SIMD multicore performance (see figure 25). This will give us an understanding of the room for improving the performance of an application. If we found that our application is compute-bound (i.e., has high arithmetic intensity) and is below the peak scalar single-core performance, we should consider forcing vectorization (see section 8.2.3) and distributing the work among multiple threads. Conversely, if an application has a low arithmetic intensity, we should seek ways to improve memory accesses (see section 8.1). The ultimate goal of optimizing performance using the Roofline model is to move the points up. Vectorization and threading move the dot up while optimizing memory accesses by increasing arithmetic intensity will move the dot to the right and also likely improve performance.

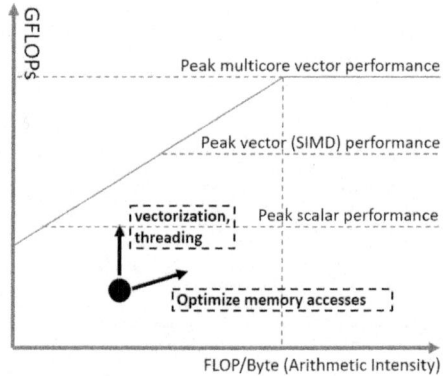

Figure 25: Roofline model.

Theoretical maximums (roof lines) can be calculated[90] based on the characteristics of the machine you are using. Usually, it is not hard to do once you know the parameters of your machine. For Intel Core i5-8259U processor, the maximum number of FLOPs (single-precision floats) with AVX2 and 2 Fused Multiply Add (FMA) units can be

---

[90] Note that often theoretical maximums are often presented in a device specification and can be easily looked up.

5.5 Roofline Performance Model

calculated as:

$$\text{Peak FLOPS} = 8 \text{ (number of logical cores)} \times \frac{256 \text{ (AVX bit width)}}{32 \text{ bit (size of float)}} \times$$
$$2 \text{ (FMA)} \times 3.8 \text{ GHz (Max Turbo Frequency)}$$
$$= 486.4 \text{ GFLOPs}$$

The maximum memory bandwidth of Intel NUC Kit NUC8i5BEH, which I used for experiments, can be calculated as:

$$\text{Peak Memory Bandwidth} = 2400 \text{ (DDR4 memory transfer rate)} \times$$
$$2 \text{ (memory channels)} \times$$
$$8 \text{ (bytes per memory access)} \times$$
$$1 \text{ (socket)} = 38.4 \text{ GiB/s}$$

Automated tools like Empirical Roofline Tool[91] and Intel Advisor[92] (see figure 26) are capable of empirically determine theoretical maximums by running a set of prepared benchmarks.

If a calculation can reuse the data in cache, much higher FLOP rates are possible. Roofline can account for that by introducing a dedicated roofline for each level of the memory hierarchy (see figure 26).

After hardware limitations are determined, we can start assessing the performance of an application against the roofline. The two most frequently used methods for automated collection of Roofline data are sampling (used by likwid[93] tool) and binary instrumentation (used by Intel Software Development Emulator (SDE[94])). Sampling incurs the lower overhead of collecting data, while binary instrumentation gives more accurate results[95]. Intel Advisor is capable of automatically building a Roofline chart and even providing hints for performance optimization of a given loop. An example of a chart generated by

---

[91] Empirical Roofline Tool - https://bitbucket.org/berkeleylab/cs-roofline-toolkit/src/master/.

[92] Intel Advisor - https://software.intel.com/content/www/us/en/develop/tools/advisor.html.

[93] Likwid - https://github.com/RRZE-HPC/likwid.

[94] Intel SDE - https://software.intel.com/content/www/us/en/develop/articles/intel-software-development-emulator.html.

[95] See a more detailed comparison between methods of collecting roofline data in this presentation: https://crd.lbl.gov/assets/Uploads/ECP20-Roofline-4-cpu.pdf.

5.5 Roofline Performance Model

Intel Advisor is presented in figure 26. Notice, Roofline charts have logarithmic scales.

Roofline methodology allows for tracking optimization progress by printing "before" and "after" points on the same chart. So, it is an iterative process that guides developers to make their applications fully utilize HW capabilities. Figure 26 reflects performance gains as a result of making two code transformations in code from Listing 8:

- Interchange two innermost loops (swap lines 4 and 5). This allows cache-friendly memory accesses (see section 8.1).
- Vectorizing innermost loop using AVX2 instructions.

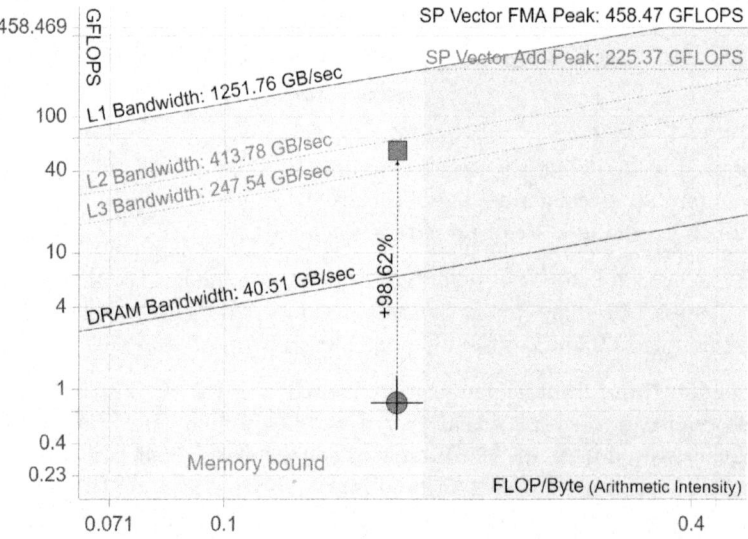

Figure 26: Roofline analysis for matrix multiplication on Intel NUC Kit NUC8i5BEH with 8GB RAM using clang 10 compiler.

In summary, the Roofline Performance Model can be helpful to:

- Identify performance bottlenecks.
- Guide software optimizations.
- Determine when we're done optimizing.
- Assess performance relative to machine capabilities.

Additional resources and links:

- NERSC Documentation, URL: https://docs.nersc.gov/development/performance-debugging-tools/roofline/.

- Lawrence Berkeley National Laboratory research, URL: https://crd.lbl.gov/departments/computer-science/par/research/roofline/
- Collection of video presentations about Roofline model and Intel Advisor, URL: https://techdecoded.intel.io/ (search "Roofline").
- Perfplot is a collection of scripts and tools that allow a user to instrument performance counters on a recent Intel platform, measure them, and use the results to generate roofline and performance plots. URL: https://github.com/GeorgOfenbeck/perfplot

5.6 Static Performance Analysis

Today we have extensive tooling for static code analysis. For C and C++ languages we have such well known tools like Clang Static Analyzer, Klocwork, Cppcheck and others[96]. They aim at checking the correctness and semantics of the code. Likewise, there are tools that try to address the performance aspect of the code. Static performance analyzers don't run the actual code. Instead, they simulate the code as if it is executed on a real HW. Statically predicting performance is almost impossible, so there are many limitations to this type of analysis.

First, it is not possible to statically analyze C/C++ code for performance since we don't know the machine code to which it will be compiled. So, static performance analysis works on assembly code.

Second, static analysis tools simulate the workload instead of executing it. It is obviously very slow, so it's not possible to statically analyze the entire program. Instead, tools take some assembly code snippet and try to predict how it will behave on real hardware. The user should pick specific assembly instructions (usually small loop) for analysis. So, the scope of static performance analysis is very narrow.

The output of the static analyzers is fairly low-level and sometimes breaks execution down to CPU cycles. Usually, developers use it for fine-grained tuning of the critical code region where every cycle matter.

---
[96] Tools for static code analysis - https://en.wikipedia.org/wiki/List_of_tools_for_static_code_analysis#C,_C++.

5.6 Static Performance Analysis

5.6.1 Static vs. Dynamic Analyzers

Static tools don't run the actual code but try to simulate the execution, keeping as many microarchitectural details as they can. They are not capable of doing real measurements (execution time, performance counters) because they don't run the code. The upside here is that you don't need to have the real HW and can simulate the code for different CPU generations. Another benefit is that you don't need to worry about consistency of the results: static analyzers will always give you stable output because simulation (in comparison with the execution on real hardware) is not biased in any way. The downside of static tools is that they usually can't predict and simulate everything inside a modern CPU: they are based on some model that may have bugs and limitations in it. Examples of static performance analyzers are IACA[97] and llvm-mca[98].

Dynamic tools are based on running the code on the real HW and collecting all sorts of information about the execution. This is the only 100% reliable method of proving any performance hypothesis. As a downside, usually, you are required to have privileged access rights to collect low-level performance data like PMCs. It's not always easy to write a good benchmark and measure what you want to measure. Finally, you need to filter the noise and different kinds of side effects. Examples of dynamic performance analyzers are Linux perf, likwid[99] and uarch-bench[100]. Examples of usage and output for the tools mentioned above can be found on easyperf blog [101].

A big collection of tools both for static and dynamic microarchitectural performance analysis is available here[102].

> **Personal Experience:** I use those tools whenever I need to explore some interesting CPU microarchitecture effect. Static and low-level dynamic analyzers (like likwid and uarch-bench) allow us to observe HW effects in practice

---

[97] IACA - https://software.intel.com/en-us/articles/intel-architecture-code-analyzer. In April 2019, the tools has reached its End Of Life and is no longer supported.
[98] LLVM MCA - https://llvm.org/docs/CommandGuide/llvm-mca.html
[99] LIKWID - https://github.com/RRZE-HPC/likwid
[100] Uarch bench - https://github.com/travisdowns/uarch-bench
[101] An article about tools for microarchitectural benchmarking - https://easyperf.net/blog/2018/04/03/Tools-for-microarchitectural-benchmarking
[102] Collection of links for C++ performance tools - https://github.com/MattPD/cpplinks/blob/master/performance.tools.md#microarchitecture.

while doing performance experiments. They are a great help for building up your mental model of how CPU works.

5.7 Compiler Optimization Reports

Nowadays, software development relies very much on compilers to do performance optimizations. Compilers play a very important role in speeding up our software. Usually, developers leave this job to compilers, interfering only when they see an opportunity to improve something compilers cannot accomplish. Fair to say, this is a good default strategy. For better interaction, compilers provide optimization reports which developers can use for performance analysis.

Sometimes you want to know if some function was inlined or loop was vectorized, unrolled, etc. If it was unrolled, what is the unroll factor? There is a hard way to know this: by studying generated assembly instructions. Unfortunately, not all people are comfortable at reading assembly language. This can be especially hard if the function is big, it calls other functions or has many loops that were also vectorized, or if the compiler created multiple versions of the same loop. Fortunately, most compilers, including GCC, ICC, and Clang, provide optimization reports to check what optimizations were done for a particular piece of code. Another example of a hint from a compiler can be Intel® ISPC[103] compiler (see more in section 8.2.3.7), which issues a number of performance warnings for code constructs that compile to relatively inefficient code.

Listing 9 shows an example of the loop that is not vectorized by clang 6.0.

To emit an optimization report in clang, you need to use -Rpass* flags:

```
$ clang -O3 -Rpass-analysis=.* -Rpass=.* -Rpass-missed=.* a.c -c
a.c:5:3: remark: loop not vectorized [-Rpass-missed=loop-vectorize]
  for (unsigned i = 1; i < N; i++) {
  ^
a.c:5:3: remark: unrolled loop by a factor of 4 with run-time trip
      count [-Rpass=loop-unroll]
  for (unsigned i = 1; i < N; i++) {
  ^
```

---
[103] ISPC - https://ispc.github.io/ispc.html.

5.7 Compiler Optimization Reports

Listing 9 a.c

```
1  void foo(float* __restrict__ a,
2           float* __restrict__ b,
3           float* __restrict__ c,
4           unsigned N) {
5    for (unsigned i = 1; i < N; i++) {
6      a[i] = c[i-1]; // value is carried over from previous iteration
7      c[i] = b[i];
8    }
9  }
```

By checking the optimization report above, we could see that the loop was not vectorized, but it was unrolled instead. It's not always easy for a developer to recognize the existence of vector dependency in the loop on line 5 in Listing 9. The value that is loaded by c[i-1] depends on the store from the previous iteration (see operations #2 and #3 in Figure 27). The dependency can be revealed by manually unrolling a few first iterations of the loop:

```
// iteration 1
  a[1] = c[0];
  c[1] = b[1]; // writing the value to c[1]
// iteration 2
  a[2] = c[1]; // reading the value of c[1]
  c[2] = b[2];
...
```

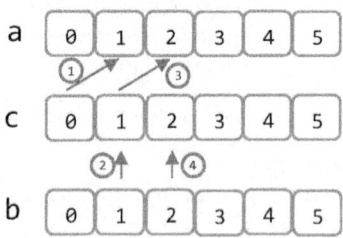

Figure 27: Visualizing the order of operations in Listing 9.

If we were to vectorize the code in Listing 9, it would result in the wrong values written in the array a. Assuming a CPU SIMD unit can process four floats at a time, we would get the code that can be expressed with the following pseudocode:

5.7 Compiler Optimization Reports

```
// iteration 1
  a[1..4] = c[0..3]; // oops, a[2..4] get the wrong values
  c[1..4] = b[1..4];
  ...
```

The code in Listing 9 cannot be vectorized because the order of operations inside the loop matter. This example can be fixed[104] by swapping lines 6 and 7 without changing the semantics of the function, as shown in Listing 10. For more information on discovering vectorization opportunities and examples using compiler optimization reports, see section 8.2.3.

Listing 10 a.c

```
1  void foo(float* __restrict__ a,
2           float* __restrict__ b,
3           float* __restrict__ c,
4           unsigned N) {
5    for (unsigned i = 1; i < N; i++) {
6      c[i] = b[i];
7      a[i] = c[i-1];
8    }
9  }
```

In the optimization report, we can see that the loop was now vectorized:

```
$ clang -O3 -Rpass-analysis=.* -Rpass=.* -Rpass-missed=.* a.c -c
a.cpp:5:3: remark: vectorized loop (vectorization width: 4,
    interleaved count: 2) [-Rpass=loop-vectorize]
  for (unsigned i = 1; i < N; i++) {
```

Compiler reports are generated per source file, which can be quite big. A user can simply search the source lines of interest in the output. Compiler Explorer[105] website has the "Optimization Output" tool for LLVM-based compilers that reports performed transformations when you hover your mouse over the corresponding line of source code.

In LTO[106] mode, some optimizations are made during the linking

---

[104] Alternatively, the code can be improved by splitting the loop into two separate loops.
[105] Compiler Explorer - https://godbolt.org/.
[106] Link-Time optimizations, also called InterProcedural Optimizations (IPO). Read more here: https://en.wikipedia.org/wiki/Interprocedural_optimization.

stage. To emit compiler reports from both compilation and linking stages, one should pass dedicated options to both the compiler and the linker. See LLVM "Remarks" guide[107] for more information.

Compiler optimization reports not only help in finding missed optimization opportunities and explain why that happened but also are useful for testing hypotheses. The compiler often decides whether a certain transformation will be beneficial based on its cost model analysis. But it doesn't always make the optimal choice, which we can be tuned further. One can detect missing optimization in a report and provide a hint to a compiler by using `#pragma`, attributes, compiler built-ins, etc. See an example of using such hints on easyperf blog[108]. As always, verify your hypothesis by measuring it in a practical environment.

> **Personal Experience:** Compiler optimization reports could be one of the key items in your toolbox. It is a fast way to check what optimizations were done for a particular hotspot and see if some important ones failed. I have found many improvement opportunities by using opt reports.

5.8 Chapter Summary

- Latency and throughput are often the ultimate metrics of the program performance. When seeking ways to improve them, we need to get more detailed information on how the application executes. Both HW and SW provide data that can be used for performance monitoring.

- Code instrumentation allows us to track many things in the program but causes relatively large overhead both on the development and runtime side. While developers do not manually instrument their code these days very often, this approach is still relevant for automated processes, e.g., PGO.

- Tracing is conceptually similar to instrumentation and is useful for exploring anomalies in the system. Tracing allows us to catch the entire sequence of events with timestamps attached to each event.

---
[107] LLVM compiler remarks - https://llvm.org/docs/Remarks.html.
[108] Using compiler optimization pragmas - https://easyperf.net/blog/2017/11/09/Multiversioning_by_trip_counts.

5.8 Chapter Summary

- Workload Characterization is a way to compare and group applications based on their runtime behavior. Once characterized, specific recipes could be followed to find optimization headrooms in the program.

- Sampling skips the large portion of the program execution and take just one sample that is supposed to represent the entire interval. Even though sampling usually gives precise enough distributions. The most well-known use case of sampling is finding hotspots in the code. Sampling is the most popular analysis approach since it doesn't require recompilation of the program and has very little runtime overhead.

- Generally, counting and sampling incur very low runtime overhead (usually below 2%). Counting gets more expensive once you start multiplexing between different events (5-15% overhead), sampling gets more expensive with increasing sampling frequency [Nowak and Bitzes, 2014]. Consider using user-mode sampling for analyzing long-running workloads or when you don't need very accurate data.

- Roofline is a throughput-oriented performance model that is heavily used in the HPC world. It allows plotting the performance of an application against hardware limitations. Roofline model helps to identify performance bottlenecks, guides software optimizations, and keeps track of optimization progress.

- There are tools that try to statically analyze the performance of the code. Such tools simulate the piece of code instead of executing it. Many limitations and constraints apply to this approach, but you get a very detailed and low-level report in return.

- Compiler Opt reports help to find missing compiler optimizations. It may also guide developers in composing new performance experiments.

6 CPU Features For Performance Analysis

The ultimate goal of performance analysis is to identify the bottleneck and locate the place in the code that associates with it. Unfortunately, there are no predetermined steps to follow, so it can be approached in many different ways.

Usually, profiling the application can give quick insights about the hotspots of the application. Sometimes it is everything developers need to do to fix performance inefficiencies. Especially high-level performance problems can often be revealed by profiling. For example, consider a situation when you profile an application with interest in a particular function. According to your mental model of the application, you expect that function to be cold. But when you open the profile, you see it consumes a lot of time and is called a large number of times. Based on that information, you can apply techniques like caching or memoization to reduce the number of calls to that function and expect to see significant performance gains.

However, when you have fixed all the major performance inefficiencies, but you still need to squeeze more performance from your application, basic information like the time spent in a particular function is not enough. Here is when you need additional support from the CPU to understand where the performance bottlenecks are. So, before using the information presented in this chapter, make sure that the application you are trying to optimize does not suffer from major performance flaws. Because if it does, using CPU performance monitoring features for low-level tuning doesn't make sense. It will likely steer you in the wrong direction, and instead of fixing real high-level performance problems, you will be tuning bad code, which is just a waste of time.

> **Personal Experience:** When I was starting with performance optimization work, I usually just profiled the app and tried to grasp through the hotspots of the benchmark, hoping to find something there. This often led me to random experiments with unrolling, vectorization, inlining, you name it. I'm not saying it's always a losing

strategy. Sometimes you can be lucky to get a big performance boost from random experiments. But usually, you need to have very good intuition and luck.

Modern CPUs are constantly getting new features that enhance performance analysis in different ways. Using those features greatly simplifies finding low-level issues like cache-misses, branch mispredictions, etc. In this chapter, we will take a look at a few HW performance monitoring capabilities available on modern Intel CPUs. Most of them also have their counterparts in CPUs from other vendors like AMD, ARM, and others. Look for more details in the corresponding sections.

- Top-Down Microarchitecture Analysis Methodology (TMA) - a powerful technique for identifying ineffective usage of CPU microarchitecture by the program. It characterizes the bottleneck of the workload and allows locating the exact place in the source code where it occurs. It abstracts away intricacies of the CPU microarchitecture and is easy to use even for inexperienced developers.
- Last Branch Record (LBR) - a mechanism that continuously logs the most recent branch outcomes in parallel with executing the program. It is used for collecting call stacks, identify hot branches, calculating misprediction rates of individual branches, and more.
- Processor Event-Based Sampling (PEBS) - a feature that enhances sampling. Among its primary advantages are: lowering the overhead of sampling and providing "Precise Events" capability, which allows pinpointing exact instruction that caused a particular performance event.
- Intel Processor Traces (PT) - a facility to record and reconstruct the program execution with a timestamp on every instruction. Its main usages are postmortem analysis and root-causing performance glitches.

The features mentioned above provide insights on the efficiency of a program from the CPU perspective and how to make it more CPU-friendly. Profiling tools leverage them to provide many different types of performance analysis.

6.1 Top-Down Microarchitecture Analysis

Top-Down Microarchitecture Analysis Methodology (TMA) is a very powerful technique for identifying CPU bottlenecks in the program. It is a robust and formal methodology that is easy to use even for inexperienced developers. The best part of this methodology is that it does not require a developer to have a deep understanding of the microarchitecture and PMCs in the system and still efficiently find CPU bottlenecks. However, it does not automatically fix problems; otherwise, this book would not exist.

At a high-level, TMA identifies what was stalling the execution of every hotspot in the program. The bottleneck can be related to one of the four components: Front End Bound, Back End Bound, Retiring, Bad Speculation. Figure 28 illustrates this concept. Here is a short guide on how to read this diagram. As we know from section 3, there are internal buffers in the CPU that keep track of information about instructions that are being executed. Whenever new instruction gets fetched and decoded, new entries in those buffers are allocated. If uop for instruction was not allocated during a particular cycle of execution, it could be for two reasons: we were not able to fetch and decode it (Front End Bound), or Back End was overloaded with work and resources for new uop could not be allocated (Back End Bound). Uop that was allocated and scheduled for execution but not retired is related to the Bad Speculation bucket. An example of such a uop can be some instruction that was executed speculatively but later was proven to be on a wrong program path and was not retired. Finally, Retiring is the bucket where we want all our uops to be, although there are exceptions. A high Retiring value for non-vectorized code may be a good hint for users to vectorize the code (see section 8.2.3). Another situation when we might see high Retiring value but slow overall performance may happen in the program that operates on denormal floating-point values making such operations extremely slow (see section 10.4).

Figure 28 gives a breakdown for every instruction in a program. However, analyzing every single instruction in the workload is definitely overkill, and of course, TMA doesn't do that. Instead, we are usually interested in knowing what is stalling the program as a whole. To accomplish this goal, TMA observes the execution of the program by collecting specific metrics (ratios of PMCs). Based on those metrics, it characterizes application by relating it to one of the four high-level buckets. There are nested categories for each high-level bucket (see

6.1 Top-Down Microarchitecture Analysis

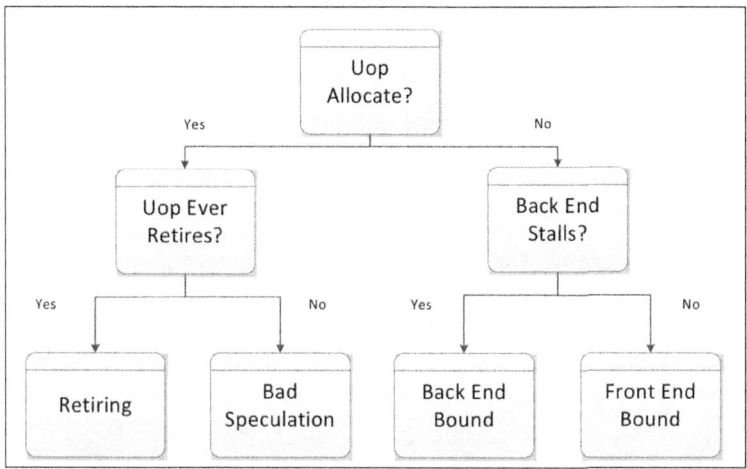

Figure 28: The concept behind TMA's top-level breakdown. © *Image from [Yasin, 2014]*

Figure 29) that give a better breakdown of the CPU performance bottlenecks in the program. We run the workload several times[109], each time focusing on specific metrics and drilling down until we get to the more detailed classification of performance bottleneck. For example, initially, we collect metrics for four main buckets: Front End Bound, Back End Bound, Retiring, Bad Speculation. Say, we found out that the big portion of the program execution was stalled by memory accesses (which is a Back End Bound bucket, see Figure 29). The next step is to run the workload again and collect metrics specific for the Memory Bound bucket only (drilling down). The process is repeated until we know the exact root cause, for example, L3 Bound.

In a real-world application, performance could be limited by multiple factors. E.g., it can experience a large number of branch mispredicts (Bad Speculation) and cache misses (Back End Bound) at the same time. In this case, TMA will drill down into multiple buckets simultaneously and will identify the impact that each type of bottleneck makes on the performance of a program. Analysis tools such as Intel VTune Profiler, AMD uprof, and Linux perf can calculate all the metrics

---

[109] In reality, it is sufficient to run the workload once to collect all the metrics required for TMA. Profiling tools achieve that by multiplexing between different performance events during a single run (see section 5.3.3).

6.1 Top-Down Microarchitecture Analysis

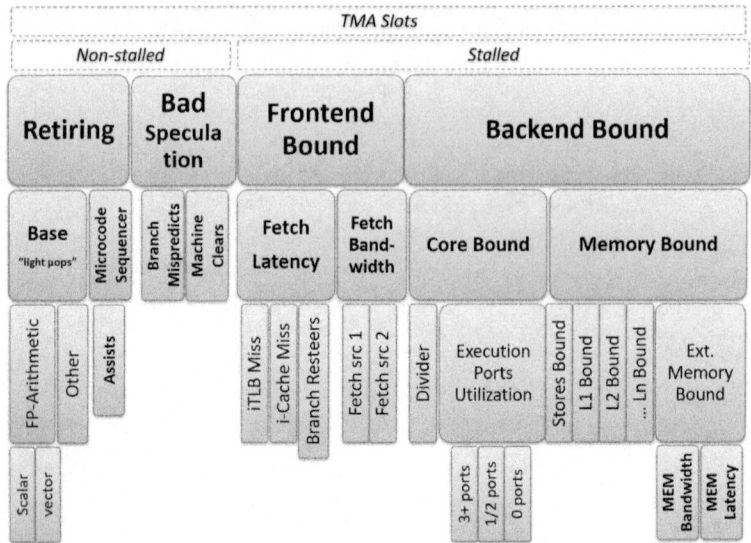

Figure 29: The TMA hierarchy of performance bottlenecks. © *Image by Ahmad Yasin.*

with a single run of the benchmark.[110]

The top two-levels of TMA metrics are expressed in the percentage of all pipeline slots (see section 4.5) that were available during the execution of the program. It allows TMA to give an accurate representation of CPU microarchitecture utilization, taking into account the full bandwidth of the processor.

After we identified the performance bottleneck in the program, we would be interested to know where exactly in the code it is happening. The second stage of TMA is locating the source of the problem down to the exact line of code and assembly instruction. Analysis methodology provides exact PMC that one should use for each category of the performance problem. Then the developer can use this PMC to find the area in the source code that contributes to the most critical performance bottleneck identified by the first stage. This correspondence

---

[110] This only is acceptable if the workload is steady. Otherwise, you would better fall back to the original strategy of multiple runs and drilling down with each run.

6.1 Top-Down Microarchitecture Analysis

can be found in TMA metrics[111] table in "Locate-with" column. For example, to locate the bottleneck associated with a high DRAM_Bound metric in an application running on the Intel Skylake processor, one should sample on MEM_LOAD_RETIRED.L3_MISS_PS performance event.

6.1.1 TMA in Intel® VTune™ Profiler

TMA is featured through the "Microarchitecture Exploration"[112] analysis in the latest Intel VTune Profiler. Figure 30 shows analysis summary for 7-zip benchmark [113]. On the diagram, you can see that a significant amount of execution time was wasted due to CPU Bad Speculation and, in particular, due to mispredicted branches.

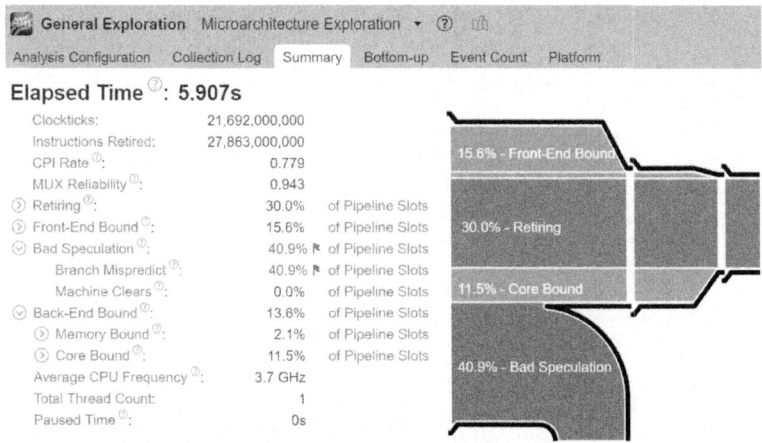

Figure 30: Intel VTune Profiler "Microarchitecture Exploration" analysis.

The beauty of the tool is that you can click on the metric you are interested in, and the tool will get you to the page that shows top functions that contribute to that particular metric. For example, if you click on the Bad Speculation metric, you will see something like what is shown in Figure 31. [114]

From there, if you double click on the LzmaDec_DecodeReal2 function, Intel® VTune™ Profiler will get you to the source level view like the

---
[111] TMA metrics - https://download.01.org/perfmon/TMA_Metrics.xlsx.
[112] VTune microarchitecture analysis - https://software.intel.com/en-us/vtune-help-general-exploration-analysis. In pre-2019 versions of Intel® VTune Profiler,

105

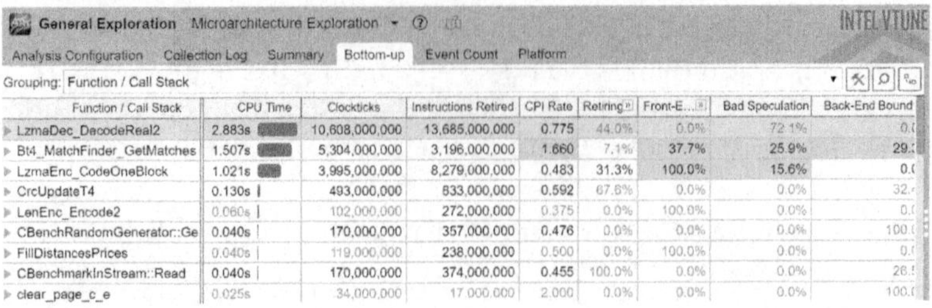

6.1 Top-Down Microarchitecture Analysis

Figure 31: "Microarchitecture Exploration" Bottom-up view.

one that is shown in Figure 32. The highlighted line contributes to the biggest number of branch mispredicts in the `LzmaDec_DecodeReal2` function.

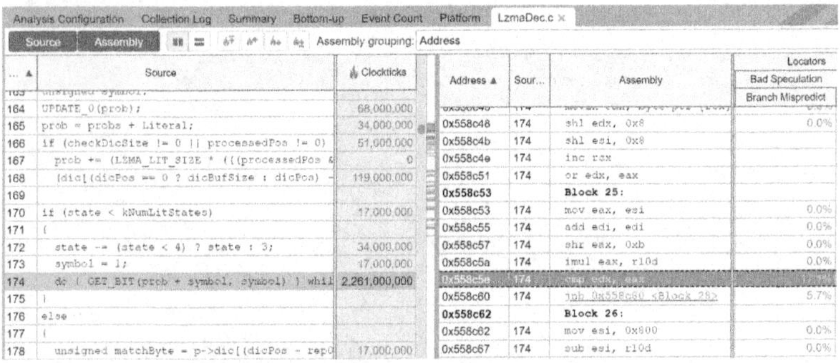

Figure 32: "Microarchitecture Exploration" source code and assembly view.

6.1.2 TMA in Linux Perf

As of Linux kernel 4.8, `perf` has an option `--topdown` used in `perf stat` command[115] that prints TMA level 1 metrics, i.e., only four high-level buckets:

---

it was called as "General Exploration" analysis.

[113] 7zip benchmark - https://github.com/llvm-mirror/test-suite/tree/master/MultiSource/Benchmarks/7zip.

[114] Per-function view of TMA metrics is a feature unique to Intel® VTune profiler.

[115] Linux `perf stat` manual page - http://man7.org/linux/man-pages/man1/perf-stat.1.html#STAT_REPORT.

106

6.1 Top-Down Microarchitecture Analysis

```
$ perf stat --topdown -a -- taskset -c 0 ./7zip-benchmark b
       retiring  bad speculat  FE bound  BE bound
S0-C0    30.8%       41.8%        8.8%     18.6%   <==
S0-C1    17.4%        2.3%       12.0%     68.2%
S0-C2    10.1%        5.8%       32.5%     51.6%
S0-C3    47.3%        0.3%        2.9%     49.6%
...
```

To get values for high-level TMA metrics, Linux `perf` requires profiling the whole system (`-a`). This is why we see metrics for all cores. But since we pinned the benchmark to core0 with `taskset -c 0`, we can only focus on the first row that corresponds to S0-C0.

To get access to Top-Down metrics level 2, 3, etc. one can use toplev[116] tool that is a part of pmu-tools[117] written by Andi Kleen. It is implemented in `Python` and invokes Linux `perf` under the hood. You will see examples of using it in the next section. Specific Linux kernel settings must be enabled to use `toplev`, check the documentation for more details. To better present the workflow, the next section provides a step-by-step example of using TMA to improve the performance of a memory-bound application.

> **Personal Experience:** Intel® VTune™ Profiler is an extremely powerful tool, no doubt about it. However, for quick experiments, I often use Linux perf that is available on every Linux distribution I'm working on. Thus, the motivation for the example in the next section being explored with Linux perf.

6.1.3 Step1: Identify the bottleneck

Suppose we have a tiny benchmark (`a.out`) that runs for 8.5 sec. The complete source code of the benchmark can be found on github[118].

```
$ time -p ./a.out
real 8.53
```

As a first step, we run our application and collect specific metrics that will help us to characterize it, i.e., we try to detect to which

---
[116] Toplev - https://github.com/andikleen/pmu-tools/wiki/toplev-manual
[117] PMU tools - https://github.com/andikleen/pmu-tools.
[118] Benchmark for TMA section - https://github.com/dendibakh/dendibakh.github.io/tree/master/_posts/code/TMAM.

6.1 Top-Down Microarchitecture Analysis

category our application belongs. Below are level-1 metrics for our benchmark:[119]

```
$ ~/pmu-tools/toplev.py --core S0-C0 -l1 -v --no-desc taskset -c 0
    ./a.out
...
# Level 1
S0-C0    Frontend_Bound:      13.81 % Slots
S0-C0    Bad_Speculation:      0.22 % Slots
S0-C0    Backend_Bound:       53.43 % Slots <==
S0-C0    Retiring:            32.53 % Slots
```

Notice, the process is pinned to CPU0 (using `taskset -c 0`), and the output of `toplev` is limited to this core only (`--core S0-C0`). By looking at the output, we can tell that performance of the application is bound by the CPU backend. Without trying to analyze it right now, let us drill one level down: [120]

```
$ ~/pmu-tools/toplev.py --core S0-C0 -l2 -v --no-desc taskset -c 0
    ./a.out
...
# Level 1
S0-C0    Frontend_Bound:                       13.92 % Slots
S0-C0    Bad_Speculation:                       0.23 % Slots
S0-C0    Backend_Bound:                        53.39 % Slots
S0-C0    Retiring:                             32.49 % Slots
# Level 2
S0-C0    Frontend_Bound.FE_Latency:            12.11 % Slots
S0-C0    Frontend_Bound.FE_Bandwidth:           1.84 % Slots
S0-C0    Bad_Speculation.Branch_Mispred:        0.22 % Slots
S0-C0    Bad_Speculation.Machine_Clears:        0.01 % Slots
S0-C0    Backend_Bound.Memory_Bound:           44.59 % Slots <==
S0-C0    Backend_Bound.Core_Bound:              8.80 % Slots
S0-C0    Retiring.Base:                        24.83 % Slots
S0-C0    Retiring.Microcode_Sequencer:          7.65 % Slots
```

We see that the application's performance is bound by memory accesses. Almost half of the CPU execution resources were wasted waiting for memory requests to complete. Now let us dig one level deeper: [121]

---

[119] Outputs in this section are trimmed to fit on the page. Do not rely on the exact format that is presented.

[120] Alternatively, we could use `-l1 --nodes Core_Bound,Memory_Bound` instead of `-l2` to limit the collection of all the metrics since we know from the first level metrics that the application is bound by CPU Backend.

[121] Alternatively, we could use `-l2 --nodes L1_Bound,L2_Bound,L3_Bound ,DRAM_Bound,Store_Bound, Divider,Ports_Utilization` option instead of `-l3` to limit collection, since we knew from the second level metrics that the application is bound by memory.

6.1 Top-Down Microarchitecture Analysis

```
$ ~/pmu-tools/toplev.py --core S0-C0 -13 -v --no-desc taskset -c 0
  ./a.out
...
# Level 1
S0-C0    Frontend_Bound:                       13.91 % Slots
S0-C0    Bad_Speculation:                       0.24 % Slots
S0-C0    Backend_Bound:                        53.36 % Slots
S0-C0    Retiring:                             32.41 % Slots
# Level 2
S0-C0    FE_Bound.FE_Latency:                  12.10 % Slots
S0-C0    FE_Bound.FE_Bandwidth:                 1.85 % Slots
S0-C0    BE_Bound.Memory_Bound:                44.58 % Slots
S0-C0    BE_Bound.Core_Bound:                   8.78 % Slots
# Level 3
S0-C0-T0 BE_Bound.Mem_Bound.L1_Bound:           4.39 % Stalls
S0-C0-T0 BE_Bound.Mem_Bound.L2_Bound:           2.42 % Stalls
S0-C0-T0 BE_Bound.Mem_Bound.L3_Bound:           5.75 % Stalls
S0-C0-T0 BE_Bound.Mem_Bound.DRAM_Bound:        47.11 % Stalls <==
S0-C0-T0 BE_Bound.Mem_Bound.Store_Bound:        0.69 % Stalls
S0-C0-T0 BE_Bound.Core_Bound.Divider:           8.56 % Clocks
S0-C0-T0 BE_Bound.Core_Bound.Ports_Util:       11.31 % Clocks
```

We found the bottleneck to be in `DRAM_Bound`. This tells us that many memory accesses miss in all levels of caches and go all the way down to the main memory. We can also confirm if we collect the absolute number of L3 cache misses (DRAM hit) for the program. For Skylake architecture, the `DRAM_Bound` metric is calculated using the `CYCLE_ACTIVITY.STALLS_L3_MISS` performance event. Let's collect it:

```
$ perf stat -e cycles,cycle_activity.stalls_l3_miss -- ./a.out
  32226253316  cycles
  19764641315  cycle_activity.stalls_l3_miss
```

According to the definition of `CYCLE_ACTIVITY.STALLS_L3_MISS`, it counts cycles when execution stalls, while the L3 cache miss demand load is outstanding. We can see that there are ~60% of such cycles, which is pretty bad.

6.1.4 Step2: Locate the place in the code

As the second step in the TMA process, we would locate the place in the code where the bottleneck occurs most frequently. In order to do so, one should sample the workload using a performance event that corresponds to the type of bottleneck that was identified during Step 1.

A recommended way to find such an event is to run `toplev` tool with the `--show-sample` option that will suggest the `perf record` command

6.1 Top-Down Microarchitecture Analysis

line that can be used to locate the issue. For the purpose of understanding the mechanics of TMA, we also present the manual way to find an event associated with a particular performance bottleneck. Correspondence between performance bottlenecks and performance events that should be used for locating the place in the code where such bottlenecks take place can be done with the help of TMA metrics[122] table introduced earlier in the chapter. The Locate-with column denotes a performance event that should be used to locate the exact place in the code where the issue occurs. For the purpose of our example, in order to find memory accesses that contribute to such a high value of the DRAM_Bound metric (miss in the L3 cache), we should sample on MEM_LOAD_RETIRED.L3_MISS_PS precise event as shown in the listing above:

```
$ perf record -e
    cpu/event=0xd1,umask=0x20,name=MEM_LOAD_RETIRED.L3_MISS/ppp
    ./a.out

$ perf report -n --stdio
...
# Samples: 33K of event 'MEM_LOAD_RETIRED.'L3_MISS
# Event count (approx.): 71363893
# Overhead    Samples   Shared Object       Symbol
# ........    .......   .................   ..............
#
   99.95%     33811     a.out               [.] foo
    0.03%        52     [kernel]            [k] get_page_from_freelist
    0.01%         3     [kernel]            [k] free_pages_prepare
    0.00%         1     [kernel]            [k] free_pcppages_bulk
```

The majority of L3 misses are caused by memory accesses in function foo inside executable a.out. In order to avoid compiler optimizations, function foo is implemented in assembly language, which is presented in Listing 11. The "driver" portion of the benchmark is implemented in the main function, as shown in Listing 12. We allocate a big enough array a to make it not fit in the L3 cache[123]. The benchmark basically generates a random index to array a and passes it to the foo function along with the address of array a. Later foo function reads this random memory location. [124]

By looking at Listing 11, we can see that all L3-Cache misses in

---

[122] TMA metrics - https://download.01.org/perfmon/TMA_Metrics.xlsx.

[123] L3 cache on the machine I was using is 38.5 MB - Intel(R) Xeon(R) Platinum 8180 CPU.

[124] According to x86 calling conventions (https://en.wikipedia.org/wiki/X86_calling_conventions), first 2 arguments land in rdi and rsi registers respectively.

6.1 Top-Down Microarchitecture Analysis

Listing 11 Assembly code of function foo.

```
$ perf annotate --stdio -M intel foo
Percent |      Disassembly of a.out for MEM_LOAD_RETIRED.L3_MISS
---------------------------------------------------------------
        :      Disassembly of section .text:
        :
        :      0000000000400a00 <foo>:
        :      foo():
   0.00 :        400a00:   nop    DWORD PTR [rax+rax*1+0x0]
   0.00 :        400a08:   nop    DWORD PTR [rax+rax*1+0x0]
                 ...
 100.00 :        400e07:   mov    rax,QWORD PTR [rdi+rsi*1] <==
                 ...
   0.00 :        400e13:   xor    rax,rax
   0.00 :        400e16:   ret
```

Listing 12 Source code of function main.

```
extern "C" { void foo(char* a, int n); }
const int _200MB = 1024*1024*200;
int main() {
  char* a = (char*)malloc(_200MB);  // 200 MB buffer
  ...
  for (int i = 0; i < 100000000; i++) {
    int random_int = distribution(generator);
    foo(a, random_int);
  }
  ...
}
```

function foo are tagged to a single instruction. Now that we know which instruction caused so many L3 misses, let's fix it.

6.1.5 Step3: Fix the issue

Because there is a time window between the moment when we get the next address that will be accessed and actual load instruction, we can add a prefetch hint[125] as shown on Listing 13. More information about memory prefetching can be found in section 8.1.2.

This hint improved execution time by 2 seconds, which is a 30% speedup. Notice 10x less value for CYCLE_ACTIVITY.STALLS_L3_MISS event:

---

[125] Documentation about __builtin_prefetch can be found at https://gcc.gnu.org/onlinedocs/gcc/Other-Builtins.html.

6.1 Top-Down Microarchitecture Analysis

Listing 13 Inserting memory prefetch into main.

```
  for (int i = 0; i < 100000000; i++) {
    int random_int = distribution(generator);
+   __builtin_prefetch ( a + random_int, 0, 1);
    foo(a, random_int);
  }
```

```
$ perf stat -e cycles,cycle_activity.stalls_l3_miss -- ./a.out
  24621931288      cycles
   2069238765      cycle_activity.stalls_l3_miss
     6,498080824 seconds time elapsed
```

TMA is an iterative process, so we now need to repeat the process starting from the Step1. Likely it will move the bottleneck into some other bucket, in this case, Retiring. This was an easy example demonstrating the workflow of TMA methodology. Analyzing real-world application is unlikely to be that easy. The next entire chapter in this book is organized in a way to be conveniently used with the TMA process. E.g., its sections are broken down to reflect each high-level category of performance bottlenecks. The idea behind such a structure is to provide some kind of checklist which developer can use to drive code changes after performance issue has been found. For instance, when developers see that the application they are working on is Memory Bound, they can look up section 8.1 for ideas.

6.1.6 Summary

TMA is great for identifying CPU performance bottlenecks in the code. Ideally, when we run it on some application, we would like to see the Retiring metric at 100%. This would mean that this application fully saturates the CPU. It is possible to achieve results close to this on a toy program. However, real-world applications are far from getting there.

Using TMA on a code that has major performance flaws is not recommended because it will likely steer you in the wrong direction, and instead of fixing real high-level performance problems, you will be tuning bad code, which is just a waste of time. Similarly, make sure the environment doesn't get in the way of profiling. For example, if you drop filesystem cache and run the benchmark under TMA, it will likely show that your application is Memory Bound, which in fact, may be false when filesystem cache is warmed up.

Workload characterization provided by the TMA can increase the scope of potential optimizations beyond source code. For example, if the application is memory bound and all possible ways to speed it up on the software level are examined, it is possible to improve the memory subsystem by using faster memory. This enables educated experiments since the money will only be spent once you found that the program is memory bound and it will benefit from faster memory.

At the time of this writing, the first level of TMA metrics is also available on AMD processors.

Additional resources and links:

- Ahmad Yasin's paper "A top-down method for performance analysis and counters architecture" [Yasin, 2014].

- Presentation "Software Optimizations Become Simple with Top-Down Analysis on Intel Skylake" by Ahmad Yasin at IDF'15, URL: https://youtu.be/kjufVhyuV_A.

- Andi Kleen's blog - pmu-tools, part II: toplev, URL: http://halobates.de/blog/p/262.

- Toplev manual, URL: https://github.com/andikleen/pmu-tools/wiki/toplev-manual.

- Understanding How General Exploration Works in Intel® VTune™ Profiler, URL: https://software.intel.com/en-us/articles/understanding-how-general-exploration-works-in-intel-vtune-amplifier-xe.

6.2 Last Branch Record

Modern Intel and AMD CPUs have a feature called Last Branch Record (LBR), where the CPU continuously logs a number of previously executed branches. But before going into the details, one might ask: *Why are we so interested in branches?* Well, because this is how we are able to determine the control flow of our program. We largely ignore other instructions in a basic block (see section 7.2) because branches are always the last instruction in a basic block. Since all instructions in the basic block are guaranteed to be executed once, we can only focus on branches that will "represent" the entire basic block. Thus, it's possible to reconstruct the entire line-by-line execution path of the program if we track the outcome of every branch. In fact, this is what Intel Processor Traces (PT) feature is capable of doing, which will be discussed in section 6.4. LBR feature predates PT and has different use cases and special features.

Thanks to the LBR mechanism, the CPU can continuously log branches to a set of model-specific registers (MSRs) in parallel with executing the program, causing minimal slowdown[126]. Hardware logs the "from" and "to" address of each branch along with some additional metadata (see Figure 33). The registers act like a ring buffer that is continuously overwritten and provides only 32 most recent branch outcomes[127]. If we collect a long enough history of source-destination pairs, we will be able to unwind the control flow of our program, just like a call stack with limited depth.

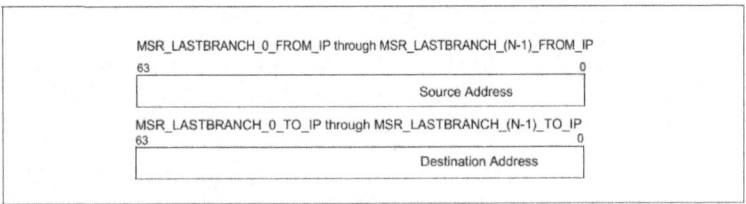

Figure 33: 64-bit Address Layout of LBR MSR. © *Image from [Int, 2020]*.

With LBRs, we can sample branches, but during each sample, look at the previous branches inside the LBR stack that were executed. This gives reasonable coverage of the control flow in the hot code paths but does not overwhelm us with too much information, as only a smaller number of the total branches are examined. It is important to keep in mind that this is still sampling, so not every executed branch can be examined. CPU generally executes too fast for that to be feasible.[Kleen, 2016]

- **Last Branch Record (LBR) Stack** — since Skylake provides 32 pairs of MSRs that store the source and destination address of recently taken branches.
- **Last Branch Record Top-of-Stack (TOS) Pointer** — contains a pointer to the MSR in the LBR stack that contains the

---

[126] Runtime overhead for the majority of LBR use cases is below 1%. [Nowak and Bitzes, 2014]

[127] Only since Skylake microarchitecture. In Haswell and Broadwell architectures LBR stack is 16 entries deep. Check the Intel manual for information about other architectures.

6.2 Last Branch Record

most recent branch, interrupt or exception recorded.

It is very important to keep in mind that only taken branches are being logged with the LBR mechanism. Below is an example that shows how branch results are tracked in the LBR stack.

```
----> 4eda10:   mov    edi,DWORD PTR [rbx]
|     4eda12:   test   edi,edi
| --- 4eda14:   jns    4eda1e              <== NOT taken
| |   4eda16:   mov    eax,edi
| |   4eda18:   shl    eax,0x7
| |   4eda1b:   lea    edi,[rax+rdi*8]
| L-> 4eda1e:   call   4edb26
|     4eda23:   add    rbx,0x4
|     4eda27:   mov    DWORD PTR [rbx-0x4],eax
|     4eda2a:   cmp    rbx,rbp
---- 4eda2d:    jne    4eda10              <== taken
```

Below is what we expect to see in the LBR stack at the moment we executed the CALL instruction. Because the JNS branch (4eda14 -> 4eda1e) was not taken, it is not logged and thus does not appear in the LBR stack:

```
FROM_IP         TO_IP
...             ...
4eda2d          4eda10
4eda1e          4edb26       <== LBR TOS
```

> **Personal Experience:** Untaken branches not being logged might add some additional burden for analysis but usually doesn't complicate it too much. We can still unwind the LBR stack since we know that the control flow was sequential from TO_IP(N-1) to FROM_IP(N).

Starting from Haswell, LBR entry received additional components to detect branch misprediction. There is a dedicated bit for it in the LBR entry (see [Int, 2020, Volume 3B, Chapter 17]). Since Skylake additional LBR_INFO component was added to the LBR entry, which has Cycle Count field that counts elapsed core clocks since the last update to the LBR stack. There are important applications to those additions, which we will discuss later. The exact format of LBR entry for a specific processor can be found in [Int, 2020, Volume 3B, Chapters 17,18].

Users can make sure LBRs are enabled on their system by doing the following command:

115

```
$ dmesg | grep -i lbr
[    0.228149] Performance Events: PEBS fmt3+, 32-deep LBR, Skylake
    events, full-width counters, Intel PMU driver.
```

6.2.1 Collecting LBR stacks

With Linux `perf`, one can collect LBR stacks using the command below:

```
$ ~/perf record -b -e cycles ./a.exe
[ perf record: Woken up 68 times to write data ]
[ perf record: Captured and wrote 17.205 MB perf.data (22089
    samples) ]
```

LBR stacks can also be collected using `perf record --call-graph lbr` command, but the amount of information collected is less than using `perf record -b`. For example, branch misprediction and cycles data is not collected when running `perf record --call-graph lbr`.

Because each collected sample captures the entire LBR stack (32 last branch records), the size of collected data (`perf.data`) is significantly bigger than sampling without LBRs. Below is the Linux perf command one can use to dump the contents of collected branch stacks:

```
$ perf script -F brstack &> dump.txt
```

If we look inside the `dump.txt` (it might be big) we will see something like as shown below:

```
...
0x4edabd/0x4edad0/P/-/-/2       0x4edaf9/0x4edab0/P/-/-/29
0x4edabd/0x4edad0/P/-/-/2       0x4edb24/0x4edab0/P/-/-/23
0x4edadd/0x4edb00/M/-/-/4       0x4edabd/0x4edad0/P/-/-/2
0x4edb24/0x4edab0/P/-/-/24      0x4edadd/0x4edb00/M/-/-/4
0x4edabd/0x4edad0/P/-/-/2       0x4edb24/0x4edab0/P/-/-/23
0x4edadd/0x4edb00/M/-/-/1       0x4edabd/0x4edad0/P/-/-/1
0x4edb24/0x4edab0/P/-/-/3       0x4edadd/0x4edb00/P/-/-/1
0x4edabd/0x4edad0/P/-/-/1       0x4edb24/0x4edab0/P/-/-/3
...
```

On the block above, we present eight entries from the LBR stack, which typically consists of 32 LBR entries. Each entry has FROM and TO addresses (hexadecimal values), predicted flag (M/P)[128], and a number of cycles (number in the last position of each entry). Components

---

[128] M - Mispredicted, P - Predicted.

marked with "-" are related to transactional memory (TSX), which we won't discuss here. Curious readers can look up the format of decoded LBR entry in the `perf script` specification[129].

There is a number of important use cases for LBR. In the next sections, we will address the most important ones.

6.2.2 Capture call graph

Discussions on collecting call graph and its importance were covered in section 5.4.3. LBR can be used for collecting call-graph information even if you compiled a program without frame pointers (controlled by compiler option `-fomit-frame-pointer`, ON by default) or debug information[130]:

```
$ perf record --call-graph lbr -- ./a.exe
$ perf report -n --stdio
# Children      Self    Samples  Command  Object   Symbol
# ........   .......   .......   .......  .......  .......
   99.96%     99.94%     65447    a.out    a.out    [.] bar
              |
              --99.94%--main
                        |
                        |--90.86%--foo
                        |         |
                        |         --90.86%--bar
                        |
                        --9.08%--zoo
                                 bar
```

As you can see, we identified the hottest function in the program (which is `bar`). Also, we found out callers that contribute to the most time spent in function `bar` (it is `foo`). In this case, we can see that 91% of samples in `bar` have `foo` as its caller function.[131]

Using the LBR feature, we can determine a Hyper Block (sometimes called Super Block), which is a chain of basic blocks executed most frequently in the whole program. Basic blocks from that chain are not necessarily laid in the sequential physical order; they're executed sequentially.

---

[129] Linux `perf script` manual page - http://man7.org/linux/man-pages/man1/perf-script.1.html.

[130] Utilized by `perf record --call-graph dwarf`.

[131] We cannot necessarily drive conclusions about function call counts in this case. For example, we cannot say that `foo` calls `bar` 10 times more than `zoo`. It could be the case that `foo` calls `bar` once, but it executes some expensive path inside `bar` while `zoo` calls `bar` lots of times but returns quickly from it.

6.2.3 Identify hot branches

The LBR feature also allows us to know what were the most frequently taken branches:

```
$ perf record -e cycles -b -- ./a.exe
[ perf record: Woken up 3 times to write data ]
[ perf record: Captured and wrote 0.535 MB perf.data (670 samples) ]
$ perf report -n --sort overhead,srcline_from,srcline_to -F
    +dso,symbol_from,symbol_to --stdio
# Samples: 21K of event 'cycles'
# Event count (approx.): 21440
# Overhead   Samples  Source Sym  Target Sym  From Line  To Line
# ........   .......  ..........  ..........  .........  .......
    51.65%     11074  [.] bar     [.] bar     a.c:4      a.c:5
    22.30%      4782  [.] foo     [.] bar     a.c:10     (null)
    21.89%      4693  [.] foo     [.] zoo     a.c:11     (null)
     4.03%       863  [.] main    [.] foo     a.c:21     (null)
```

From this example, we can see that more than 50% of taken branches are inside the `bar` function, 22% of branches are function calls from `foo` to `bar`, and so on. Notice how `perf` switched from `cycles` events to analyzing LBR stacks: only 670 samples were collected, yet we have an entire LBR stack captured with every sample. This gives us `670 * 32 = 21440` LBR entries (branch outcomes) for analysis.[132]

Most of the time, it's possible to determine the location of the branch just from the line of code and target symbol. However, theoretically, one could write code with two `if` statements written on a single line. Also, when expanding the macro definition, all the expanded code gets the same source line, which is another situation when this might happen. This issue does not totally block the analysis but only makes it a little more difficult. In order to disambiguate two branches, you likely need to analyze raw LBR stacks yourself (see example on easyperf[133] blog).

6.2.4 Analyze branch misprediction rate

It's also possible to know the misprediction rate for hot branches [134]:

---

[132] The report header generated by perf confuses users because it says `21K of event cycles`. But there are 21K LBR entries, not `cycles`.

[133] Analyzing raw LBR stacks - https://easyperf.net/blog/2019/05/06/Estimating-branch-probability.

[134] Adding `-F +srcline_from,srcline_to` slows down building report. Hopefully, in newer versions of perf, decoding time will be improved.

```
$ perf record -e cycles -b -- ./a.exe
$ perf report -n --sort symbol_from,symbol_to -F
   +mispredict,srcline_from,srcline_to --stdio
# Samples: 657K of event 'cycles'
# Event count (approx.): 657888
# Overhead  Samples  Mis  From Line  To Line    Source Sym  Target Sym
# ........  .......  ...  .........  ........   ..........  ..........
  46.12%    303391    N   dec.c:36   dec.c:40   LzmaDec     LzmaDec
  22.33%    146900    N   enc.c:25   enc.c:26   LzmaFind    LzmaFind
   6.70%     44074    N   lz.c:13    lz.c:27    LzmaEnc     LzmaEnc
   6.33%     41665    Y   dec.c:36   dec.c:40   LzmaDec     LzmaDec
```

In this example[135], lines that correspond to function `LzmaDec` are of particular interest to us. Using the reasoning from section 6.2.3, we can conclude that the branch on source line `dec.c:36` is the most executed branch in the benchmark. In the output that Linux `perf` provides, we can spot two entries that correspond to the `LzmaDec` function: one with `Y` and one with `N` letters. Analyzing those two entries together gives us a misprediction rate of the branch. In this case, we know that the branch on line `dec.c:36` was predicted `303391` times (corresponds to `N`) and was mispredicted `41665` times (corresponds to `Y`), which gives us 88% prediction rate.

Linux `perf` calculates the misprediction rate by analyzing each LBR entry and extracting misprediction bits from it. So that for every branch, we have a number of times it was predicted correctly and a number of mispredictions. Again, due to the nature of sampling, it is possible that some branches might have an `N` entry but no corresponding `Y` entry. It could mean that there are no LBR entries for that branch being mispredicted, but it doesn't necessarily mean that the prediction rate equals to 100%.

6.2.5 Precise timing of machine code

As it was discussed in section 6.2, starting from Skylake architecture, LBR entries have Cycle Count information. This additional field gives us a number of cycles elapsed between two taken branches. If the target address in the previous LBR entry is the beginning of some basic block (BB) and the source address of the current LBR entry is the last instruction of the same basic block, then the cycle count is the latency of this basic block. For example:

---

[135] This example is taken from the real-world application, 7-zip benchmark: https://github.com/llvm-mirror/test-suite/tree/master/MultiSource/Benchmarks/7zip. Although the output of perf report is trimmed a little bit to fit nicely on a page.

```
400618:    movb $0x0, (%rbp,%rdx,1)    <= start of a BB
40061d:    add $0x1, %rdx
400621:    cmp $0xc800000, %rdx
400628:    jnz 0x400644                <= end of a BB
```

Suppose we have two entries in the LBR stack:

```
FROM_IP    TO_IP     Cycle Count
...        ...       ...
40060a     400618    10
400628     400644    5           <== LBR TOS
```

Given that information, we know that there was one occurrence when the basic block that starts at offset 400618 was executed in 5 cycles. If we collect enough samples, we could plot a probability density function of the latency for that basic block (see figure 34). This chart was compiled by analyzing all LBR entries that satisfy the rule described above. For example, the basic block was executed in ~75 cycles only 4% of the time, but more often, it was executed between 260 and 314 cycles. This block has a random load inside a huge array that doesn't fit in CPU L3 cache, so the latency of the basic block largely depends on this load. There are two important spikes on the chart that is shown in Figure 34: first, around 80 cycles corresponds to the L3 cache hit, and the second spike, around 300 cycles, corresponds to L3 cache miss where the load request goes all the way down to the main memory.

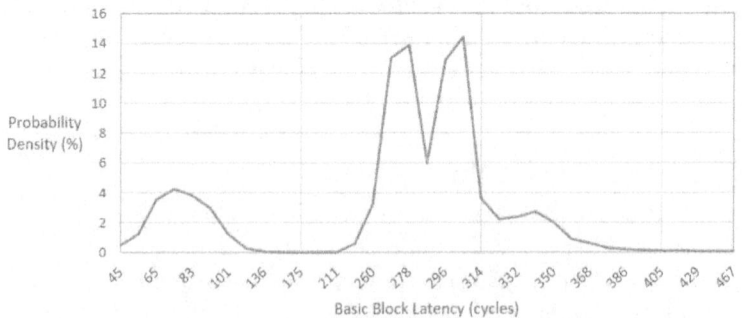

Figure 34: Probability density function for latency of the basic block that starts at address 0x400618.

This information can be used for further fine-grained tuning of this basic block. This example might benefit from memory prefetching, which we will discuss in section 8.1.2. Also, this cycle information

6.2 Last Branch Record

can be used for timing loop iterations, where every loop iteration ends with a taken branch (back edge).

An example of how one can build a probability density function for the latency of an arbitrary basic block can be found on easyperf blog[136]. However, in newer versions of Linux perf, getting this information is much easier. For example[137]:

```
$ perf record -e cycles -b -- ./a.exe
$ perf report -n --sort symbol_from,symbol_to -F
   +cycles,srcline_from,srcline_to --stdio
# Samples: 658K of event 'cycles'
# Event count (approx.): 658240
# Overhead  Samples  BBCycles  FromSrcLine  ToSrcLine
# ........  .......  ........  ...........  ...........
   2.82%     18581      1       dec.c:325    dec.c:326
   2.54%     16728      2       dec.c:174    dec.c:174
   2.40%     15815      4       dec.c:174    dec.c:174
   2.28%     15032      2       find.c:375   find.c:376
   1.59%     10484      1       dec.c:174    dec.c:174
   1.44%      9474      1       enc.c:1310   enc.c:1315
   1.43%      9392     10       7zCrc.c:15   7zCrc.c:17
   0.85%      5567     32       dec.c:174    dec.c:174
   0.78%      5126      1       enc.c:820    find.c:540
   0.77%      5066      1       enc.c:1335   enc.c:1325
   0.76%      5014      6       dec.c:299    dec.c:299
   0.72%      4770      6       dec.c:174    dec.c:174
   0.71%      4681      2       dec.c:396    dec.c:395
   0.69%      4563      3       dec.c:174    dec.c:174
   0.58%      3804     24       dec.c:174    dec.c:174
```

Several not significant lines were removed from the output of perf record in order to make it fit on the page. If we now focus on the branch in which source and destination is dec.c:174[138], we can find multiple lines associated with it. Linux perf sorts entries by overhead first, which requires us to manually filter entries for the branch which we are interested in. In fact, if we filter them, we will get the latency distribution for the basic block that ends with this branch, as shown in the table 5. Later user can plot this data and get a chart similar to Figure 34.

---

[136] Building a probability density function for the latency of an arbitrary basic block - https://easyperf.net/blog/2019/04/03/Precise-timing-of-machine-code-with-Linux-perf.

[137] Adding -F +srcline_from,srcline_to slows down building report. Hopefully, in newer versions of perf, decoding time will be improved.

[138] In the source code, line dec.c:174 expands a macro that has a self-contained branch. That's why the source and destination happen to be on the same line.

121

Table 5: Probability density for basic block latency.

Cycles	Number of samples	Probability density
1	10484	17.0%
2	16728	27.1%
3	4563	7.4%
4	15815	25.6%
6	4770	7.7%
24	3804	6.2%
32	5567	9.0%

Currently, timed LBR is the most precise cycle-accurate source of timing information in the system.

6.2.6 Estimating branch outcome probability

Later in section 7, we will discuss the importance of code layout for performance. Going forward a little bit, having a hot path in a fall through manner[139] generally improves the performance of the program. Considering a single branch, knowing that `condition` 99% of the time is false or true is essential for a compiler to make better optimizing decisions.

LBR feature allows us to get this data without instrumenting the code. As the outcome from the analysis, the user will get a ratio between true and false outcomes of the condition, i.e., how many times the branch was taken and how much not taken. This feature especially shines when analyzing indirect jumps (switch statement) and indirect calls (virtual calls). One can find examples of using it on a real-world application on easyperf blog[140].

6.2.7 Other use cases

- **Profile guided optimizations**. LBR feature can provide profiling feedback data for optimizing compilers. LBR can be a better choice as opposed to static code instrumentation when runtime overhead is considered.

---

[139] I.e., when outcomes of branches are not taken.
[140] Analyzing raw LBR stacks - https://easyperf.net/blog/2019/05/06/Estimating-branch-probability.

- **Capturing function arguments.** When LBR features is used together with PEBS (see section 6.3), it is possible to capture function arguments, since according to x86 calling conventions[141] first few arguments of a callee land in registers which are captured by PEBS record. [Int, 2020, Appendix B, Chapter B.3.3.4]
- **Basic Block Execution Counts.** Since all the basic blocks between a branch IP (source) and the previous target in the LBR stack are executed exactly once, it's possible to evaluate the execution rate of basic blocks inside a program. This process involves building a map of starting addresses of each basic block and then traversing collected LBR stacks backward. [Int, 2020, Appendix B, Chapter B.3.3.4]

6.3 Processor Event-Based Sampling

The Processor Event-Based Sampling (PEBS) is another very useful feature in CPUs that provides many different ways to enhance performance analysis. Similar to Last Branch Record (see section 6.2), PEBS is used while profiling the program to capture additional data with every collected sample. In Intel processors, the PEBS feature was introduced in NetBurst microarchitecture. A similar feature on AMD processors is called Instruction Based Sampling (IBS) and is available starting with the Family 10h generation of cores (code-named "Barcelona" and "Shanghai").

The set of additional data has a defined format, which is called the PEBS record. When a performance counter is configured for PEBS, the processor saves the contents of the PEBS buffer, which is later stored in memory. The record contains the architectural state of the processor, for instance, the state of the general-purpose registers (EAX, EBX, ESP, etc.), instruction pointer register (EIP), flags register (EFLAGS) and more. The content layout of a PEBS record varies across different implementations that support PEBS. See [Int, 2020, Volume 3B, Chapter 18.6.2.4 Processor Event-Based Sampling (PEBS)] for details of enumerating PEBS record format. PEBS Record Format for Intel Skylake CPU is shown in Figure 35.

Users can check if PEBS is enabled by executing `dmesg`:

---

[141] X86 calling conventions - https://en.wikipedia.org/wiki/X86_calling_conventions

6.3 Processor Event-Based Sampling

Byte Offset	Field	Byte Offset	Field
00H	R/EFLAGS	68H	R11
08H	R/EIP	70H	R12
10H	R/EAX	78H	R13
18H	R/EBX	80H	R14
20H	R/ECX	88H	R15
28H	R/EDX	90H	Applicable Counter
30H	R/ESI	98H	Data Linear Address
38H	R/EDI	A0H	Data Source Encoding
40H	R/EBP	A8H	Latency value (core cycles)
48H	R/ESP	B0H	EventingIP
50H	R8	B8H	TX Abort Information (Section 18.3.6.5.1)
58H	R9	C0H	TSC
60H	R10		

Figure 35: PEBS Record Format for 6th Generation, 7th Generation and 8th Generation Intel Core Processor Families. © *Image from [Int, 2020, Volume 3B, Chapter 18]*.

```
$ dmesg | grep PEBS
[    0.061116] Performance Events: PEBS fmt1+, IvyBridge events,
    16-deep LBR, full-width counters, Intel PMU driver.
```

Linux `perf` doesn't export the raw PEBS output as it does for LBR[142]. Instead, it processes PEBS records and extracts only the subset of data depending on a particular need. So, it's not possible to access the collection of raw PEBS records with Linux `perf`. Although, Linux `perf` provides some PEBS data processed from raw samples, which can be accessed by `perf report -D`. To dump raw PEBS records, one can use `pebs-grabber`[143] tool.

There is a number of benefits that the PEBS mechanism brings to performance monitoring, which we will discuss in the next section.

6.3.1 Precise events

One of the major problems in profiling is pinpointing the exact instruction that caused a particular performance event. As discussed in section 5.4, interrupt-based sampling is based on counting specific performance events and waiting until it overflows. When an overflow interrupt happens, it takes a processor some amount of time to

---

[142] For LBR, Linux perf dumps entire contents of LBR stack with every collected sample. So, it's possible to analyze raw LBR dumps collected by Linux perf.

[143] PEBS grabber tool - https://github.com/andikleen/pmu-tools/tree/master/pebs-grabber. Requires root access.

6.3 Processor Event-Based Sampling

stop the execution and tag instruction that caused the overflow. This is especially difficult for modern complex out-of-order CPU architectures.

It introduces the notion of a skid, which is defined as the distance between the IP that caused the event to the IP where the event is tagged (in the IP field inside the PEBS record). Skid makes it difficult to discover the instruction, which is actually causing the performance issue. Consider an application with a big number of cache misses and the hot assembly code that looks like this:

```
; load1
; load2
; load3
```

The profiler might attribute load3 as the instruction that causes a large number of cache misses, while in reality, load1 is the instruction to blame. This usually causes a lot of confusion for beginners. Interested readers could learn more about underlying reasons for such issues on Intel Developer Zone website[144].

The problem with the skid is mitigated by having the processor itself store the instruction pointer (along with other information) in a PEBS record. The EventingIP field in the PEBS record indicates the instruction that caused the event. This needs to be supported by the hardware and is typically available only for a subset of supported events, called "Precise Events". A complete list of precise events for specific microarchitecture can be found in [Int, 2020, Volume 3B, Chapter 18]. Below listed precise events for the Skylake Microarchitecture:

```
INST_RETIRED.*
OTHER_ASSISTS.*
BR_INST_RETIRED.*
BR_MISP_RETIRED.*
FRONTEND_RETIRED.*
HLE_RETIRED.*
RTM_RETIRED.*
MEM_INST_RETIRED.*
MEM_LOAD_RETIRED.*
MEM_LOAD_L3_HIT_RETIRED.*
```

, where .* means that all sub-events inside a group can be configured as precise events.

---

[144] Hardware event skid - https://software.intel.com/en-us/vtune-help-hardware-event-skid.

TMA methodology (see section 6.1) heavily relies on precise events to locate the source of inefficient execution of the code. An example of using precise events to mitigate skid can be found on easyperf blog[145]. Users of Linux `perf` should add `ppp` suffix to the event to enable precise tagging:

```
$ perf record -e
    cpu/event=0xd1,umask=0x20,name=MEM_LOAD_RETIRED.L3_MISS/ppp --
    ./a.exe
```

6.3.2 Lower sampling overhead

Frequently generating interrupts and having an analysis tool itself capture program state inside the interrupt service routine is very costly since it involves OS interaction. This is why some hardware allows automatically sampling multiple times to a dedicated buffer without any interrupts. Only when the dedicated buffer is full, the processor raises interrupt, and the buffer gets flushed to memory. This has a lower overhead than traditional interrupt-based sampling.

When a performance counter is configured for PEBS, an overflow condition in the counter will arm the PEBS mechanism. On the subsequent event following overflow, the processor will generate a PEBS event. On a PEBS event, the processor stores the PEBS record in the PEBS buffer area, clears the counter overflow status and reloads the counter with the initial value. If the buffer is full, the CPU will raise an interrupt. [Int, 2020, Volume 3B, Chapter 18]

Note that the PEBS buffer itself is located in the main memory, and its size is configurable. Again, it is the job of a performance analysis tool to allocate and configure the memory area for the CPU to be able to dump PEBS records in it.

6.3.3 Analyzing memory accesses

Memory accesses are a critical factor for the performance of many applications. With PEBS, it is possible to gather detailed information about memory accesses in the program. The feature that allows this to happen is called Data Address Profiling. To provide additional information about sampled loads and stores, it leverages the following fields inside the PEBS facility (see Figure 35):

---

[145] Performance skid - https://easyperf.net/blog/2018/08/29/Understanding-performance-events-skid.

- Data Linear Address (0x98)
- Data Source Encoding (0xA0)
- Latency value (0xA8)

If the performance event supports Data Linear Address (DLA) facility, and it is enabled, CPU will dump memory addresses and latency of the sampled memory access. Keep in mind; this feature does not trace all the stores and loads. Otherwise, the overhead would be too big. Instead, it samples on memory accesses, i.e., analyzes only one from 1000 accesses or so. It is customizable how much samples per second you want.

One of the most important use cases for this PEBS extension is detecting True/False sharing[146], which we will discuss in section 11.7. Linux perf c2c tool heavily relies on DLA data to find contested memory accesses, which could experience True/False sharing.

Also, with the help of Data Address Profiling, user can get general statistics about memory accesses in the program:

```
$ perf mem record -- ./a.exe
$ perf mem -t load report --sort=mem --stdio
# Samples: 656   of event  'cpu/mem-loads,ldlat=30/P'
# Total weight : 136578
# Overhead        Samples    Memory access
# ........     ............  .........................
    44.23%          267      LFB or LFB hit
    18.87%          111      L3 or L3 hit
    15.19%           78      Local RAM or RAM hit
    13.38%           77      L2 or L2 hit
     8.34%          123      L1 or L1 hit
```

From this output, we can see that 8% of the loads in the application were satisfied with L1 cache, 15% from DRAM, and so on.

6.4 Intel Processor Traces

The Intel Processor Traces (PT) is a CPU feature that records the program execution by encoding packets in a highly compressed binary format that can be used to reconstruct execution flow with a timestamp on every instruction. PT has extensive coverage and relatively small overhead[147], which is usually below 5%. Its main usages are postmortem analysis and root-causing performance glitches.

---
[146] False sharing - https://en.wikipedia.org/wiki/False_sharing.
[147] See more information on overhead in [Sharma and Dagenais, 2016].

6.4.1 Workflow

Similar to sampling techniques, PT does not require any modifications to the source code. All you need to collect traces is just to run the program under the tool that supports PT. Once PT is enabled and the benchmark launches, the analysis tool starts writing tracing packets to DRAM.

Similar to LBR, Intel PT works by recording branches. At runtime, whenever a CPU encounters any branch instruction, PT will record the outcome of this branch. For a simple conditional jump instruction, a CPU will record whether it was taken (T) or not taken (NT) using just 1 bit. For an indirect call, PT will record the destination address. Note that unconditional branches are ignored since we statically know their targets.

An example of encoding for a small instruction sequence is shown in Figure 36. Instructions like PUSH, MOV, ADD, and CMP are ignored because they don't change the control flow. However, JE instruction may jump to .label, so its result needs to be recorded. Later there is an indirect call for which destination address is saved.

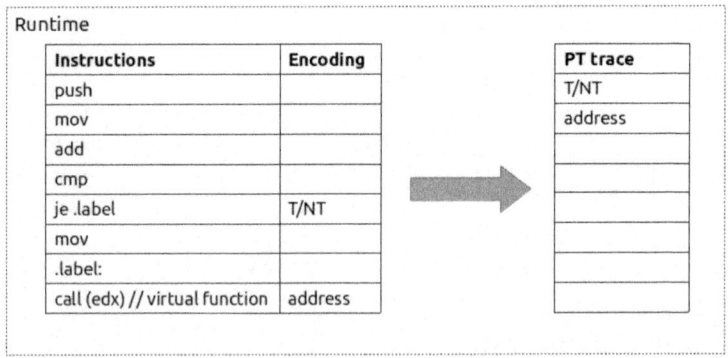

Figure 36: Intel Processor Traces encoding

At the time of analysis, we bring together the application binary and collected PT trace. SW decoder needs the application binary file in order to reconstruct the execution flow of the program. It starts from the entry point and then uses collected traces as a lookup reference to determine the control flow. Figure 37 shows an example of decoding Intel Processor Traces. Suppose that the PUSH instruction is an entry

6.4 Intel Processor Traces

point of the application binary file. Then PUSH, MOV, ADD, and CMP are reconstructed as-is without looking into encoded traces. Later SW decoder encounters JE instruction, which is a conditional branch and for which we need to look up the outcome. According to the traces on fig. 37, JE was taken (T), so we skip the next MOV instruction and go to the CALL instruction. Again, CALL(edx) is an instruction that changes the control flow, so we look up the destination address in encoded traces, which is 0x407e1d8. Instructions highlighted in yellow were executed when our program was running. Note that this is *exact* reconstruction of program execution; we did not skip any instruction. Later we can map assembly instructions back to the source code by using debug information and have a log of source code that was executed line by line.

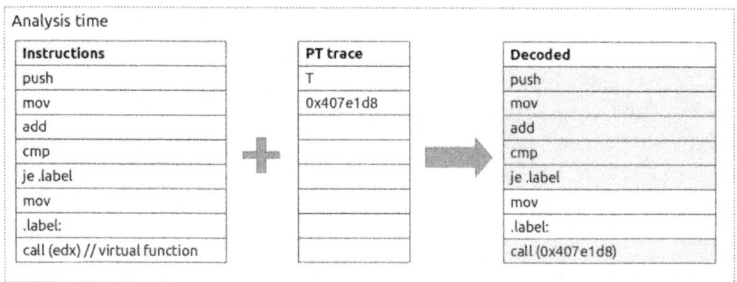

Figure 37: Intel Processor Traces decoding

6.4.2 Timing Packets

With Intel PT, not only execution flow can be traced but also timing information. In addition to saving jump destinations, PT can also emit timing packets. Figure 38 provides a visualization of how time packets can be used to restore timestamps for instructions. As in the previous example, we first see that JNZ was not taken, so we update it and all the instructions above with timestamp 0ns. Then we see a timing update of 2ns and JE being taken, so we update it and all the instructions above JE (and below JNZ) with timestamp 2ns. After that, there is an indirect call, but no timing packet is attached to it, so we do not update timestamps. Then we see that 100ns elapsed, and JB was not taken, so we update all the instructions above it with the timestamp of 102ns.

6.4 Intel Processor Traces

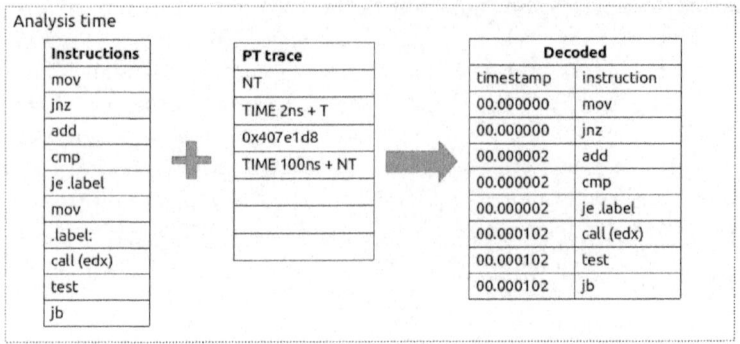

Figure 38: Intel Processor Traces timings

In the example shown in figure 38, instruction data (control flow) is perfectly accurate, but timing information is less accurate. Obviously, CALL(edx), TEST, and JB instructions were not happening at the same time, yet we do not have more accurate timing information for them. Having timestamps allows us to align the time interval of our program with some other event in the system, and it's easy to compare to wall clock time. Trace timing in some implementations can further be improved by a cycle-accurate mode, in which the hardware keeps a record of cycle counts between normal packets (see more details in [Int, 2020, Volume 3C, Chapter 36]).

6.4.3 Collecting and Decoding Traces

Intel PT traces can be easily collected with the Linux `perf` tool:

```
$ perf record -e intel_pt/cyc=1/u ./a.out
```

In the command line above, we asked the PT mechanism to update timing information every cycle. But likely, it will not increase our accuracy greatly since timing packets will only be sent when paired with some other control flow packet (see section 6.4.2).

After collecting, raw PT traces can be obtained by executing:

```
$ perf report -D > trace.dump
```

PT bundles up to 6 conditional branches before it emits a timing packet. Since the Intel Skylake CPU generation, timing packets have

6.4 Intel Processor Traces

cycle count elapsed from the previous packet. If we then look into the `trace.dump`, we might see something like the following:

```
000073b3: 2d 98 8c    TIP 0x8c98         // target address (IP)
000073b6: 13          CYC 0x2            // timing update
000073b7: c0          TNT TNNNNN (6)     // 6 conditional branches
000073b8: 43          CYC 0x8            // 8 cycles passed
000073b9: b6          TNT NTTNTT (6)
```

Above we showed the raw PT packets, which are not very useful for performance analysis. To decode processor traces to human-readable form, one can execute:

```
$ perf script --ns --itrace=i1t -F time,srcline,insn,srccode
```

Below is the example of decoded traces one might get:

```
timestamp        srcline     instruction        srccode
...
253.555413143:   a.cpp:24    call 0x35c         foo(arr, j);
253.555413143:   b.cpp:7     test esi, esi      for(int i=0; i<=n; i++)
253.555413508:   b.cpp:7     js 0x1e
253.555413508:   b.cpp:7     movsxd rsi, esi
...
```

Above is shown just a small snippet from the long execution log. In this log, **we have traces of every instruction executed while our program was running**. We can literally observe every step that was made by the program. It is a very strong foundation for further analysis.

6.4.4 Usages

Here are some of the cases when PT can be useful:

1. **Analyze performance glitches**. Because PT captures the entire instruction stream, it is possible to analyze what was going on during the small-time period when the application was not responding. More detailed examples can be found in an article[148] on easyperf blog.
2. **Postmortem debugging**. PT traces can be replayed by traditional debuggers like `gdb`. In addition to that, PT provides call stack information, which is *always* valid even if the stack is

---
[148] Analyze performance glitches with Intel PT - https://easyperf.net/blog/2019/09/06/Intel-PT-part3.

corrupted[149]. PT traces could be collected on a remote machine once and then analyzed offline. This is especially useful when the issue is hard to reproduce or access to the system is limited.
  3. **Introspect execution of the program**.
     - We can immediately tell if some code path was never executed.
     - Thanks to timestamps, it's possible to calculate how much time was spent waiting while spinning on a lock attempt, etc.
     - Security mitigation by detecting specific instruction pattern.

6.4.5 Disk Space and Decoding Time

Even taking into account the compressed format of the traces, encoded data can consume a lot of disk space. Typically, it's less than 1 byte per instruction, however taking into account the speed at which CPU executes instructions, it is still a lot. Depending on a workload, it's very common for CPU to encode PT at a speed of 100 MB/s. Decoded traces might easily be ten times more (~1GB/s). This makes PT not practical for using on long-running workloads. But it is affordable to run it for a small period of time, even on a big workload. In this case, the user can attach to the running process just for the period of time when the glitch happened. Or they can use a circular buffer, where new traces will overwrite old ones, i.e., always having traces for the last 10 seconds or so.

Users can limit collection even further in several ways. They can limit collecting traces only on user/kernel space code. Also, there is an address range filter, so it's possible to opt-in and opt-out of tracing dynamically to limit the memory bandwidth. This allows us to trace just a single function or even a single loop. [150]

Decoding PT traces can take a long time. On an Intel Core i5-8259U machine, for a workload that runs for 7 milliseconds, encoded PT trace takes around 1MB. Decoding this trace using `perf script` takes ~20 seconds. The decoded output from `perf script -F time,ip,sym,symoff,insn` takes ~1.3GB of disk space.

---

[149] Postmortem debugging with Intel PT - https://easyperf.net/blog/2019/08/30/Intel-PT-part2.
[150] Cheat sheet for Intel PT - http://halobates.de/blog/p/410.

Personal Experience: Intel PT is supposed to be an end game for performance analysis. With its low runtime overhead, it is a very powerful analysis feature. However, right now (February 2020), decoding traces with 'perf script -F' with '+srcline' or '+srccode' gets extremely slow and is not practical for daily usage. The implementation of Linux perf might be improved. Intel VTune Profiler support for PT is still experimental.

References and links
- Intel publication "Processor Tracing", URL: https://software.intel.com/en-us/blogs/2013/09/18/processor-tracing.
- Intel® 64 and IA-32 Architectures Software Developer Manuals [Int, 2020, Volume 3C, Chapter 36].
- Whitepaper "Hardware-assisted instruction profiling and latency detection" [Sharma and Dagenais, 2016].
- Andi Kleen article on LWN, URL: https://lwn.net/Articles/648154.
- Intel PT Micro Tutorial, URL: https://sites.google.com/site/intelptmicrotutorial/.
- simple_pt: Simple Intel CPU processor tracing on Linux, URL: https://github.com/andikleen/simple-pt/.
- Intel PT documentation in the Linux kernel, URL: https://github.com/torvalds/linux/blob/master/tools/perf/Documentation/intel-pt.txt.
- Cheatsheet for Intel Processor Trace, URL: http://halobates.de/blog/p/410.

6.5 Chapter Summary

- Utilizing HW features for low-level tuning is recommended only once all high-level performance issues are fixed. Tuning poorly designed algorithms is a bad investment of a developer's time. Once all the major performance problems get eliminated, one can use CPU performance monitoring features to analyze and further tune their application.
- Top-Down Microarchitecture Analysis (TMA) methodology is a very powerful technique for identifying ineffective usage of CPU microarchitecture by the program. It is a robust and formal methodology that is easy to use even for inexperienced developers. TMA is an iterative process that consists of multiple

6.5 Chapter Summary

steps, including characterizing the workload and locating the exact place in the source code where the bottleneck occurs. We advise that TMA should be a starting point of analysis for every low-level tuning effort. TMA is available on Intel and AMD[151] processors.
- Last Branch Record (LBR) mechanism continuously logs the most recent branch outcomes in parallel with executing the program, causing a minimal slowdown. It allows us to have a deep enough call stack for every sample we collect while profiling. Also, LBR helps identify hot branches, misprediction rates and allows for precise timing of machine code. LBR is supported on Intel and AMD processors.
- Processor Event-Based Sampling (PEBS) feature is another enhancement for profiling. It lowers the sampling overhead by automatically sampling multiple times to a dedicated buffer without interrupts. However, PEBS are more widely known for introducing "Precise Events", which allow pinpointing exact instruction that caused a particular performance event. The feature is supported on Intel processors. AMD CPUs have a similar feature called Instruction Based Sampling (IBS).
- Intel Processor Traces (PT) is a CPU feature that records the program execution by encoding packets in a highly compressed binary format that can be used to reconstruct execution flow with a timestamp on every instruction. PT has extensive coverage and relatively small overhead. Its main usages are postmortem analysis and finding the root cause(s) of performance glitches. Processors based on ARM architecture also have a tracing capability called CoreSight[152], but it is mostly used for debugging rather than for performance analysis.

Performance profilers leverage HW features presented in this chapter to enable many different types of analysis.

---

[151] Although at the time of writing, AMD processors only support the first level of TMA metrics, i.e., Front End Bound, Back End Bound, Retiring, and Bad Speculation.

[152] ARM CoreSight: https://developer.arm.com/ip-products/system-ip/coresight-debug-and-trace

Part2. Source Code Tuning For CPU

In part 2, we will take a look at how to use CPU monitoring features (see section 6) to find the places in the code which can be tuned for execution on a CPU. For performance-critical applications like large distributed cloud services, scientific HPC software, 'AAA' games, etc. it is very important to know how underlying HW works. It is a fail-from-the-start when the program is being developed without HW focus.

Standard algorithms and data structures don't always work well for performance-critical workloads. For example, a linked list is pretty much deprecated in favor of 'flat' data structures. Traditionally every new node of the linked list is dynamically allocated. Besides invoking many costly[153] memory allocations, this will likely result in a situation where all the elements of the list are scattered in memory. Traversing such a data structure requires random memory access for every element. Even though algorithmic complexity is still O(N), in practice, the timings will be much worse than of a plain array. Some data structures, like binary trees, have natural linked-list-like representation, so it might be tempting to implement them in a pointer chasing manner. However, more efficient "flat" versions of those data structures exist, see `boost::flat_map`, `boost::flat_set`.

Even though the algorithm you choose is best known for a particular problem, it might not work best for your particular case. For example, a binary search is optimal for finding an element in a sorted array. However, this algorithm usually suffers from branch mispredictions since every test of the element value has a 50% chance of being true. This is why on a small-sized (less than 20 elements) array of integers, linear search is usually better.

Performance engineering is an art. And like in any art, the set of possible scenarios is endless. This chapter tries to address optimizations specific to CPU microarchitecture without trying to cover all existing optimization opportunities one can imagine. Still, I think it is important to at least name some high-level ones:

---

[153] By default, memory allocation involves an expensive system call (`malloc`), which can be especially costly in a multithreaded context.

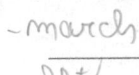

- If a program is written using interpreted languages (python, javascript, etc.), rewrite its performance-critical portion in a language with less overhead.
- Analyze the algorithms and data structures used in the program, see if you can find better ones.
- Tune compiler options. Check that you use at least these three compiler flags: -O3 (enables machine-independent optimizations), -march (enables optimizations for particular CPU generation), -flto (enables inter-procedural optimizations).
- If a problem is a highly parallelizable computation, make it threaded, or consider running it on a GPU.
- Use async IO to avoid blocking while waiting for IO operations.
- Leverage using more RAM to reduce the amount of CPU and IO you have to use (memoization, look-up tables, caching of data, compression, etc.)

Data-Driven Optimizations

One of the most important techniques for tuning is called "Data-Driven" optimization that is based on introspecting the data the program is working on. The approach is to focus on the layout of the data and how it is transformed throughout the program.[154] A classic example of such an approach is Structure-Of-Array to Array-Of-Structures (SOA-to-AOS[155]) transformation, which is shown on Listing 14.

The answer to the question of which layout is better depends on how the code is accessing the data. If the program iterates over the data structure and only accesses field b, then SOA is better because all memory accesses will be sequential (spatial locality). However, if the program iterates over the data structure and does excessive operations on all the fields of the object (i.e. a, b, c), then AOS is better because it's likely that all the members of the structure will reside in the same cache line. It will additionally better utilize the memory bandwidth since fewer cache line reads will be required.

This class of optimizations is based on knowing the data on which the program operates, how it is laid out, and modifying the program accordingly.

---

[154] Data-Driven optimizations - https://en.wikipedia.org/wiki/Data-oriented_design.
[155] AoS to SoA transformation - https://en.wikipedia.org/wiki/AoS_and_SoA.

Listing 14 SOA to AOS transformation.

```
struct S {
  int a[N];
  int b[N];
  int c[N];
  // many other fields
};

<=>

struct S {
  int a;
  int b;
  int c;
  // many other fields
};
S s[N];
```

> **Personal Experience:** In fact, we can say that all optimizations are data-driven in some sense. Even the transformations that we will look at in the next sections are based on some feedback we receive from the execution of the program: function call counts, profiling data, performance counters, etc.

Another very important example of data-driven optimization is "Small Size optimization". Its idea is to preallocate some amount of memory for a container to avoid dynamic memory allocations. It is especially useful for small and medium-sized containers when the upper limit of elements can be well-predicted. This approach was successfully deployed across the whole LLVM infrastructure and provided significant performance benefits (search `SmallVector`, for example). The same concept is implemented in `boost::static_vector`.

Obviously, it's not a complete list of data-driven optimizations, but as was written earlier, there was no attempt to list them all. Readers can find some more examples on easyperf blog[156].

Modern CPU is a very complicated device, and it's nearly impossible to predict how certain pieces of code will perform. Instruction

---
[156] Examples of data-driven tuning - https://easyperf.net/blog/2019/11/27/data-driven-tuning-specialize-indirect-call and https://easyperf.net/blog/2019/11/22/data-driven-tuning-specialize-switch.

execution by the CPU depends on many factors, and the number of moving parts is too big for a human mind to overlook. Hopefully, knowing how your code looks like from a CPU perspective is possible thanks to all the performance monitoring capabilities we discussed in section 6.

Note that optimization that you implement might not be beneficial for every platform. For example, loop blocking[157] very much depends on the characteristics of the memory hierarchy in the system, especially L2 and L3 cache sizes. So, an algorithm tuned for CPU with particular sizes of L2 and L3 caches might not work well for CPUs with smaller caches[158]. It is important to test the change on the platforms your application will be running on.

The next three chapters are organized in the most convenient way to be used with TMA (see section 6.1). The idea behind this classification is to offer some kind of checklist which engineers can use in order to effectively eliminate inefficiencies that TMA reveals. Again, this is not supposed to be a complete list of transformations one can come up with. However, this is an attempt to describe the typical ones.

---

[157] Loop nest optimizations - https://en.wikipedia.org/wiki/Loop_nest_optimization.

[158] Alternatively, one can use cache-oblivious algorithms whose goal is to work reasonably well for any size of the cache. See https://en.wikipedia.org/wiki/Cache-oblivious_algorithm.

7 CPU Front-End Optimizations

CPU Front-End (FE) component is discussed in section 3.8.1. Most of the time, inefficiencies in CPU FE can be described as a situation when Back-End is waiting for instructions to execute, but FE is not able to provide them. As a result, CPU cycles are wasted without doing any actual useful work. Because modern processors are 4-wide (i.e., they can provide four uops every cycle), there can be a situation when not all four available slots are filled. This can be a source of inefficient execution as well. In fact, `IDQ_UOPS_NOT_DELIVERED`[159] performance event is counting how many available slots were not utilized due to a front-end stall. TMA uses this performance counter value to calculate its "Front-End Bound" metric[160].

The reasons for why FE could not deliver instructions to the execution units can be plenty. But usually, it boils down to caches utilization and inability to fetch instructions from memory. It's recommended to start looking into optimizing code for CPU FE only when TMA points to a high "Front-End Bound" metric.

> **Personal Experience:** Most of the real-world applications will experience a non-zero "Front-End Bound" metric, meaning that some percentage of running time will be lost on suboptimal instruction fetching and decoding. Luckily it is usually below 10%. If you see the "Front-End Bound" metric being around 20%, it's definitely worth to spend time on it.

7.1 Machine code layout

When a compiler translates your source code into machine code (binary encoding), it generates a serial byte sequence. For example, for the following C code:

```
if (a <= b)
  c = 1;
```

---

[159] See more information about this performance event here: https://easyperf.n et/blog/2018/12/29/Understanding-IDQ_UOPS_NOT_DELIVERED
[160] See exact formulas in TMA metrics table: https://download.01.org/perfmo n/TMA_Metrics.xlsx.

the compiler could generate assembly like this:

```
; a is in rax
; b is in rdx
; c is in rcx
cmp rax, rdx
jg .label
mov rcx, 1
.label:
```

Assembly instructions will be encoded and laid out in memory consequently:

```
400510   cmp rax, rdx
400512   jg 40051a
400514   mov rcx, 1
40051a   ...
```

This is what is called *machine code layout*. Note that for the same program, it's possible to lay out the code in many different ways. For example, given two functions: `foo` and `bar`, we can place `bar` first in the binary and then `foo` or reverse the order. This affects offsets at which instructions will be placed in memory, which in turn affects the performance of the generated binary. For the rest of this chapter, we will take a look at some typical optimizations for the machine code layout.

7.2 Basic Block

A basic block is a sequence of instructions with a single entry and single exit. Figure 39 shows a simple example of a basic block, where `MOV` instruction is an entry, and `JA` is an exit instruction. While basic block can have one or many predecessors and successors, no instruction in the middle can exit the block.

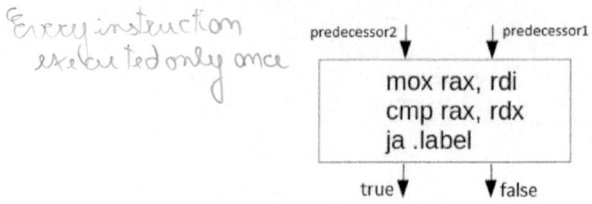

Figure 39: Basic Block of assembly instructions.

It is guaranteed that every instruction in the basic block will be executed exactly once. This is a very important property that is utilized

140

by many compiler transformations. For example, it greatly reduces the problem of control flow graph analysis and transformations since, for some class of problems, we can treat all instructions in the basic block as one entity.

7.3 Basic block placement

Likely/unlikely

Suppose we have a hot path in the program that has some error handling code (`coldFunc`) in between:

```
// hot path
if (cond)
  coldFunc();
// hot path again
```

Figure 40 shows two possible physical layouts for this snippet of code. Figure 40a is the layout most compiler will emit by default, given no hints provided. The layout that is shown in figure 40b can be achieved if we invert the condition `cond` and place hot code as a fall-through.

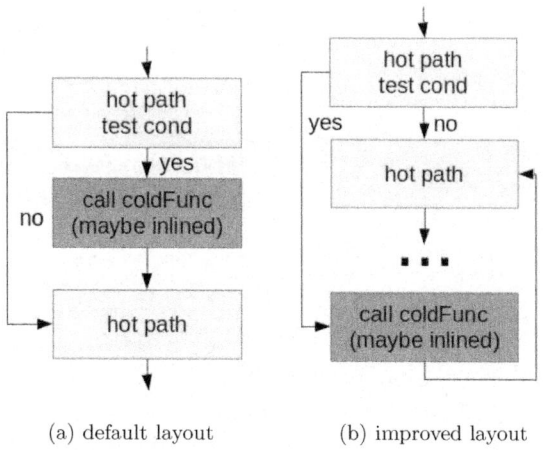

(a) default layout   (b) improved layout

Figure 40: Two different machine code layouts.

Which layout is better in the common case greatly depends on whether `cond` is usually true or not. If `cond` is usually true, then we would better choose the default layout because otherwise, we would be doing two jumps instead of one. Also, in the general case, we want to inline

7.3 Basic block placement

the function that is guarded under cond. However, in this particular example, we know that coldFunc is an error handling function and is likely not executed very often. By choosing layout 40b, we maintain fall through between hot pieces of the code and convert taken branch into not taken one.

There are a few reasons why for the code presented earlier in this section, layout 40b performs better. First of all, not taken branches are fundamentally cheaper than taken. In the general case, modern Intel CPUs can execute two untaken branches per cycle but only one taken branch every two cycles. [161]

Secondly, layout 40b makes better use of the instruction and uop-cache (DSB, see section 3.8.1). With all hot code contiguous, there is no cache line fragmentation: all the cache lines in the L1I-cache are used by hot code. The same is true for the uop-cache since it caches based on the underlying code layout as well.

Finally, taken branches are also more expensive for the fetch unit. It fetches contiguous chunks of 16 bytes, so every taken jump means the bytes after the jump are useless. This reduces the maximum effective fetch throughput.

In order to suggest the compiler to generate an improved version of the machine code layout, one can provide a hint using `__builtin_expect`[162] construct:

```
// hot path
if (__builtin_expect(cond, 0)) // NOT likely to be taken
  coldFunc();
// hot path again
```

Developers usually write LIKELY helper macros to make the code more readable, so more often, you can find the code that looks like the one shown below. Since C++20, there is a standard `[[likely]]`[163] attribute, which should be preferred.

```
#define LIKELY(EXPR)    __builtin_expect((bool)(EXPR), true)
#define UNLIKELY(EXPR)  __builtin_expect((bool)(EXPR), false)
if (LIKELY(ptr != nullptr))
  // do something with ptr
```

---

[161] There is a special small loop optimization that allows very small loops to have one taken branch per cycle.

[162] More about builtin-expect here: https://llvm.org/docs/BranchWeightMetadata.html#builtin-expect.

[163] C++ standard `[[likely]]` attribute: https://en.cppreference.com/w/cpp/language/attributes/likely.

Optimizing compilers will not only improve code layout when they encounter LIKELY/UNLIKELY hints. They will also leverage this information in other places. For example, when UNLIKELY hint is applied to our original example in this section, the compiler will prevent inlining coldFunc as it now knows that it is unlikely to be executed often and it's more beneficial to optimize it for size, i.e., just leave a CALL to this function. Inserting __builtin_expect hint is also possible for a switch statement as presented in Listing 15.

Listing 15 Built-in expect hint for switch statement

```
for (;;) {
  switch (__builtin_expect(instruction, ADD)) {
    // handle different instructions
  }
}
```

Using this hint, a compiler will be able to reorder code a little bit differently and optimize the hot switch for faster processing ADD instructions. More details about this transformation is available on easyperf[164] blog.

7.4 Basic block alignment

Sometimes performance can significantly change depending on the offset at which instructions are laid out in memory. Consider a simple function presented in Listing 16.

Listing 16 Basic block alignment

```
void benchmark_func(int* a) {
  for (int i = 0; i < 32; ++i)
    a[i] += 1;
}
```

A decent optimizing compiler might come up with machine code for Skylake architecture that may look like below:

---

[164] Using __builtin_expect for a switch statement - https://easyperf.net/blog/2019/11/22/data-driven-tuning-specialize-switch.

7.4 Basic block alignment

```
00000000004046a0 <_Z14benchmark_funcPi>:
  4046a0:    mov      rax,0xffffffffffffff80
  4046a7:    vpcmpeqd ymm0,ymm0,ymm0
  4046ab:    nop      DWORD PTR [rax+rax*1+0x0]
  4046b0:    vmovdqu  ymm1,YMMWORD PTR [rdi+rax*1+0x80]   # loop begins
  4046b9:    vpsubd   ymm1,ymm1,ymm0
  4046bd:    vmovdqu  YMMWORD PTR [rdi+rax*1+0x80],ymm1
  4046c6:    add      rax,0x20
  4046ca:    jne      4046b0                              # loop ends
  4046cc:    vzeroupper
  4046cf:    ret
```

The code itself is pretty reasonable[165] for Skylake architecture, but its layout is not perfect (see Figure 41a). Instructions that correspond to the loop are highlighted in yellow. As well as for data caches, instruction cache lines are usually 64 bytes long. On Figure 41 thick boxes denote cache line borders. Notice that the loop spans multiple cache lines: it begins on the cache line 0x80 - 0xBF and ends in the cache-line 0xC0 - 0xFF. Those kinds of situations usually cause performance problems for the CPU Front-End, especially for the small loops like presented above.

To fix this, we can shift the loop instructions forward by 16 bytes using NOPs so that the whole loop will reside in one cache line. Figure 41b shows the effect of doing this with NOP instructions highlighted in blue. Note that since the benchmark runs nothing but this hot loop, it is pretty much guaranteed that both cache lines will remain in L1I-cache. The reason for the better performance of the layout 41b is not trivial to explain and will involve a fair amount of microarchitectural details[166], which we will avoid in this book.

Even though CPU architects try hard to hide such kind of bottlenecks in their designs, there are still cases when code placement (alignment) can make a difference in performance.

By default, the LLVM compiler recognizes loops and aligns them at 16B boundaries, as we saw in Figure 41a. To reach the desired code placement for our example, as shown in Figure 41b, one should use the `-mllvm -align-all-blocks` option[167]. However, be careful with using this option, as it can easily degrade performance. Inserting NOPs

---
[165] Loop unrolling is disabled for illustrating the idea of the section.
[166] Interested readers can find more information in the article on easyperf blog Code alignment issues.
[167] For other available options to control code placement, one can take a look at the article on easyperf blog: Code alignment options in llvm.

7.5 Function splitting

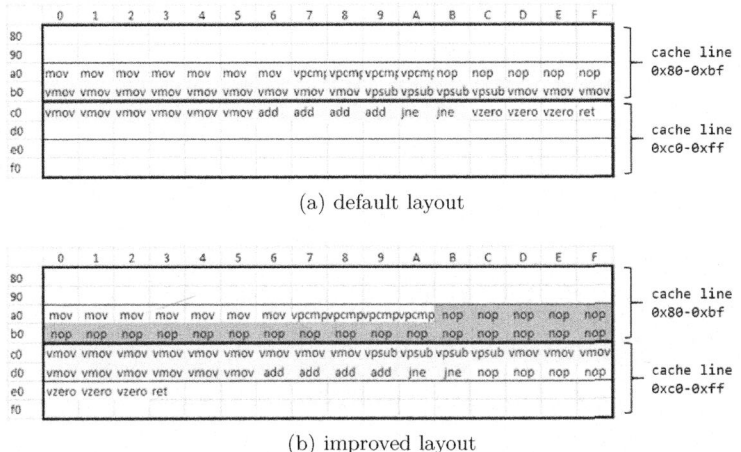

(a) default layout

(b) improved layout

Figure 41: Two different alignments for the loop.

that will be executed can add overhead to the program, especially if they stand on a critical path. NOPs do not require execution; however, they still require to be fetched from memory, decoded, and retired. The latter additionally consumes space in FE data structures and buffers for bookkeeping, similar to all other instructions.

In order to have fine-grained control over alignment, it is also possible to use `ALIGN`[168] assembler directives. For experimental purposes, the developer can emit assembly listing and then insert the `ALIGN` directive:

```
; will place the .loop at the beginning of 256 bytes boundary
ALIGN 256
.loop
    dec rdi
    jnz rdi
```

7.5 Function splitting

The idea behind function splitting[169] is to separate hot code from the cold. This optimization is beneficial for relatively big functions

---

[168] x86 assembler directives manual - https://docs.oracle.com/cd/E26502_01/html/E28388/eoiyg.html. This example uses MASM. Otherwise, you will see the `.align` directive.

[169] Such transformation is also often called "outlining". Readers can find LLVM implementation of this functionality in lib/Transforms/IPO/HotColdSplitting.cpp.

7.5 Function splitting

with complex CFG and big pieces of cold code inside a hot path. An example of code when such transformation might be profitable is shown on Listing 17. To remove cold basic blocks from the hot path, we could cut and put them into its own new function and create a call to it (see Listing 18).

Listing 17 Function splitting: baseline version.

```
void foo(bool cond1, bool cond2) {
  // hot path
  if (cond1) {
    // large amount of cold code (1)
  }
  // hot path
  if (cond2) {
    // large amount of cold code (2)
  }
}
```

Listing 18 Function splitting: cold code outlined.

```
void foo(bool cond1, bool cond2) {
  // hot path
  if (cond1)
    cold1();
  // hot path
  if (cond2)
    cold2();
}

void cold1() __attribute__((noinline)) { // cold code (1) }
void cold2() __attribute__((noinline)) { // cold code (2) }
```

prevent inlining

Figure 42 gives a graphical representation of this transformation. Because we left just the CALL instruction inside the hot path, it's likely that the next hot instruction will reside in the same cache line. This improves the utilization of CPU Front-End data structures like I-cache and DSB.

This transformation contains another important idea: disable inlining of cold functions. Even if we create a new function for the cold code, the compiler may decide to inline it, which will effectively undo our transformation. This is why we want to use the `noinline` function attribute to prevent inlining. Alternatively, we could apply the UNLIKELY macro (see section 7.3) on both `cond1` and `cond2` branches

7.6 Function grouping

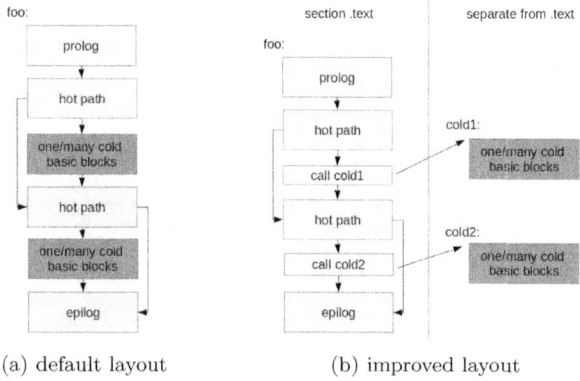

(a) default layout   (b) improved layout

Figure 42: Splitting cold code into a separate function.

to convey to the compiler that inlining `cold1` and `cold2` functions is not desired.

Finally, new functions should be created outside of .text segment, for example in .text.cold. This may improve memory footprint if the function is never called since it won't be loaded into memory in the runtime.

7.6 Function grouping

Following the principles described in previous sections, hot functions can be grouped together to further improve the utilization of caches in the CPU Front-End. When hot functions are grouped together, they might share the same cache line, which reduces the number of cache lines the CPU needs to fetch.

Figure 43 gives a graphical representation of grouping `foo`, `bar`, and `zoo`. The default layout (see fig. 43a) requires four cache line reads, while in the improved version (see fig. 43b), code of `foo`, `bar` and `zoo` fits in only three cache lines. Additionally, when we call `zoo` from `foo`, the beginning of `zoo` is already in the I-cache since we fetched that cache line already.

Similar to previous optimizations, function grouping improves the utilization of I-cache and DSB-cache. This optimization works best when there are many small hot functions.

7.6 Function grouping

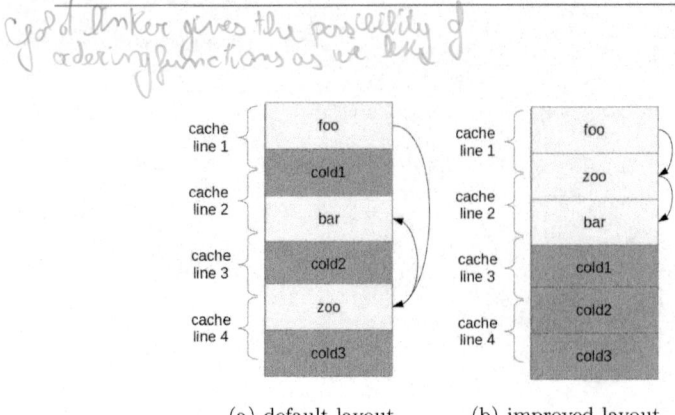

Figure 43: Grouping hot functions together.

The linker is responsible for laying out all the functions of the program in the resulting binary output. While developers can try to reorder functions in a program themselves, there is no guarantee on the desired physical layout. For decades people have been using linker scripts to achieve this goal. Still, this is the way to go if you are using the GNU linker. The Gold linker (ld.gold) has an easier approach to this problem. To get the desired ordering of functions in the binary with the Gold linker, one can first compile the code with the -ffunction-sections flag, which will put each function into a separate section. Then --section-ordering-file=order.txt option should be used to provide a file with a sorted list of function names that reflects the desired final layout. The same feature exists in the LLD linker, which is a part of LLVM compiler infrastructure and is accessible via the --symbol-ordering-file option.

An interesting approach to solving the problem of grouping hot functions together is implemented in the tool called HFSort[170]. It is a tool that generates the section ordering file automatically based on profiling data [Ottoni and Maher, 2017]. Using this tool, Facebook engineers got a 2% performance speedup of large distributed cloud applications like Facebook, Baidu, and Wikipedia. Right now, HFSort is integrated into Facebook's HHVM project and is not available as a standalone tool. The LLD linker employs implementation[171] of the

---

[170] HFSort - https://github.com/facebook/hhvm/tree/master/hphp/tools/hfsort.

[171] HFSort in LLD - https://github.com/llvm-project/lld/blob/master/ELF/CallGraphSort.cpp.

148

HFSort algorithm, which sorts sections based on the profiling data.

7.7 Profile Guided Optimizations

Compiling a program and generating optimal assembly listing is all about heuristics. Code transformation algorithms have many corner cases that aim for optimal performance in specific situations. For a lot of decisions that compiler makes, it tries to guess the best choice based on some typical cases. For example, when deciding whether a particular function should be inlined, the compiler could take into account the number of times this function will be called. The problem is that compiler doesn't know that beforehand.

Here is when profiling information becomes handy. Given profiling information compiler can make better optimization decisions. There is a set of transformations in most compilers that can adjust their algorithms based on profiling data fed back to them. This set of transformations is called Profile Guided Optimizations (PGO). Sometimes in literature, one can find the term Feedback Directed Optimizations (FDO), which essentially refers to the same thing as PGO. Often times a compiler will rely on profiling data when it is available. Otherwise, it will fall back to using its standard algorithms and heuristics.

It is not uncommon to see real workloads performance increase by up to 15% from using Profile Guided Optimizations. PGO does not only improve inlining and code placement but also improves register allocation[172] and more.

Profiling data can be generated based on two different ways: code instrumentation (see section 5.1) and sample-based profiling (see section 5.4). Both are relatively easy to use and have associated benefits and drawbacks discussed in section 5.8.

The first method can be utilized in the LLVM compiler by building the program with the `-fprofile-instr-generate` option. This will instruct the compiler to instrument the code, which will collect profiling information at runtime. After that LLVM compiler can consume profiling data with the `-fprofile-instr-use` option to recompile the program and output PGO-tuned binary. The guide for using PGO in

---
[172] because with PGO compiler can put all the hot variables into registers, etc.

clang is described in the documentation[173]. GCC compiler uses different set of options -fprofile-generate and -fprofile-use as described in GCC documentation.

The second method, which is generating profiling data input for the compiler based on sampling, can be utilized thanks to AutoFDO[174] tool, which converts sampling data generated by Linux perf into a format that compilers like GCC and LLVM can understand. [Chen et al., 2016]

Keep in mind that the compiler "blindly" uses the profile data you provided. The compiler assumes that all the workloads will behave the same, so it optimizes your app just for that single workload. Users of PGO should be careful about choosing the workload to profile because while improving one use case of the application, other might be pessimized. Luckily, it doesn't have to be exactly a single workload since profile data from different workloads can be merged together to represent a set of use cases for the application.

In the mid-2018, Facebook open-sourced its binary relinker tool called BOLT. BOLT works on the already compiled binary. It first disassembles the code, then it uses profile information to do various layout transformations (including basic blocks reordering, function splitting, and grouping) and generates optimized binary [Panchenko et al., 2018]. A similar tool was developed at Google called Propeller, which serves a similar purpose as BOLT but claim certain advantages over it. It is possible to integrate optimizing relinker into the build system and enjoy an extra 5-10% performance speedup from the optimized code layout. The only thing one needs to worry about is to have a representative and meaningful workload for collecting profiling information.

7.8 Optimizing for ITLB

Another important area of tuning FE efficiency is virtual-to-physical address translation of memory addresses. Primarily those translations are served by TLB (see section 3), which caches most recently used memory page translations in dedicated entries. When TLB cannot serve translation request, a time-consuming page walk of the kernel page table takes place to calculate the correct physical address for

---
[173] PGO in Clang - https://clang.llvm.org/docs/UsersManual.html#profiling-with-instrumentation.
[174] AutoFDO - https://github.com/google/autofdo.

each referenced virtual address. When TMA points to a high ITLB Overhead [175], the advice in this section may become handy.

ITLB pressure can be reduced by mapping the portions of the performance-critical code of an application onto large pages. This requires relinking the binary to align text segments at the proper page boundary in preparation for large page mapping (see guide[176] to libhugetlbfs). For general discussion on large pages, see section 8.1.3.

Besides from employing large pages, standard techniques for optimizing I-cache performance can be used for improving ITLB performance; namely, reordering functions so that hot functions are more collocated, reducing the size of hot regions via LTO/IPO [177], using profile-guided optimization, and less aggressive inlining.

7.9 Chapter Summary

Summary of CPU Front-End optimizations is presented in table 6.

Table 6: Summary of CPU Front-End optimizations.

Transform	How transformed?	Why helps?	Works best for	Done by
Basic block placement	maintain fall through hot code	not taken branches are cheaper; better cache utilization	any code, especially with a lot of branches	compiler
Basic block alignment	shift the hot code using NOPS	better cache utilization	hot loops	compiler

---

[175] ITLB Overhead - https://software.intel.com/content/www/us/en/develop/documentation/vtune-help/top/reference/cpu-metrics-reference/front-end-bound/itlb-overhead.html
[176] libhugetlbfs guide - https://github.com/libhugetlbfs/libhugetlbfs/blob/master/HOWTO.
[177] Interprocedural optimizations - https://en.wikipedia.org/wiki/Interprocedural_optimization.

151

7.9 Chapter Summary

Transform	How transformed?	Why helps?	Works best for	Done by
Function splitting	split cold blocks of code and place them in separate functions	better cache utilization	functions with complex CFG when there are big blocks of cold code between hot parts	compiler
Function grouping	group hot functions together	better cache utilization	many small hot functions	linker

Personal Experience: I think code layout improvements are often underestimated and end up being omitted and forgotten. I agree that you might want to start with low hanging fruits like loop unrolling and vectorization opportunities. But knowing that you might get an extra 5-10% just from better laying out the machine code is still useful. It is usually the best option to use PGO if you can come up with a set of typical use cases for your application.

8 CPU Back-End Optimizations

CPU Back-End (BE) component is discussed in section 3.8.2. Most of the time, inefficiencies in CPU BE can be described as a situation when FE has fetched and decoded instructions, but BE is overloaded and can't handle new instructions. Technically speaking, it is a situation when FE cannot deliver uops due to a lack of required resources for accepting new uops in the Backend. An example of it may be a stall due to data-cache miss or a stall due to the divider unit being overloaded.

I want to emphasize to the reader that it's recommended to start looking into optimizing code for CPU BE only when TMA points to a high "Back-End Bound" metric. TMA further divides the Backend Bound metric into two main categories: Memory Bound and Core Bound, which we will discuss next.

Large number of memory accesses

8.1 Memory Bound

When an application executes a large number of memory accesses and spends significant time waiting for them to finish, such an application is characterized as being bounded by memory. It means that to further improve its performance, we likely need to improve how we access memory, reduce the number of such accesses or upgrade the memory subsystem itself.

The statement that memory hierarchy performance is very important is backed by Figure 44. It shows the growth of the gap in performance between memory and processors. The vertical axis is on a logarithmic scale and shows the growth of the CPU-DRAM performance gap. The memory baseline is the latency of memory access of 64 KB DRAM chips from 1980. Typical DRAM performance improvement is 7% per year, while CPUs enjoy 20-50% improvement per year.[Hennessy and Patterson, 2011]

In TMA, Memory Bound estimates a fraction of slots where the CPU pipeline is likely stalled due to demand load or store instructions. The first step to solving such a performance problem is to locate the memory accesses that contribute to the high Memory Bound metric (see section 6.1.4). Once guilty memory access is identified, several optimization strategies could be applied. Below we will discuss a few

153

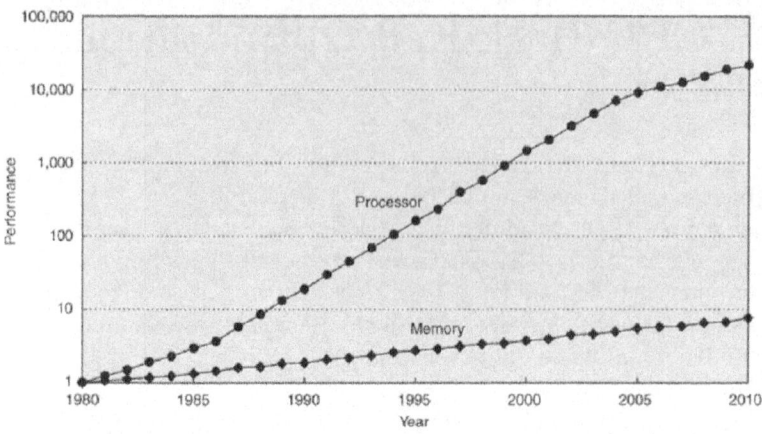

Figure 44: The gap in performance between memory and processors. © Image from [Hennessy and Patterson, 2011].

typical cases.

8.1.1 Cache-Friendly Data Structures

A variable can be fetched from the cache in just a few clock cycles, but it can take more than a hundred clock cycles to fetch the variable from RAM memory if it is not in the cache. There is a lot of information written on the importance of writing cache-friendly algorithms and data structures, as it is one of the key items in the recipe for a well-performing application. The key pillar of cache-friendly code is the principles of temporal and spatial locality (see section 3.5), which goal is to allow efficient fetching of required data from caches. When designing a cache-friendly code, it's helpful to think in terms of cache lines, not only individual variables and their places in memory.

8.1.1.1 Access data sequentially. The best way to exploit the spatial locality of the caches is to make sequential memory accesses. By doing so, we allow the HW prefetcher (see section 3.5.1.5.1) to recognize the memory access pattern and bring in the next chunk of data ahead of time. An example of a C-code that does such cache-friendly accesses is shown on Listing 19. The code is "cache-friendly" because it accesses the elements of the matrix in the order in which they are laid out in memory (row-major traversal[178]). Swapping the order of indexes in the array (i.e., `matrix[column][row]`) will result in column-major order traversal of the matrix, which does not exploit spatial locality and hurts performance.

Listing 19 Cache-friendly memory accesses.

```
for (row = 0; row < NUMROWS; row++)
  for (column = 0; column < NUMCOLUMNS; column++)
    matrix[row][column] = row + column;
```

The example presented in Listing 19 is classical, but usually, real-world applications are much more complicated than this. Sometimes you need to go an additional mile to write cache-friendly code. For instance, the standard implementation of binary search in a sorted large array does not exploit spatial locality since it tests elements in different locations that are far away from each other and do not share the same cache line. The most famous way of solving this problem is storing elements of the array using the Eytzinger layout [Khuong and Morin, 2015]. The idea of it is to maintain an implicit binary search tree packed into an array using the BFS-like layout, usually seen with binary heaps. If the code performs a large number of binary searches in the array, it may be beneficial to convert it to the Eytzinger layout.

8.1.1.2 Use appropriate containers. There is a wide variety of ready-to-use containers in almost any language. But it's important to know their underlying storage and performance implications. A good step-by-step guide for choosing appropriate C++ containers can be found in [Fog, 2004, Chapter 9.7 Data structures, and container classes].

Additionally, choose the data storage, bearing in mind what the code will do with it. Consider a situation when there is a need to choose between storing objects in the array versus storing pointers to those objects while the object size is big. An array of pointers take less amount of memory. This will benefit operations that modify the array since an array of pointers requires less memory being transferred. However, a linear scan through an array will be faster when keeping

---

[178] Row- and column-major order - https://en.wikipedia.org/wiki/Row-_and_column-major_order.

the objects themselves since it is more cache-friendly and does not require indirect memory accesses.[179]

8.1.1.3 Packing the data.
Memory hierarchy utilization can be improved by making the data more compact. There are many ways to pack data. One of the classic examples is to use bitfields. An example of code when packing data might be profitable is shown on Listing 20. If we know that a, b, and c represent enum values which take a certain number of bits to encode, we can reduce the storage of the struct s (see Listing 21).

Listing 20 Packing Data: baseline struct.

```
struct S {
  unsigned a;
  unsigned b;
  unsigned c;
}; // S is sizeof(unsigned int) * 3
```

Listing 21 Packing Data: packed struct.

```
struct S {
  unsigned a:4;
  unsigned b:2;
  unsigned c:2;
}; // S is only 1 byte
```

This greatly reduces the amount of memory transferred back and forth and saves cache space. Keep in mind that this comes with the cost of accessing every packed element. Since the bits of b share the same machine word with a and c, compiler need to perform a >> (shift right) and & (AND) operation to load it. Similarly, << (shift left) and | (OR) operations are needed to store the value back. Packing the data is beneficial in places where additional computation is cheaper than the delay caused by inefficient memory transfers.

Also, a programmer can reduce the memory usage by rearranging fields in a struct or class when it avoids padding added by a compiler (see example in Listing 22). The reason for a compiler to insert unused bytes of memory (pads) is to allow efficient storing and fetching of

---

[179] Blog article "Vector of Objects vs Vector of Pointers" by B. Filipek - https://www.bfilipek.com/2014/05/vector-of-objects-vs-vector-of-pointers.html.

individual members of a struct. In the example, the size of S1 can be reduced if its members are declared in the order of decreasing their sizes.

Listing 22 Avoid compiler padding.

```
struct S1 {
  bool b;
  int i;
  short s;
}; // S1 is sizeof(int) * 3

struct S2 {
  int i;
  short s;
  bool b;
}; // S2 is sizeof(int) * 2
```

8.1.1.4 Aligning and padding. Another technique to improve the utilization of the memory subsystem is to align the data. There could be a situation when an object of size 16 bytes occupies two cache lines, i.e., it starts on one cache line and ends in the next cache line. Fetching such an object requires two cache line reads, which could be avoided would the object be aligned properly. Listing 23 shows how memory objects can be aligned using C++11 `alignas` keyword.

Listing 23 Aligning data using the "alignas" keyword.

```
// Make an aligned array
alignas(16) int16_t a[N];

// Objects of struct S are aligned at cache line boundaries
#define CACHELINE_ALIGN alignas(64)
struct CACHELINE_ALIGN S {
  //...
};
```

A variable is accessed most efficiently if it is stored at a memory address, which is divisible by the size of the variable. For example, a double takes 8 bytes of storage space. It should, therefore, preferably be stored at an address divisible by 8. The size should always be a power of 2. Objects bigger than 16 bytes should be stored at an address divisible by 16. [Fog, 2004]

8.1 Memory Bound

Alignment can cause holes of unused bytes, which potentially decreases memory bandwidth utilization. If, in the example above, struct S is only 40 bytes, the next object of S starts at the beginning of the next cache line, which leaves 64 - 40 = 24 unused bytes in every cache line which holds objects of struct S.

Sometimes padding data structure members is required to avoid edge cases like cache contentions [Fog, 2004, Chapter 9.10 Cache contentions] and false sharing (see section 11.7.3). For example, false sharing issues might occur in multithreaded applications when two threads, A and B, access different fields of the same structure. An example of code when such a situation might happen is shown on Listing 24. Because a and b members of struct S could potentially occupy the same cache line, cache coherency issues might significantly slow down the program. In order to resolve the problem, one can pad S such that members a and b do not share the same cache line as shown in Listing 25.

Listing 24 Padding data: baseline version.

```
struct S {
  int a; // written by thread A
  int b; // written by thread B
};
```

Listing 25 Padding data: improved version.

```
#define CACHELINE_ALIGN alignas(64)
struct S {
  int a; // written by thread A
  CACHELINE_ALIGN int b; // written by thread B
};
```

When it comes to dynamic allocations via malloc, it is guaranteed that the returned memory address satisfies the target platform's minimum alignment requirements. Some applications might benefit from a stricter alignment. For example, dynamically allocating 16 bytes with a 64 bytes alignment instead of the default 16 bytes alignment. In order to leverage this, users of POSIX systems can use memalign[180] API. Others can roll their own like described here[181].

---
[180] Linux manual page for memalign - https://linux.die.net/man/3/memalign.
[181] Generating aligned memory - https://embeddedartistry.com/blog/2017/02/22/generating-aligned-memory/.

One of the most important areas for alignment considerations is the SIMD code. When relying on compiler auto-vectorization, the developer doesn't have to do anything special. However, when you write the code using compiler vector intrinsics (see section 10.2), it's pretty common that they require addresses divisible by 16, 32, or 64. Vector types provided by the compiler intrinsic header files are already annotated to ensure the appropriate alignment. [Fog, 2004]

```
// ptr will be aligned by alignof(__m512) if using C++17
__m512 * ptr = new __m512[N];
```

8.1.1.5 Dynamic memory allocation. First of all, there are many drop-in replacements for `malloc`, which are faster, more scalable[182], and address fragmentation[183] problems better. You can have a few percent performance improvement just by using a non-standard memory allocator. A typical issue with dynamic memory allocation is when at startup threads race with each other trying to allocate their memory regions at the same time[184]. One of the most popular memory allocation libraries are jemalloc[185] and tcmalloc[186].

Secondly, it is possible to speed up allocations using custom allocators, for example, arena allocators[187]. One of the main advantages is their low overhead since such allocators don't execute system calls for every memory allocation. Another advantage is its high flexibility. Developers can implement their own allocation strategies based on the memory region provided by the OS. One simple strategy could be to maintain two different allocators with their own arenas (memory regions): one for the hot data and one for the cold data. Keeping hot data together creates opportunities for it to share cache lines, which improves memory bandwidth utilization and spatial locality. It also improves TLB utilization since hot data occupies less amount of memory pages. Also, custom memory allocators can use thread-local storage to implement per-thread allocation and get rid of any synchronization between threads. This becomes useful when an

---

[182] Typical `malloc` implementation involves synchronization in case multiple threads would try to dynamically allocate the memory
[183] Fragmentation - https://en.wikipedia.org/wiki/Fragmentation_(computing).
[184] The same applies to memory deallocation.
[185] jemalloc - http://jemalloc.net/.
[186] tcmalloc - https://github.com/google/tcmalloc
[187] Region-based memory management - https://en.wikipedia.org/wiki/Region-based_memory_management

application is based on a thread pool and does not spawn a large number of threads.

8.1.1.6 Tune the code for memory hierarchy.
The performance of some applications depends on the size of the cache on a particular level. The most famous example here is improving matrix multiplication with loop blocking (tiling). The idea is to break the working size of the matrix into smaller pieces (tiles) such that each tile will fit in the L2 cache[188]. Most of the architectures provide CPUID-like instruction[189], which allows us to query the size of caches. Alternatively, one can use cache-oblivious algorithms[190] whose goal is to work reasonably well for any size of the cache.

Intel CPUs have Data Linear Address HW feature (see section 6.3.3) that supports cache blocking as described on easyperf blogpost[191].

8.1.2 Explicit Memory Prefetching

Often, in general-purpose workloads, there are situations when data accesses have no clear pattern or are random, so hardware can't effectively prefetch the data ahead of time (see information about HW prefetchers in section 3.5.1.5.1). Those are cases when cache misses could not be eliminated by choosing a better data structure either. An example of code when such transformation might be profitable is shown on Listing 26. Suppose `calcNextIndex` returns random values that significantly differ from each other. In this situation, we would have a subsequent load `arr[j]` go to a completely new place in memory and will frequently miss in caches. When the `arr` array is big enough[192], the HW prefetcher won't be able to catch the pattern and fail to pull the required data ahead of time. In the example in Listing 26, there is some time window between the index `j` is calculated, and the element `arr[j]` is requested. Thanks

---

[188] Usually, people tune for the size of the L2 cache since it is not shared between the cores.

[189] In Intel processors CPUID instruction is described in [Int, 2020, Volume 2]

[190] Cache-oblivious algorithm - https://en.wikipedia.org/wiki/Cache-oblivious_algorithm.

[191] Blog article "Detecting false sharing" - https://easyperf.net/blog/2019/12/17/Detecting-false-sharing-using-perf#2-tune-the-code-for-better-utilization-of-cache-hierarchy.

[192] For this example, we define "big enough" to be more than this size of L3 cache inside a typical desktop CPU, which, at the time of writing, varies from 5 to 20 MB.

to that, we can manually add explicit prefetching instructions with __builtin_prefetch[193] as shown on Listing 27.

Listing 26 Memory Prefetching: baseline version.

```
for (int i = 0; i < N; ++i) {
  int j = calcNextIndex();
  // ...
  doSomeExtensiveComputation();
  // ...
  x = arr[j]; // this load misses in L3 cache a lot
}
```

Listing 27 Memory Prefetching: using built-in prefetch hints.

```
for (int i = 0; i < N; ++i) {
  int j = calcNextIndex();
  __builtin_prefetch(a + j, 0, 1); // well before the load
  // ...
  doSomeExtensiveComputation();
  // ...
  x = arr[j];
}
```

For prefetch hints to take effect, be sure to insert it well ahead of time so that by the time the loaded value will be used in other calculations, it will be already in the cache. Also, do not insert it too early since it may pollute the cache with the data that is not used for some time. In order to estimate the prefetch window, use the method described in section 6.2.5. [194]

The most common scenario where engineers use explicit memory prefetching is to get the data required for the next iteration of the loop. However, linear function prefetching can also be very helpful, e.g., when you know the address of the data ahead of time but request the data with some delay (prefetch window).

Explicit memory prefetching is not portable, meaning that if it gives performance gains on one platform, it doesn't guarantee similar speedups on another platform. Even worse, when used badly, it can

---

[193] GCC builtins - https://gcc.gnu.org/onlinedocs/gcc/Other-Builtins.html.
[194] Readers can also find an example of estimating the prefetch window in the article: https://easyperf.net/blog/2019/04/03/Precise-timing-of-machine-code-with-Linux-perf#application-estimating-prefetch-window.

worsen the performance of caches. When using the wrong size of a memory block or requesting prefetches too often, it can force other useful data to be evicted from the caches.

While software prefetching gives programmer control and flexibility, it's not always easy to get it right. Consider a situation when we want to insert a prefetch instruction into the piece of code that has average IPC=2, and every DRAM access takes 100 cycles. To have the best effect, we would need to insert prefetching instruction 200 instructions before the load. It is not always possible, especially if the load address is computed right before the load itself. The pointer chasing problem can be a good example when explicit prefetching is helpless. [Nima Honarmand]

Finally, an explicit prefetch instruction increases code size and adds pressure on the CPU Front-End. The prefetch instruction is just like any other instruction: it consumes CPU resources, and when using it wrong, it can pessimize the performance of a program.

8.1.3 Optimizing For DTLB

As described in section 3, the TLB is a fast but finite per-core cache for virtual-to-physical address translations of memory addresses. Without it, every memory access by an application would require a time-consuming page walk of the kernel page table to calculate the correct physical address for each referenced virtual address.

TLB hierarchy typically consists of L1 ITLB (instructions), L1 DTLB (data), and L2 STLB (unified cache for instructions and data). A miss in the L1 (first level) ITLBs results in a very small penalty that can usually be hidden by the Out of Order (OOO) execution. A miss in the STLB results in the page walker being invoked. This penalty can be noticeable in the runtime because, during this process, the CPU is stalled [Suresh Srinivas, 2019]. Assuming the default page size in Linux kernel is 4KB, modern L1 level TLB caches can keep only up to a few hundred most recently used page-table entries, which covers address space of ~1MB, while L2 STLB can hold up to a few thousand page-table entries. Exact numbers for a specific processor can be found at https://ark.intel.com.

On Linux and Windows systems, applications are loaded into memory into 4KB pages, which is the default on most systems. Allocating many small pages is expensive. If an application actively references

8.1 Memory Bound

tens or hundreds of GBs of memory, that would require many 4KB-sized pages, each of which will contend for a limited set of TLB entries. Using large 2MB pages, 20MB of memory can be mapped with just ten pages, whereas with 4KB pages, 5120 pages are required. This means fewer TLB entries are needed, in turn reducing the number of TLB misses. Both Windows and Linux allow applications to establish large-page memory regions. HugeTLB subsystem support depends on the architecture, while AMD64 and Intel 64 architecture support both 2 MB (huge) and 1 GB (gigantic) pages.

As we just learned, one way to reduce the number of ITLB misses is to use the larger page size. Thankfully, TLB is capable of caching entries for 2MB and 1GB pages as well. If the aforementioned application employed 2MB pages instead of the default 4KB pages, it would reduce TLB pressure by a factor of 512. Likewise, if it updated from using 2MB pages to 1GB pages, it would reduce TLB pressure by yet another factor of 512. That is quite an improvement! Using a larger page size may be beneficial for some applications because less space is used in the cache for storing translations, allowing more space to be available for the application code. Huge pages typically lead to fewer page walks, and the penalty for walking the kernel page table in the event of a TLB miss is reduced since the table itself is more compact.

Large pages can be used for code, data, or both. Large pages for data are good to try if your workload has a large heap. Large memory applications such as relational database systems (e.g., MySQL, PostgreSQL, Oracle, etc.) and Java applications configured with large heap regions frequently benefit from using large pages. One example of using huge pages for optimizing runtimes is presented in [Suresh Srinivas, 2019], showing how this feature improves performance and reduces ITLB misses (up to 50%) in three applications in three environments. However, as it is with many other features, large pages are not for every application. An application that wants to allocate only one byte of data would be better off using a 4k page rather than a huge one; that way, memory is used more efficiently.

On Linux OS, there are two ways of using large pages in an application: Explicit and Transparent Huge Pages.

8.1.3.1 Explicit Hugepages.

Are available as a part of the system memory, exposed as a huge page file system (`hugetlbfs`), applications can access it using system calls, e.g., `mmap`. One can check

Huge Pages appropriately configured on the system through `cat /proc/meminfo` and look at `HugePages_Total` entries. Huge pages can be reserved at boot time or at run time. Reserving at boot time increases the possibility of success because the memory has not yet been significantly fragmented. Exact instructions for reserving huge pages can be found in Red Hat Performance Tuning Guide.

There is an option to dynamically allocate memory on top of large pages with libhugetlbfs[195] library that overrides `malloc` calls used in existing dynamically linked binary executables. It doesn't require modifying the code or even relink the binary; end-users just need to configure several environment variables. It can use both explicitly reserved huge pages as well as transparent ones. See libhugetlbfs how-to documentation[196] for more details.

For more fine-grained control over accesses to large pages from the code (i.e., not affecting every memory allocation), developers have the following alternatives:

- `mmap` using the `MAP_HUGETLB` flag (exampe code[197]).
- `mmap` using a file from a mounted `hugetlbfs` filesystem (exampe code[198]).
- `shmget` using the `SHM_HUGETLB` flag (exampe code[199]).

8.1.3.2 Transparent Hugepages. Linux also offers Transparent Hugepage Support (THP), which manages large pages[200] automatically and is transparent for applications. Under Linux, you can enable THP, which dynamically switches to huge pages when large blocks of memory are needed. The THP feature has two modes of operation: system-wide and per-process. When THP is enabled system-wide, the kernel tries to assign huge pages to any process when it is possible to allocate such, so huge pages do not need to be reserved manually. If THP is enabled per-process, the kernel only assigns huge pages to individual processes' memory areas attributed to the

---

[195] libhugetlbfs - https://github.com/libhugetlbfs/libhugetlbfs.
[196] libhugetlbfs "how-to" page - https://github.com/libhugetlbfs/libhugetlbfs/blob/master/HOWTO.
[197] MAP_HUGETLB example - https://elixir.bootlin.com/linux/latest/source/tools/testing/selftests/vm/map_hugetlb.c.
[198] Mounted `hugetlbfs` filesystem - https://elixir.bootlin.com/linux/latest/source/tools/testing/selftests/vm/hugepage-mmap.c.
[199] SHM_HUGETLB example - https://elixir.bootlin.com/linux/latest/source/tools/testing/selftests/vm/hugepage-shm.c.
[200] Note that the THP feature only supports 2MB pages.

`madvise` system call. You can check if THP enabled in the system with:

```
$ cat /sys/kernel/mm/transparent_hugepage/enabled
always [madvise] never
```

If the values are `always` (system-wide) or `madvise` (per-process), then THP is available for your application. With the `madvise` option, THP is enabled only inside memory regions attributed with `MADV_HUGEPAGE` via `madvise` system call. Complete specification for every option can be found in Linux kernel documentation[201] regarding THP.

8.1.3.3 Explicit vs. Transparent Hugepages.

Whilst Explicit Huge Pages (EHP) are reserved in virtual memory upfront, THPs are not. In the background, the kernel attempts to allocate a THP, and if it fails, it will default to the standard 4k page. This all happens transparently to the user. The allocation process can potentially involve a number of kernel processes responsible for making space in the virtual memory for a future THP (which may include swapping memory to the disk, fragmentation, or compacting pages[202]). Background maintenance of transparent huge pages incurs non-deterministic latency overhead from the kernel as it manages the inevitable fragmentation and swapping issues. EHP is not subject to memory fragmentation and cannot be swapped to the disk.

Secondly, EHP is available for use on all segments of an application, including text segments (i.e., benefits both DTLB *and* ITLB), while THP is only available for dynamically allocated memory regions.

One advantage of THP is that less OS configuration effort is required than with EHP, which enables faster experiments.

8.2 Core Bound

The second type of CPU Back-End bottleneck is `Core Bound`. Generally speaking, this metric represents all the stalls inside a CPU Out-Of-Order execution engine that was not caused by memory issues. There are two main categories that represent Core Bound metric:

---

[201] Linux kernel THP documentation - https://www.kernel.org/doc/Documentation/vm/transhuge.txt

[202] E.g., compacting 4KB pages into 2MB, breaking 2MB pages back into 4KB, etc.

8.2 Core Bound

- Shortage in hardware compute resources. It indicates that certain execution units are overloaded (execution port contention). This can happen when a workload frequently performs lots of heavy instructions. For example, division and square root operations are served by the Divider unit and can take considerably longer latency than other instructions.
- Dependencies between software's instructions. It indicates that dependencies in the program's data- or instruction-flow are limiting the performance. For example, floating-point dependent long-latency arithmetic operations lead to low Instruction Level Parallelism (ILP).

In this subsection, we will take a look at the most well-known optimizations like function inlining, vectorization, and loop optimizations. Those optimizations aim at reducing the total amount of executed instructions, which, technically, is also helpful when the workload experience a high Retiring metric. But the author believes that it is appropriate to discuss them here.

8.2.1 Inlining Functions

Function inlining is replacing a call to a function F with the code for F specialized with the actual arguments of the call. Inlining is one of the most important compiler optimizations. Not only because it eliminates the overhead of calling a function[203], but also it enables other optimizations. This happens because when a compiler inlines a function, the scope of compiler analysis widens to a much larger chunk of code. However, there are disadvantages as well: inlining can potentially increase the code size and compile time[204].

The primary mechanism for function inlining in many compilers relies on some sort of a cost model. For example, for the LLVM compiler, it is based on computing cost and a threshold for each function call (callsite). Inlining happens if the cost is less than the threshold. Generally, the cost of inlining a function call is based on the number and type of instructions in that function. A threshold is usually fixed; however, it can be varied under certain circumstances[205]. There are

---

[203] Overhead of calling a function usually consists of executing CALL, PUSH, POP, and RET instructions. Series of PUSH instructions are called "Prologue", and series of POP instructions are called "Epilogue".
[204] See the article: https://aras-p.info/blog/2017/10/09/Forced-Inlining-Might-Be-Slow/.
[205] For example, 1) when a function declaration has a hint for inlining, 2) when

8.2 Core Bound

many heuristics that surround that general cost model. For instance:
- Tiny functions (wrappers) are almost always inlined.
- Functions with a single callsite are preferred candidates for inlining.
- Large functions usually are not inlined as they bloat the code of the caller function.

Also, there are situations when inlining is problematic:
- A recursive function cannot be inlined into itself.
- Function that is referred to through a pointer can be inlined in place of a direct call but has to stay in the binary, i.e., cannot be fully inlined and eliminated. The same is true for functions with external linkage.

As we said earlier, compilers tend to use a cost model approach when making a decision about inlining a function, which typically works well in practice. In general, it is a good strategy to rely on the compiler for making all the inlining decisions and adjust if needed. The cost model cannot account for every possible situation, which leaves room for improvement. Sometimes compilers require special hints from the developer. One way to find potential candidates for inlining in a program is by looking at the profiling data, and in particular, how hot is the prologue and the epilogue[206] of the function. Below is an example[207] of a function profile with prologue and epilogue consuming ~50% of the function time:

```
Overhead |  Source code & Disassembly
   (%)   |  of function `foo`
-----------------------------------------
   3.77 :    418be0:   push    r15        # prologue
   4.62 :    418be2:   mov     r15d,0x64
   2.14 :    418be8:   push    r14
   1.34 :    418bea:   mov     r14,rsi
   3.43 :    418bed:   push    r13
   3.08 :    418bef:   mov     r13,rdi
   1.24 :    418bf2:   push    r12
   1.14 :    418bf4:   mov     r12,rcx
   3.08 :    418bf7:   push    rbp
   3.43 :    418bf8:   mov     rbp,rdx
```

there is profiling data for the function, or 3) when a compiler optimizes for size (-Os) rather than performance (-O2).

[206] Inlining a function with hot prologue and epilogue - https://en.wikipedia.org/wiki/Function_prologue.
[207] https://easyperf.net/blog/2019/05/28/Performance-analysis-and-tuning-contest-3#inlining-functions-with-hot-prolog-and-epilog-265.

```
1.94 :   418bfb:   push   rbx
0.50 :   418bfc:   sub    rsp,0x8
 ...
 #                         # function body
 ...
4.17 :   418d43:   add    rsp,0x8   # epilogue
3.67 :   418d47:   pop    rbx
0.35 :   418d48:   pop    rbp
0.94 :   418d49:   pop    r12
4.72 :   418d4b:   pop    r13
4.12 :   418d4d:   pop    r14
0.00 :   418d4f:   pop    r15
1.59 :   418d51:   ret
```

This might be a strong indicator that the time consumed by the prologue and epilogue of the function might be saved if we inline the function. Note that even if the prologue and epilogue are hot, it doesn't necessarily mean it will be profitable to inline the function. Inlining triggers a lot of different changes, so it's hard to predict the outcome. Always measure the performance of the changed code to confirm the need to force inlining.

For GCC and Clang compilers, one can make a hint for inlining foo with the help of C++11 [[gnu::always_inline]] attribute[208] as shown in the code example below. For the MSVC compiler, one can use the __forceinline keyword.

```
[[gnu::always_inline]] int foo() {
    // foo body
}
```

8.2.2 Loop Optimizations

Loops are the heart of nearly all high performance (HPC) programs. Since loops represent a piece of code that is executed a large number of times, they are where the majority of the execution time is spent. Small changes in such a critical piece of code may have a high impact on the performance of a program. That's why it is so important to carefully analyze the performance of hot loops in a program and know possible options to improve them.

To effectively optimize a loop, it is crucial to know what is the bottleneck of the loop. Once you find the loops that are using the most time, try to determine their bottlenecks. Usually, the

---
[208] For earlier C++ standards one can use __attribute__((always_inline)).

8.2 Core Bound

performance of the loops is limited by one or many of the following: memory latency, memory bandwidth, or compute capabilities of a machine. Roofline Performance Model (section 5.5) is a good starting point for assessing the performance of different loops against the HW theoretical maximums. Top-Down Microarchitecture Analysis (section 6.1) can be another good source of information about the bottlenecks.

In this section, we will take a look at the most well-known loop optimizations that address the types of bottlenecks mentioned above. We first discuss low-level optimizations that only move code around in a single loop. Such optimizations typically help make computations inside the loop more effective. Next, we will take a look at high-level optimizations that restructure loops, which often affects multiple loops. The second class of optimizations generally aims at improving memory accesses eliminating memory bandwidth and memory latency issues. Note, this is not a complete list of all discovered loop transformations. For more detailed information on each of the transformations discussed below, readers can refer to [Cooper and Torczon, 2012].

Compilers can automatically recognize an opportunity to perform a certain loop transformation. However, sometimes developer's interference may be required to reach the desired outcome. In the second part of this section, we will take a look at possible ways to discover performance improvement opportunities in the loops. Understanding what transformations were performed on a given loop and what optimizations compiler failed to do is one of the keys to successful performance tuning. In the end, we will consider an alternative way of optimizing loops with polyhedral frameworks.

8.2.2.1 Low-level optimizations.

First, we will consider simple loop optimizations that transform the code inside a single loop: Loop Invariant Code Motion, Loop Unrolling, Loop Strength Reduction, and Loop Unswitching. Such optimizations usually help improve the performance of loops with high arithmetic intensity (see section 5.5), i.e., when a loop is bound by CPU compute capabilities. Generally, compilers are good at doing such transformations; however, there are still cases when a compiler might need a developer's support. We will talk about that in subsequent sections.

Loop Invariant Code Motion (LICM). Expressions evaluated in a loop that never change are called loop invariants. Since their value doesn't change across loop iterations, we can move loop invariant expressions outside of the loop. We do so by storing the result in a temporary and just use the temporary inside the loop (see Listing 28).

Listing 28 Loop Invariant Code motion

```
for (int i = 0; i < N; ++i)        for (int i = 0; i < N; ++i) {
  for (int j = 0; j < N; ++j)        auto temp = c[i];
    a[j] = b[j] * c[i];       =>     for (int j = 0; j < N; ++j)
                                       a[j] = b[j] * temp;
                                   }
```

Loop Unrolling. An induction variable is a variable in a loop, whose value is a function of the loop iteration number. For example, $v = f(i)$, where i is an iteration number. Modifying the induction variable in each iteration can be expensive. Instead, we can unroll a loop and perform multiple iterations for each increment of the induction variable (see Listing 29).

Listing 29 Loop Unrolling

```
for (int i = 0; i < N; ++i)        for (int i = 0; i < N; i+=2) {
  a[i] = b[i] * c[i];       =>       a[i] = b[i] * c[i];
                                     a[i+1] = b[i+1] * c[i+1];
                                   }
```

The primary benefit of loop unrolling is to perform more computations per iteration. At the end of each iteration, the index value must be incremented, tested, and the control is branched back to the top of the loop if it has more iterations to process. This work can be considered as loop "tax", which can be reduced. By unrolling the loop in Listing 29 by a factor of 2, we reduce the number of executed compare and branch instructions by half.

Loop unrolling is a well-known optimization; still, many people are confused about it and try to unroll the loops manually. I suggest that no developer should unroll any loop by hand. First, compilers are very good at doing this and usually do loop unrolling quite optimally. The second reason is that processors have an "embedded unroller" thanks to their out-of-order speculative execution engine (see section 3). While the processor is waiting for the load from the first iteration to finish, it may speculatively start executing the load from the second iteration. This spans to multiple iterations

8.2 Core Bound

ahead, effectively unrolling the loop in the instruction Reorder Buffer (ROB).

Loop Strength Reduction (LSR). The idea of LSR is to replace expensive instructions with cheaper ones. Such transformation can be applied to all expressions that use an induction variable. Strength reduction is often applied to array indexing. Compilers perform LSR by analyzing how the value of a variable evolves[209] across the loop iterations (see Listing 30).

Listing 30 Loop Strength Reduction

```
for (int i = 0; i < N; ++i)          int j = 0;
  a[i] = b[i * 10] * c[i];      =>   for (int i = 0; i < N; ++i) {
                                       a[i] = b[j] * c[i];
                                       j += 10;
                                     }
```

Loop Unswitching. If a loop has a conditional inside and it is invariant, we can move it outside of the loop. We do so by duplicating the body of the loop and placing a version of it inside each of the `if` and `else` clauses of the conditional (see Listing 31). While the loop unswitching may double the amount of code written, each of these new loops may now be separately optimized.

Listing 31 Loop Unswitching

```
for (i = 0; i < N; i++) {            if (c)
  a[i] += b[i];                        for (i = 0; i < N; i++) {
  if (c)                      =>         a[i] += b[i];
    b[i] = 0;                            b[i] = 0;
}                                      }
                                     else
                                       for (i = 0; i < N; i++) {
                                         a[i] += b[i];
                                       }
```

8.2.2.2 High-level optimizations.

There is another class of loop transformations that change the structure of loops and often affect multiple nested loops. We will take a look at Loop Interchange, Loop Blocking (Tiling), and Loop Fusion and Distribution (Fission). This set of transformations aims at improving memory accesses and

---

[209] In LLVM, it is known as Scalar Evolution (SCEV).

eliminating memory bandwidth and memory latency bottlenecks. From a compiler perspective, doing high-level loop transformations legally and automatically is very difficult. It is often hard to justify the benefit of making any of the optimizations mentioned in this paragraph. In that sense, developers are in a better position since they only have to care about the legality of the transformation in their particular piece of code, not about every possible scenario that may happen. Unfortunately, that also means that often times, we have to do such transformations manually.

Loop Interchange. It is a process of exchanging the loop order of nested loops. The induction variable used in the inner loop switches to the outer loop, and vice versa. Listing 32 shows an example of interchanging nested loops for i and j. The major purpose of loop interchange is to perform sequential memory accesses to the elements of a multi-dimensional array. By following the order in which elements are laid out in memory, we can improve the spatial locality of memory accesses and make our code more cache-friendly (see section 8.1.1). This transformation helps to eliminate memory bandwidth and memory latency bottlenecks.

Listing 32 Loop Interchange

```
for (i = 0; i < N; i++)              for (j = 0; j < N; j++)
  for (j = 0; j < N; j++)    =>        for (i = 0; i < N; i++)
    a[j][i] += b[j][i] * c[j][i];        a[j][i] += b[j][i] * c[j][i];
```

Loop Blocking (Tiling). The idea of this transformation is to split the multi-dimensional execution range into smaller chunks (blocks or tiles) so that each block will fit in the CPU caches[210]. If an algorithm works with large multi-dimensional arrays and performs strided accesses to their elements, there is a high chance of poor cache utilization. Every such access may push the data that will be requested by future accesses out of the cache (cache eviction). By partitioning an algorithm in smaller multi-dimensional blocks, we ensure the data used in a loop stays in the cache until it is reused.

In the example shown in Listing 33, an algorithm performs row-major traversal of elements of array a while doing column-major traversal of array b. The loop nest can be partitioned into smaller blocks in

---

[210] Typically, engineers optimize a tiled algorithm for the size of the L2 cache since it is private for each CPU core.

8.2 Core Bound

order to maximize the reuse of elements of the array b.

Listing 33 Loop Blocking

```
// linear traversal              // traverse in 8*8 blocks
for (int i = 0; i < N; i++)      for (int ii = 0; ii < N; ii+=8)
  for (int j = 0; j < N; j++) => for (int jj = 0; jj < N; jj+=8)
    a[i][j] += b[j][i];            for (int i = ii; i < ii+8; i++)
                                     for (int j = jj; j < jj+8; j++)
                                       a[i][j] += b[j][i];
```

Loop Blocking is a widely known method of optimizing GEneral Matrix Multiplication (GEMM) algorithms. It enhances the cache reuse of the memory accesses and improves both memory bandwidth and memory latency of an algorithm.

Loop Fusion and Distribution (Fission). Separate loops can be fused together when they iterate over the same range and do not reference each other's data. An example of a Loop Fusion is shown in Listing 34. The opposite procedure is called Loop Distribution (Fission) when the loop is split into separate loops.

Listing 34 Loop Fusion and Distribution

```
for (int i = 0; i < N; i++)              for (int i = 0; i < N; i++) {
  a[i].x = b[i].x;                         a[i].x = b[i].x;
                               <=>         a[i].y = b[i].y;
for (int j = 0; j < N; j++)              }
  a[i].y = b[i].y;
```

Loop Fusion helps to reduce the loop overhead (see discussion in Loop Unrolling) since both loops can use the same induction variable. Also, loop fusion can help to improve the temporal locality of memory accesses. In Listing 34, if both x and y members of a structure happen to reside on the same cache line, it is better to fuse the two loops since we can avoid loading the same cache line twice. This will reduce the cache footprint and improve memory bandwidth utilization.

However, loop fusion does not always improve performance. Sometimes it is better to split a loop into multiple passes, pre-filter the data, sort and reorganize it, etc. By distributing the large loop into multiple smaller ones, we limit the amount of data required for each iteration of the loop, effectively increasing the temporal locality of memory accesses. This helps in situations with a high cache contention, which typically happens in large loops. Loop distribution also reduces register pressure since, again, fewer operations are being done within each iteration of the loop. Also, breaking a big loop into multiple smaller ones will likely be beneficial for the performance of the CPU Front-End because of better instruction cache utilization (see section 7). Finally, when distributed, each small loop can be further optimized separately by the compiler.

8.2.2.3 Discovering loop optimization opportunities. As we discussed at the beginning of this section, compilers will do the heavy-lifting part of optimizing your loops. You can count on them on making all the obvious improvements in the code of your loops, like eliminating unnecessary work, doing various peephole optimizations, etc. Sometimes a compiler is clever enough to generate the fast versions of the loops by default, and other times we have to do some rewriting ourselves to help the compiler. As we said earlier, from a compiler's perspective, doing loop transformations legally and automatically is very difficult. Often, compilers have to be conservative when they cannot prove the legality of a transformation.

Consider a code in Listing 35. A compiler cannot move the expression `strlen(a)` out of the loop body. So, the loop checks if we reached the end of the string on each iteration, which is obviously slow. The reason why a compiler cannot hoist the call is that there could be a situation when the memory regions of arrays a and b overlap. In this case, it would be illegal to move `strlen(a)` out of the loop body. If developers are sure that the memory regions do not overlap, they can declare both parameters of function `foo` with the `restrict` keyword, i.e., `char* __restrict__ a`.

Listing 35 Cannot move strlen out of the loop

```
void foo(char* a, char* b) {
  for (int i = 0; i < strlen(a); ++i)
    b[i] = (a[i] == 'x') ? 'y' : 'n';
}
```

Sometimes compilers can inform us about failed transformations via compiler optimization remarks (see section 5.7). However, in this case, neither Clang 10.0.1 nor GCC 10.2 were able to explicitly tell that the expression `strlen(a)` was not hoisted out of the loop. The only way to find this out is to examine hot parts of the generated assembly code according to the profile of the application. Analyzing machine code requires the basic ability to read assembly language, but it is a highly rewarding activity.

It is a reasonable strategy to try to get the low-hanging fruits first. Developers could use compiler optimizations reports or examine the machine code of a loop to search for easy improvements. Sometimes, it's possible to adjust compiler transformations using user directives. For example, when we find out that the compiler unrolled our loop by a factor of 4, we may check if using a higher unrolling factor will benefit performance. Most compilers support `#pragma unroll(8)`, which will instruct a compiler to use the unrolling factor specified by the user. There are other pragmas that control certain transformations, like loop vectorization, loop distribution, and others. For a complete list of user directives, we invite the user to check the compiler's manual.

Next, developers should identify the bottlenecks in the loop and assess performance against the HW theoretical maximum. Start with the Roofline Performance Model (section 5.5), which will reveal the bottlenecks that developers should try to address. The performance of the loops is limited by one or many of the following factors: memory latency, memory bandwidth, or compute capabilities of a machine. Once the bottlenecks of the loop were identified, developers can try to apply one of the transformations we discussed earlier in this section.

> **Personal Experience:** Even though there are well-known optimization techniques for a particular set of computational problems, for a large part, loop optimizations are sort of "black art" that comes with experience. I recommend you to rely on a compiler and only complement it with making needed transformations yourself. Finally, keep the code as simple as possible and do not introduce unreasonable complicated changes if the performance benefits are negligible.

8.2.2.4 Use Loop Optimization Frameworks

Over the years, researchers have developed techniques to determine the legality of loop transformations and automatically transform the loops. One such invention is the polyhedral framework[211]. GRAPHITE[212] was among the first set of polyhedral tools that were integrated into a production compiler. GRAPHITE performs a set of classical loop optimizations based on the polyhedral information, extracted from GIMPLE, GCC's low-level intermediate representation. GRAPHITE has demonstrated the feasibility of the approach.

LLVM-based compilers employ their own polyhedral framework: Polly[213]. Polly is a high-level loop and data-locality optimizer and optimization infrastructure for LLVM. It uses an abstract mathematical representation based on integer polyhedral to analyze and optimize the memory access pattern of a program. Polly performs classical loop transformations, especially tiling and loop fusion, to improve data-locality. This framework has shown significant speedups on a number of well-known benchmarks [Grosser et al., 2012]. Below we show an example of how Polly can give an almost 30 times speedup of a GEneral Matrix-Multiply (GEMM) kernel from Polybench 2.0[214] benchmark suite:

```
$ clang -O3 gemm.c -o gemm.clang
$ time ./gemm.clang
real    0m6.574s
$ clang -O3 gemm.c -o gemm.polly -mllvm -polly
$ time ./gemm.polly
real    0m0.227s
```

Polly is a powerful framework for loop optimizations; however, it still misses out on some common and important situations[215]. It is not enabled in the standard optimization pipeline in the LLVM infrastructure and requires that the user provide an explicit compiler option for using it (`-mllvm -polly`). Using polyhedral frameworks is a viable option when searching for a way to speed up your loops.

8.2.3 Vectorization

On modern processors, the use of SIMD instructions can result in a great speedup over regular un-vectorized (scalar) code. When doing

---
[211] Polyhedral framework - https://en.wikipedia.org/wiki/Loop_optimization#The_polyhedral_or_constraint-based_framework.
[212] GRAPHITE polyhedral framework - https://gcc.gnu.org/wiki/Graphite.
[213] Polly - https://polly.llvm.org/.
[214] Polybench - https://web.cse.ohio-state.edu/~pouchet.2/software/polybench/.
[215] Why not Polly? - https://sites.google.com/site/parallelizationforllvm/why-not-polly.

performance analysis, one of the top priorities of the software engineer is to ensure that the hot parts of the code are vectorized by the compiler. This section is supposed to guide engineers towards discovering vectorization opportunities. To recap on general information about the SIMD capabilities of modern CPUs, readers can take a look at section 3.7.

Most vectorization happens automatically without any intervention of the user (Autovectorization). That is when a compiler automatically recognizes the opportunity to produce SIMD machine code from the source code. It is a good strategy to rely on autovectorization since modern compilers generate fast vectorized code for a wide variety of source code inputs. Echoing advice given earlier, the author recommends to let the compiler do its job and only interfere when it is needed.

In rather rare cases, software engineers need to adjust autovectorization, based on the feedback[216] that they get from a compiler or profiling data. In such cases, programmers need to tell the compiler that some code region is vectorizable or that vectorization is profitable. Modern compilers have extensions that allow power users to control the vectorizer directly and make sure that certain parts of the code are vectorized efficiently. There will be several examples of using compiler hints in the subsequent sections.

It is important to note that there is a range of problems where SIMD is invaluable and where autovectorization just does not work and is not likely to work in the near future (one can find an example in [Muła and Lemire, 2019]). If it is not possible to make a compiler generate desired assembly instructions, a code snippet can be rewritten with the help of compiler intrinsics. In most cases, compiler intrinsics provide a 1-to-1 mapping into assembly instruction (see section 10.2).

> **Personal Opinion:** Even though in some cases developers need to mess around with compiler intrinsics, I recommend to mostly rely on compiler auto-vectorization and only use intrinsics when necessary. A code that uses compiler intrinsics resembles inline assembly and quickly becomes unreadable. Compiler auto-vectorization can often be adjusted using pragmas and other hints.

---

[216] For example, compiler optimization reports, see section 5.7.

Generally, three kinds of vectorization are done in a compiler: inner loop vectorization, outer loop vectorization, and SLP (Superword-Level Parallelism) vectorization. In this section, we will mostly consider inner loop vectorization since this is the most common case. We provide general information about the outer loop and SLP vectorization in appendix B.

8.2.3.1 Compiler Autovectorization. Multiple hurdles can prevent auto-vectorization, some of which are inherent to the semantics of programming languages. For example, the compiler must assume that unsigned loop-indices may overflow, and this can prevent certain loop transformations. Another example is the assumption that the C programming language makes: pointers in the program may point to overlapping memory regions, which can make the analysis of the program very difficult. Another major hurdle is the design of the processor itself. In some cases processors, don't have efficient vector instructions for certain operations. For example, performing predicated (bitmask-controlled) load and store operations are not available on most processors. Another example is vector-wide format conversion between signed integers to doubles because the result operates on vector registers of different sizes. Despite all of the challenges, the software developer can work around many of the challenges and enable vectorization. Later in the section, we provide guidance on how to work with the compiler and ensure that the hot code is vectorized by the compiler.

The vectorizer is usually structured in three phases: legality-check, profitability-check, and transformation itself:

- **Legality-check**. In this phase, the compiler checks if it is legal to transform the loop (or some other code region) into using vectors. The loop vectorizer checks that the iterations of the loop are consecutive, which means that the loop progresses linearly. The vectorizer also ensures that all of the memory and arithmetic operations in the loop can be widened into consecutive operations. That the control flow of the loop is uniform across all lanes and that the memory access patterns are uniform. The compiler has to check or ensure somehow that the generated code won't touch memory that it is not supposed to and that the order of operations will be preserved. The compiler needs to analyze the possible range of pointers, and if it has some missing information, it has to assume that the transformation is illegal. The legality phase collects a list of requirements that need to happen for vectorization of the loop to be legal.

- **Profitability-check.** Next, the vectorizer checks if a transformation is profitable. It compares different vectorization factors and figures out which vectorization factor would be the fastest to execute. The vectorizer uses a cost model to predict the cost of different operations, such as scalar add or vector load. It needs to take into account the added instructions that shuffle data into registers, predict register pressure, and estimate the cost of the loop guards that ensure that preconditions that allow vectorizations are met. The algorithm for checking profitability is simple: 1) add-up the cost of all of the operations in the code, 2) compare the costs of each version of the code, 3) divide the cost by the expected execution count. For example, if the scalar code costs 8 cycles, and the vectorized code costs 12 cycles, but performs 4 loop iterations at once, then the vectorized version of the loop is probably faster.

- **Transformation.** Finally, after the vectorizer figures out that the transformation is legal and profitable, they transform the code. This process also includes the insertion of guards that enable vectorization. For example, most loops use an unknown iteration count, so the compiler has to generate a scalar version of the loop, in addition to the vectorized version of the loop, to handle the last few iterations. The compiler also has to check if pointers don't overlap, etc. All of these transformations are done using information that is collected during the legality check phase.

8.2.3.2 Discovering vectorization opportunities.
Amdahl's law[217] teaches us that we should spend time analyzing only those parts of code that are used the most during the execution of a program. Thus, the performance engineer should focus on hot parts of the code that were highlighted by a profiling tool (see section 5.4). As mentioned earlier, vectorization is most frequently applied to loops.

Discovering opportunities for improving vectorization should start by analyzing hot loops in the program and checking what optimizations

---
[217] Amdahl's_law - https://en.wikipedia.org/wiki/Amdahl's_law.

were performed by the compiler to them. Checking compiler vectorization remarks (see section 5.7) is the easiest way to know that. Modern compilers can report whether a certain loop was vectorized, provide additional details, like vectorization factor (VF). In the case when the compiler cannot vectorize a loop, it is also able to tell the reason why it failed.

An alternative way to using compiler optimization reports is to check assembly output. It is best to analyze the output from a profiling tool that shows the correspondence between the source code and generated assembly instructions for a given loop. However, this method requires the ability to read and understand assembly language. It may take some time to figure out the semantics of the instructions generated by the compiler[218]. But this skill is highly rewarding and often provide additional insights. For example, one can spot suboptimal generated code, such as lack of vectorization, suboptimal vectorization factor, performing unnecessary computations, etc.

There are a few common cases that developers frequently run into when trying to accelerate vectorizable code. Below we present four typical scenarios and give general guidance on how to proceed in each case.

8.2.3.3 Vectorization is illegal.
In some cases, the code that iterates over elements of an array is simply not vectorizable. Vectorization remarks are very effective at explaining what went wrong and why the compiler can't vectorize the code. Listing 36 shows an example of dependence inside a loop that prevents vectorization[219].

Listing 36 Vectorization: read-after-write dependence.
```
void vectorDependence(int *A, int n) {
  for (int i = 1; i < n; i++)
    A[i] = A[i-1] * 2;
}
```

While some loops cannot be vectorized due to the hard limitations

---
[218] Although one can quickly tell if the code was vectorized or not just by looking at instruction mnemonics or at register names used by those instructions. Vector instructions operate on packed data (thus have P in their name) and use XMM, YMM, or ZMM registers.
[219] It is easy to spot read-after-write dependency once you unroll a couple of iterations of the loop. See example in section 5.7.

8.2 Core Bound

described above, others could be vectorized when certain constraints are relaxed. There are situations when the compiler cannot vectorize a loop because it simply cannot prove it is legal to do so. Compilers are generally very conservative and only do transformations when they are sure it doesn't break the code. Such soft limitations could be relaxed by providing additional hints to the compiler. For example, when transforming the code that performs floating-point arithmetic, vectorization may change the behavior of the program. The floating-point addition and multiplication are commutative, which means that you can swap the left-hand side and the right-hand side without changing the result: (a + b == b + a). However, these operations are not associative, because rounding happens at different times: ((a + b) + c) != (a + (b + c)). The code in Listing 37 cannot be auto vectorized by the compiler. The reason is that vectorization would change the variable sum into a vector accumulator, and this will change the order of operations and may lead to different rounding decisions and a different result.

Listing 37 Vectorization: floating-point arithmetic.

```
// a.cpp
float calcSum(float* a, unsigned N) {
  float sum = 0.0f;
  for (unsigned i = 0; i < N; i++) {
    sum += a[i];
  }
  return sum;
}
```

However, if the program can tolerate a bit of inaccuracy in the final result (which usually is the case), we can convey this information to the compiler to enable vectorization. Clang and GCC compilers have a flag, -ffast-math[220], that allows this kind of transformation:

```
$ clang++ -c a.cpp -O3 -march=core-avx2 -Rpass-analysis=.*
...
a.cpp:5:9: remark: loop not vectorized: cannot prove it is safe to
    reorder floating-point operations; allow reordering by
    specifying '#pragma clang loop vectorize(enable)' before the
    loop or by providing the compiler option '-ffast-math'.
    [-Rpass-analysis=loop-vectorize]
...
```

---

[220] The compiler flag -Ofast enables -ffast-math as well as the -O3 compilation mode.

```
$ clang++ -c a.cpp -O3 -ffast-math -Rpass=.*
...
a.cpp:4:3: remark: vectorized loop (vectorization width: 4,
    interleaved count: 2) [-Rpass=loop-vectorize]
...
```

Let's look at another typical situation when a compiler may need support from a developer to perform vectorization. When compilers cannot prove that a loop operates on arrays with non-overlapping memory regions, they usually choose to be on the safe side. Let's revisit the example from Listing 9 provided in section 5.7. When the compiler tries to vectorize the code presented in Listing 38, it generally cannot do this because the memory regions of arrays a, b, and c can overlap.

Listing 38 a.c

```
1  void foo(float* a, float* b, float* c, unsigned N) {
2    for (unsigned i = 1; i < N; i++) {
3      c[i] = b[i];
4      a[i] = c[i-1];
5    }
6  }
```

Here is the optimization report (enabled with `-fopt-info`) provided by GCC 10.2:

```
$ gcc -O3 -march=core-avx2 -fopt-info
a.cpp:2:26: optimized: loop vectorized using 32 byte vectors
a.cpp:2:26: optimized:  loop versioned for vectorization because of
    possible aliasing
```

GCC has recognized potential overlap between memory regions of arrays a, b, and c, and created multiple versions of the same loop. The compiler inserted runtime checks[221] for detecting if the memory regions overlap. Based on that checks, it dispatches between vectorized and scalar[222] versions. In this case, vectorization comes with the cost of inserting potentially expensive runtime checks. If a developer knows that memory regions of arrays a, b, and c do not overlap, it can insert `#pragma GCC ivdep`[223] right before the loop or use

---

[221] See example on easyperf blog: https://easyperf.net/blog/2017/11/03/Multi versioning_by_DD.
[222] But the scalar version of the loop still may be unrolled.
[223] It is GCC specific pragma. For other compilers, check the corresponding manuals.

the `__restrict__` keyword as shown in Listing 10. Such compiler hints will eliminate the need for the GCC compiler to insert runtime checks mentioned earlier.

By their nature, compilers are static tools: they only reason based on the code they work with. For example, some of the dynamic tools, such as Intel Advisor, can detect if issues like cross-iteration dependence or access to arrays with overlapping memory regions actually occur in a given loop. But be aware that such tools only provide a suggestion. Carelessly inserting compiler hints can cause real problems.

8.2.3.4 Vectorization is not beneficial.
In some cases, the compiler can vectorize the loop but figures that doing so is not profitable. In the code presented on Listing 39, the compiler could vectorize the memory access to array A but would need to split the access to array B into multiple scalar loads. The scatter/gather pattern is relatively expensive, and compilers that can simulate the cost of operations often decide to avoid vectorizing code with such patterns.

Listing 39 Vectorization: not beneficial.
```
1 // a.cpp
2 void stridedLoads(int *A, int *B, int n) {
3   for (int i = 0; i < n; i++)
4     A[i] += B[i * 3];
5 }
```

Here is the compiler optimization report for the code in Listing 39:

```
$ clang -c -O3 -march=core-avx2 a.cpp -Rpass-missed=loop-vectorize
a.cpp:3:3: remark: the cost-model indicates that vectorization is
    not beneficial [-Rpass-missed=loop-vectorize]
  for (int i = 0; i < n; i++)
```

Users can force the Clang compiler to vectorize the loop by using the `#pragma` hint, as shown in Listing 40. However, keep in mind that the true fact of whether vectorization is profitable or not largely depends on the runtime data, for example, the number of iterations of the loop. Compilers don't have this information available[224], so they

---
[224] Besides Profile Guided Optimizations (see section 7.7).

often tend to be conservative. Developers can use such hints when searching for performance headrooms.

Listing 40 Vectorization: not beneficial.

```
1  // a.cpp
2  void stridedLoads(int *A, int *B, int n) {
3  #pragma clang loop vectorize(enable)
4    for (int i = 0; i < n; i++)
5      A[i] += B[i * 3];
6  }
```

Developers should be aware of the hidden cost of using vectorized code. Using AVX and especially AVX512 vector instructions would lead to a big frequency downclocking. The vectorized portion of the code should be hot enough to justify using AVX512.[225]

8.2.3.5 Loop vectorized but scalar version used.
In some cases, the compiler can successfully vectorize the code, but the vectorized code does not show in the profiler. When inspecting the corresponding assembly of a loop, it is usually easy to find the vectorized version of the loop body because it uses the vector registers, which are not commonly used in other parts of the program, and the code is unrolled and filled with checks and multiple versions for enabling different edge cases.

If the generated code is not executed, one possible reason for this is that the code that the compiler has generated assumes loop trip counts that are higher than what the program uses. For example, to vectorize efficiently on a modern CPU, programmers need to vectorize and utilize AVX2 and also unroll the loop 4-5 times in order to generate enough work for the pipelined FMA units. This means that each loop iteration needs to process around 40 elements. Many loops may run with loop trip counts that are below this value and may fall back to use the scalar remainder loop. It is easy to detect these cases because the scalar remainder loop would light up in the profiler, and the vectorized code would remain cold.

The solution to this problem is to force the vectorizer to use a lower vectorization factor or unroll count, to reduce the number of elements that loops process and enable more loops with lower trip counts to

---
[225] For more details read this blog post: https://travisdowns.github.io/blog/2020/01/17/avxfreq1.html.

visit the fast vectorized loop body. Developers can achieve that with the help of #pragma hints. For Clang compiler one can use #pragma clang loop vectorize_width(N) as shown in the article[226] on easyperf blog.

8.2.3.6 Loop vectorized in a suboptimal way.
When you see a loop being vectorized and is executed at runtime, likely this part of the program already performs well. However, there are exceptions. Sometimes human experts can come up with the code that outperforms the one generated by the compiler.

The optimal vectorization factor can be unintuitive because of several factors. First, it is difficult for humans to simulate the operations of the CPU in their heads, and there is no alternative to actually trying multiple configurations. Vector shuffles that touch multiple vector lanes could be more or less expensive than expected, depending on many factors. Second, at runtime, the program may behave in unpredictable ways, depending on port pressure and many other factors. The advice here is to try to force the vectorizer to pick one specific vectorization factor and unroll factor and measure the result. Vectorization pragmas can help the user enumerate different vectorization factors and figure out the most performant one. There are relatively few possible configurations for each loop, and running the loop on typical inputs is something that humans can do that compilers can't.

Finally, there are situations when the scalar un-vectorized version of a loop performs better than the vectorized one. This could happen due to expensive vector operations like gather/scatter loads, masking, shuffles, etc. which compiler is required to use in order to make vectorization happen. Performance engineers could also try to disable vectorization in different ways. For the Clang compiler, it can be done via compiler options -fno-vectorize and -fno-slp-vectorize, or with a hint specific for a particular loop, e.g. #pragma clang loop vectorize(enable).

8.2.3.7 Use languages with explicit vectorization.
Vectorization can also be achieved by rewriting parts of a program in a programming language that is dedicated to parallel computing. Those languages use special constructs and knowledge of the program's data

---
[226] Using Clang's optimization pragmas - https://easyperf.net/blog/2017/11/09/Multiversioning_by_trip_counts

to compile the code efficiently into parallel programs. Originally such languages were mainly used to offload work to specific processing units such as graphics processing units (GPU), digital signal processors (DSP), or field-programmable gate arrays (FPGAs). However, some of those programming models can also target your CPU (such as OpenCL and OpenMP).

One such parallel language is Intel® Implicit SPMD Program Compiler (ISPC)[227], which we will cover a bit in this section. The ISPC language is based on the C programming language and uses the LLVM compiler infrastructure to emit optimized code for many different architectures. The key feature of ISPC is the "close to the metal" programming model and performance portability across SIMD architectures. It requires a shift from the traditional thinking of writing programs but gives programmers more control over CPU resource utilization.

Another advantage of ISPC is its interoperability and ease of use. ISPC compiler generates standard object files that can be linked with the code generated by conventional C/C++ compilers. ISPC code can be easily plugged in any native project since functions written with ISPC can be called as if it was C code.

Listing 41 shows a simple example of a function that we presented earlier in Listing 37, rewritten with ISPC. ISPC considers that the program will run in parallel instances, based on the target instruction set. For example, when using SSE with `floats`, it can compute 4 operations in parallel. Each program instance would operate on vector values of `i` being (0,1,2,3), then (4,5,6,7), and so on, effectively computing 4 sums at a time. As you can see, a few keywords not typical for C and C++ are used:

- The `export` keyword means that the function can be called from a C-compatible language.
- The `uniform` keyword means that a variable is shared between program instances.
- The `varying` keyword means that each program instance has its own local copy of the variable.
- The `foreach` is the same as a classic `for` loop except that it will distribute the work across the different program instances.

---

[227] ISPC compiler: https://ispc.github.io/.

Listing 41 ISPC version of summing elements of an array.

```
export uniform float calcSum(const uniform float array[],
                             uniform ptrdiff_t count)
{
    varying float sum = 0;
    foreach (i = 0 ... count)
        sum += array[i];
    return reduce_add(sum);
}
```

Since function `calcSum` must return a single value (a `uniform` variable) and our `sum` variable is a `varying`, we then need to *gather* the values of each program instance using the `reduce_add` function. ISPC also takes care of generating peeled and remainder loops as needed to take into account the data that is not correctly aligned or that is not a multiple of the vector width.

"Close to the metal" programming model. One of the problems with traditional C and C++ languages is that compiler doesn't always vectorize critical parts of code. Often times programmers resort to using compiler intrinsics (see section 10.2), which bypasses compiler autovectorization but is generally difficult and requires updating when new instruction sets come along. ISPC helps to resolve this problem by assuming every operation is SIMD by default. For example, the ISPC statement `sum += array[i]` is implicitly considered as a SIMD operation that makes multiple additions in parallel. ISPC is not an autovectorizing compiler, and it does not automatically discover vectorization opportunities. Since the ISPC language is very similar to C and C++, it is much better than using intrinsics as it allows you to focus on the algorithm rather than the low-level instructions. Also, it has reportedly matched[Pharr and Mark, 2012] or beaten[228] hand-written intrinsics code in terms of performance.

Performance portability. ISPC can automatically detect features of your CPU to fully utilize all the resources available. Programmers can write ISPC code once and compile to many vector instruction sets, such as SSE4, AVX, and AVX2. ISPC can also emit code for different architectures like x86 CPU, ARM NEON, and has experimental

---
[228] Some parts of the Unreal Engine which used SIMD intrinsics were rewritten using ISPC, which gave speedups: https://software.intel.com/content/www/us/en/develop/articles/unreal-engines-new-chaos-physics-system-screams-with-in-depth-intel-cpu-optimizations.html.

support for GPU offloading.

8.3 Chapter Summary

- Most of the real-world applications experience performance bottlenecks that can be related to the CPU Backend. It is not surprising since all the memory-related issues, as well as inefficient computations, belong to this category.
- Performance of the memory subsystem is not growing as fast as CPU performance. Yet, memory accesses are a frequent source of performance problems in many applications. Speeding up such programs requires revising the way they access memory.
- In section 8.1, we discussed some of the popular recipes for cache-friendly data structures, memory prefetching, and utilizing large memory pages to improve DTLB performance.
- Inefficient computations also represent a significant portion of the bottlenecks in real-world applications. Modern compilers are very good at removing unnecessary computation overhead by performing many different code transformations. Still, there is a high chance that we can do better than what compilers can offer.
- In section 8.2, we showed how one could search performance headrooms in a program by forcing certain code optimizations. We discussed such popular transformations as function inlining, loop optimizations, and vectorization.

9 Optimizing Bad Speculation

The speculation feature in modern CPUs is described in section 3.3.3. Mispredicting a branch can add a significant speed penalty when it happens regularly. When such an event happens, a CPU is required to clear all the speculative work that was done ahead of time and later was proven to be wrong. It also needs to flush the whole pipeline and start filling it with instructions from the correct path. Typically, modern CPUs experience a 15-20 cycles penalty as a result of a branch misprediction.

Nowadays, processors are very good at predicting branch outcomes. They not only can follow static prediction rules[229] but also detect dynamic patterns. Usually, branch predictors save the history of previous outcomes for the branches and try to guess what will be the next result. However, when the pattern becomes hard for the CPU branch predictor to follow, it may hurt performance. One can find out how much a program suffers from branch mispredictions by looking at TMA Bad Speculation metric.

> **Personal Experience:** The program will always experience some number of branch mispredictions. It is normal for general purpose applications to have a "Bad Speculation" rate in the range of 5-10%. My recommendation is to pay attention to this metric if it goes higher than 10%.

Since the branch predictors are good at finding patterns, old advice for optimizing branch prediction is no longer valid. One could provide a prediction hint to the processor in the form of a prefix to the branch instruction (0x2E: Branch Not Taken, 0x3E: Branch Taken). While this technique can improve performance on older platforms, it won't produce gains on newer ones[230].

Perhaps, the only direct way to get rid of branch mispredictions is to get rid of the branch itself. In the two subsequent sections, we will take a look at how branches can be replaced with lookup tables and predication.

---

[229] For example, a backward jump is usually taken, since most of the time, it represents the loop backedge.
[230] Anything newer than Pentium 4.

9.1 Replace branches with lookup

Frequently branches can be avoided by using lookup tables. An example of code when such transformation might be profitable is shown in Listing 42. Function `mapToBucket` maps values into corresponding buckets. For uniformly distributed values of `v`, we will have an equal probability for `v` to fall into any of the buckets. In generated assembly for the baseline version, we will likely see many branches, which could have high misprediction rates. Hopefully, it's possible to rewrite the function `mapToBucket` using a single array lookup, as shown in Listing 43.

Listing 42 Replacing branches: baseline version.

```
int mapToBucket(unsigned v) {
  if (v >= 0  && v < 10) return 0;
  if (v >= 10 && v < 20) return 1;
  if (v >= 20 && v < 30) return 2;
  if (v >= 30 && v < 40) return 3;
  if (v >= 40 && v < 50) return 4;
  return -1;
}
```

Listing 43 Replacing branches: lookup version.

```
int buckets[256] = {
    0, 0, 0, 0, 0, 0, 0, 0, 0, 0,
    1, 1, 1, 1, 1, 1, 1, 1, 1, 1,
    2, 2, 2, 2, 2, 2, 2, 2, 2, 2,
    3, 3, 3, 3, 3, 3, 3, 3, 3, 3,
    4, 4, 4, 4, 4, 4, 4, 4, 4, 4,
    5, 5, 5, 5, 5, 5, 5, 5, 5, 5,
   -1, -1, -1, -1, -1, -1, -1, -1, -1, -1,
   -1, -1, -1, -1, -1, -1, -1, -1, -1, -1,
   ... };

int mapToBucket(unsigned v) {
  if (v < (sizeof (buckets) / sizeof (int)))
    return buckets[v];
  return -1;
}
```

The assembly code of the `mapToBucket` function from Listing 43 should be using only one branch instead of many. A typical hot path through this function will execute the untaken branch and one load instruction. Since we expect most of the input values to fall into the range covered by the buckets array, the branch that guards out-of-bounds access will be well-predicted by CPU. Also, the buckets array is relatively small, so we can expect it to reside in CPU caches, which should allow for fast accesses to it.[Lemire, 2020]

If we have a need to map a bigger range of values, allocating a very large array is not practical. In this case, we might use interval map data structures that accomplish that goal using much less memory but logarithmic lookup complexity. Readers can find existing implementations of interval map container in Boost[231] and LLVM [232].

9.2 Replace branches with predication

Some branches could be effectively eliminated by executing both parts of the branch and then selecting the right result (predication). Example[233] of code when such transformation might be profitable is shown on Listing 44. If TMA suggests that the `if (cond)` branch has a very high number of mispredictions, one can try to eliminate the branch by doing the transformation shown on Listing 45.

Listing 44 Predicating branches: baseline version.

```
int a;
if (cond) { // branch has high misprediction rate
  a = computeX();
} else {
  a = computeY();
}
```

Listing 45 Predicating branches: branchless version.

```
int x = computeX();
int y = computeY();
int a = cond ? x : y;
```

[231] C++ Boost `interval_map` - https://www.boost.org/doc/libs/1_65_0/libs/icl/doc/html/boost/icl/interval_map.html
[232] LLVM's `IntervalMap` - https://llvm.org/doxygen/IntervalMap_8h_source.html
[233] Example of replacing branches with CMOV - https://easyperf.net/blog/2019/04/10/Performance-analysis-and-tuning-contest-2#fighting-branch-mispredictions-9

191

9.2 Replace branches with predication

For the version of code in Listing 45, the compiler can get rid of the branch and generate `CMOV` instruction[234] instead. The `CMOVcc` instructions check the state of one or more of the status flags in the `EFLAGS` register (`CF`, `OF`, `PF`, `SF` and `ZF`) and perform a move operation if the flags are in a specified state (or condition). [Int, 2020, Volume 2] Below are the two assembly listings for the baseline and improved version, respectively:

```
# baseline version
400504:   test    edi,edi
400506:   je      400514          # branch on cond
400508:   mov     eax,0x0
40050d:   call    <computeX>
400512:   jmp     40051e
400514:   mov     eax,0x0
400519:   call    <computeY>
40051e:   mov     edi,eax

=>

# branchless version
400537:   mov     eax,0x0
40053c:   call    <computeX>      # compute x
400541:   mov     ebp,eax         # assign x to a
400543:   mov     eax,0x0
400548:   call    <computeY>      # compute y
40054d:   test    ebx,ebx         # test cond
40054f:   cmovne  eax,ebp         # override a with y if needed
```

The modified assembly sequence doesn't have original branch instruction. However, in the second version, both x and y are calculated independently, and then only one of the values is selected. While this transformation eliminates the penalty of branch mispredictions, it is potentially doing more work than the original code. Performance improvement, in this case, very much depends on the characteristics of `computeX` and `computeY` functions. If the functions are small and the compiler is able to inline them, then it might bring noticeable performance benefits. If the functions are big, it might be cheaper to take the cost of a branch misprediction than to execute both functions.

It is important to note that predication does not always benefit the performance of the application. The issue with predication is that it limits the parallel execution capabilities of the CPU. For the code

---

[234] Similar transformation can be done for floating-point numbers with `FCMOVcc`, `VMAXSS`/`VMINSS` instruction.

9.2 Replace branches with predication

snippet in Listing 44, the CPU can choose, say, `true` branch of the `if` condition, and continue speculative execution of the code with the value of `a = computeX()`. If, for example, there is a subsequent load that uses `a` to index an element in an array, this load can be issued well before we know the true outcome of the `if` branch. This type of speculation is not possible for the code in the Listing 45 since the CPU cannot issue a load that uses `a` before the `CMOVNE` instruction completes.

The typical example of the tradeoffs involved when choosing between the standard and the branchless versions of the code is binary search[235]:

- For a search over a large array that doesn't fit in CPU caches, a branch-based binary search version performs better because the penalty of a branch misprediction is low comparing to the latency of memory accesses (which are high because of the cache misses). Because of the branches in place, the CPU can speculate on their outcome, which allows loading the array element from the current iteration and the next at the same time. It doesn't end there: the speculation continues, and you might have multiple loads in flight at the same time.
- The situation is reversed for small arrays that fit in CPU caches. The branchless search still has all the memory accesses serialized, as explained earlier. But this time, the load latency is small (only a handful of cycles) since the array fits in CPU caches. The branch-based binary search suffers constant mispredictions, which cost on the order of ~20 cycles. In this case, the cost of misprediction is much more than the cost of memory access, so that the benefits of speculative execution are hindered. The branchless version usually ends up being faster in this case.

The binary search is a neat example that shows how one can reason about when choosing between standard and branchless implementation. The real-world scenario can be more difficult to analyze, so again, measure to find out if it would be beneficial to replace branches in your case.

---

[235] See more detailed discussion here: https://stackoverflow.com/a/54273248.

9.3 Chapter Summary

- Modern processors are very good at predicting branch outcomes. So, I recommend starting the work on fixing branch mispredictions only when the TMA report points to a high `Bad Speculation` metric.
- When the outcome pattern becomes hard for the CPU branch predictor to follow, the performance of the application may suffer. In this case, the branchless version of an algorithm can be better. In this chapter, we showed how branches could be replaced with lookup tables and predication. In some situations, it is also possible to use compiler intrinsics to eliminate branches, as shown in [Kapoor, 2009].
- Branchless algorithms are not universally beneficial. Always measure to find out if that works better in your case.

10 Other Tuning Areas

In this chapter, we will take a look at some of the optimization topics not specifically related to any of the categories covered in the previous three chapters, still important enough to find their place in this book.

10.1 Compile-Time Computations

If a portion of a program does some calculations that don't depend on the input, it can be precomputed ahead of time instead of doing it in the runtime. Modern optimizing compilers already move a lot of computations into compile-time, especially trivial cases like `int x = 2 * 10` into `int x = 20`. Although, they cannot handle more complicated calculations at compile time if they involve branches, loops, function calls. C++ language provides features that allow us to make sure that certain calculations happen at compile time.

In C++, it's possible to move computations into compile-time with various metaprogramming techniques. Before `C++11/14`, developers were using templates to achieve this result. It is theoretically possible to express any algorithm with template metaprogramming; however, this method tends to be syntactically obtuse and often compile quite slowly. Still, it was a success that enabled a new class of optimizations. Fortunately, metaprogramming gradually becomes a lot simpler with every new C++ standard. The `C++14` standard allows having `constexpr` functions, and the `C++17` standard provides compile-time branches with the `if constexpr` keyword. This new way of metaprogramming allows doing many computations in compile-time without sacrificing code readability. [Fog, 2004, Chapter 15 Metaprogramming]

An example of optimizing an application by moving computations into compile-time is shown in Listing 46. Suppose a program involves a test for a number being prime. If we know that a large portion of tested numbers is less than `1024`, we can precompute the results ahead of time and keep them in a `constexpr` array `primes`. At runtime, most of the calls of `isPrime` will involve just one load from the `primes` array, which is much cheaper than computing it at runtime.

Listing 46 Precomputing prime numbers in compile-time

```
constexpr unsigned N = 1024;

// function pre-calculates first N primes in compile-time
constexpr std::array<bool, N> sieve() {
  std::array<bool, N> Nprimes{true};
  Nprimes[0] = Nprimes[1] = false;
  for(long i = 2; i < N; i++)
    Nprimes[i] = true;
  for(long i = 2; i < N; i++) {
    if (Nprimes[i])
      for(long k = i + i; k < N; k += i)
        Nprimes[k] = false;
  }
  return Nprimes;
}

constexpr std::array<bool, N> primes = sieve();

bool isPrime(unsigned value) {
  // primes is accessible both in compile-time and runtime
  static_assert(primes[97], "");
  static_assert(!primes[98], "");
  if (value < N)
    return primes[value];
  // fall back to computing in runtime
}
```

10.2 Compiler Intrinsics

There are types of applications that have very few hotspots that call for tuning them heavily. However, compilers do not always do what we want in terms of generated code in those hot places. For example, a program does some computation in a loop which the compiler vectorizes in a suboptimal way. It usually involves some tricky or specialized algorithms, for which we can come up with a better sequence of instructions. It can be very hard or even impossible to make the compiler generate the desired assembly code using standard constructs of the C and C++ languages.

Hopefully, it's possible to force the compiler to generate particular assembly instructions without writing in low-level assembly language. To achieve that, one can use compiler intrinsics, which in turn are translated into specific assembly instructions. Intrinsics provide the same benefit as using inline assembly, but also they improve

10.2 Compiler Intrinsics

code readability, allow compiler type checking, assist instruction scheduling, and help reduce debugging. Example in Listing 47 shows how the same loop in function `foo` can be coded via compiler intrinsics (function `bar`).

Listing 47 Compiler Intrinsics

```
1  void foo(float *a, float *b, float *c, unsigned N) {
2    for (unsigned i = 0; i < N; i++)
3      c[i] = a[i] + b[i];
4  }
5
6  #include <xmmintrin.h>
7
8  void bar(float *a, float *b, float *c, unsigned N) {
9    __m128 rA, rB, rC;
10   for (int i = 0; i < N; i += 4){
11     rA = _mm_load_ps(&a[i]);
12     rB = _mm_load_ps(&b[i]);
13     rC = _mm_add_ps(rA,rB);
14     _mm_store_ps(&c[i], rC);
15   }
16 }
```

Both functions in Listing 47 generate similar assembly instructions. However, there are several caveats. First, when relying on autovectorization, the compiler will insert all necessary runtime checks. For instance, it will ensure that there are enough elements to feed the vector execution units. Secondly, function `foo` will have a fallback scalar version of the loop for processing the remainder of the loop. And finally, most vector intrinsics assume aligned data, so `movaps` (aligned load) is generated for `bar`, while `movups` (unaligned load) is generated for `foo`. Keeping that in mind, developers using compiler intrinsics have to take care of safety aspects themselves.

When writing code using non-portable platform-specific intrinsics, developers should also provide a fallback option for other architectures. A list of all available intrinsics for the Intel platform can be found in this reference[236].

---
[236] Intel Intrinsics Guide - https://software.intel.com/sites/landingpage/IntrinsicsGuide/.

10.3 Cache Warming

Instruction and data caches, and the performance impact of each, were explained in section 7 and section 8.1.1, along with specific techniques to get the most benefit from each. However, in some application workloads, the portions of code that are most latency-sensitive are the least frequently executed. This results in the function blocks and associated data from aging out of the I-cache and D-cache after some time. Then, just when we need that critical piece of rarely executed code to execute, we take I-cache and D-cache miss penalties, which may exceed our target performance budget.

An example of such a workload might be a high-frequency trading application that continuously reads market data signals from the stock exchange and, once a favorable market signal is detected, sends a BUY order to the exchange. In the aforementioned workload, the code paths involved with reading the market data is most commonly executed, while the code paths for executing a BUY order is rarely executed. If we want our BUY order to reach the exchange as fast as possible and to take advantage of the favorable signal detected in the market data, then the last thing we want is to incur cache misses right at the moment we decide to execute that critical piece of code. This is where the technique of Cache Warming would be helpful.

Cache Warming involves periodically exercising the latency-sensitive code to keep it in the cache while ensuring it does not follow all the way through with any unwanted actions. Exercising the latency-sensitive code also "warms up" the D-cache by bringing latency-sensitive data into it. In fact, this technique is routinely employed for trading applications like the one described in CppCon 2018 lightning talk[237].

10.4 Detecting Slow FP Arithmetic

For applications that operate with floating-point values, there is some probability of hitting an exceptional scenario when the FP values become denormalized[238]. Operations on denormal values could be easy 10 times slower or more. When CPU handles instruction that tries to do arithmetic operation on denormal FP values, it requires special treatment for such cases. Since it is exceptional situation,

---

[237] Cache Warming technique - https://www.youtube.com/watch?v=XzRxikGgaHI.
[238] Denormal number - https://en.wikipedia.org/wiki/Denormal_number.

CPU requests a microcode assist[239]. Microcode Sequencer (MSROM) will then feed the pipeline with lots of uops (see section 4.4) for handling such a scenario.

TMA methodology classifies such bottlenecks under the Retiring category. This is one of the situations when high Retiring doesn't mean a good thing. Since operations on denormal values likely represent unwanted behavior of the program, one can just collect the FP_ASSIST.ANY performance counter. The value should be close to zero. An example of a program that does denormal FP arithmetics and thus experiences many FP assists is presented on easyperf blog[240]. C++ developers can prevent their application fall into operations with subnormal values by using std::isnormal()[241] function. Alternatively, one can change the mode of SIMD floating-point operations, enabling "flush-to-zero" (FTZ) and "denormals-are-zero" (DAZ) flags in the CPU control register[242], preventing SIMD instructions from producing denormalized numbers[243]. Disabling denormal floats at the code level can be done using dedicated macros, which can vary for different compilers[244].

10.5 System Tuning

After successfully completing all the hard work of tuning an application to exploit all the intricate facilities of the CPU microarchitecture, the last thing we want is for the system firmware, the OS, or the kernel to destroy all our efforts. The most highly tuned application will mean very little if it is intermittently disrupted by a System Management Interrupt (SMI), a BIOS interrupt that halts the entire OS in order to execute firmware code. Such interrupt might run for up to 10s to 100s of milliseconds at a time.

Fair to say, developers usually have little to no control over the en-

---

[239] CPU assists - https://software.intel.com/en-us/vtune-help-assists.
[240] Denormal FP arithmetics - https://easyperf.net/blog/2018/11/08/Using-denormal-floats-is-slow-how-to-detect-it.
[241] std::isnormal() - https://en.cppreference.com/w/cpp/numeric/math/isnormal.
[242] See more about FTZ and DAZ modes here: https://software.intel.com/content/www/us/en/develop/articles/x87-and-sse-floating-point-assists-in-ia-32-flush-to-zero-ftz-and-denormals-are-zero-daz.html.
[243] However, FTZ and DAZ modes make such operations not being compliant with the IEEE standard.
[244] See this wiki page as a starting point: https://en.wikipedia.org/wiki/Denormal_number#Disabling_denormal_floats_at_the_code_level.

vironment in which the application is executed. When we ship the product, it's unrealistic to tune every setup a customer might have. Usually, large-enough organizations have separate Operations (Ops) Teams, which handles such sort of issues. Nevertheless, when communicating with members of such teams, it's important to understand what else can limit the application to show its best performance.

As shown in section 2.1, there are many things to tune in the modern system, and avoiding system-based interference is not an easy task. An example of a performance tuning manual of x86-based server deployments is Red Hat guidelines[245]. There, you will find tips for eliminating or significantly minimizing cache disrupting interrupts from sources like the system BIOS, the Linux kernel, and from device drivers, among many other sources of application interference. These guidelines should serve as a baseline image for all new server builds before any application is deployed into a production environment.

When it comes to tuning a specific system setting, it is not always an easy 'yes' or 'no' answer. For example, it's not clear upfront whether your application will benefit from the Simultaneous Multi-Threading (SMT) feature enabled in the environment in which your SW is running. The general guideline is to enable SMT only for heterogenous workloads[246] that exhibit a relatively low IPC. On the other hand, CPU manufacturers these days offer processors with such high core counts that SMT is far less necessary than it was in the past. However, this is just a general guideline, and as with everything stressed so far in this book, it is best to measure for yourself.

Most out-of-the-box platforms are configured for optimal throughput while saving power when it's possible. But there are industries with real-time requirements, which care more about having lower latency than everything else. An example of such an industry can be robots operating in automotive assembly lines. Actions performed by such robots are triggered by external events and usually have a predetermined time budget to finish because the next interrupt will come shortly (it is usually called "control loop"). Meeting real-time goals for such a platform may require sacrificing the overall throughput of the machine or allowing it to consume more energy. One of the popular techniques in that area is to disable processor

---

[245] Red Hat low latency tuning guidelines - https://access.redhat.com/sites/default/files/attachments/201501-perf-brief-low-latency-tuning-rhel7-v2.1.pdf
[246] I.e., when sibling threads execute differing instruction patterns

10.5 System Tuning

sleeping states[247] to keep it ready to react immediately. Another interesting approach is called Cache Locking[248], where portions of the CPU cache is reserved for a particular set of data; it helps to streamline the memory latencies within an application.

---

[247] Power Management States: P-States, C-States. See details here: https://software.intel.com/content/www/us/en/develop/articles/power-management-states-p-states-c-states-and-package-c-states.html.

[248] Cache Locking. Survey of cache locking techniques [Mittal, 2016]. Example of pseudo-locking a portion of the cache, which is exposed as a character device in Linux filesystem available for mmaping from: https://events19.linuxfoundation.org/wp-content/uploads/2017/11/Introducing-Cache-Pseudo-Locking-to-Reduce-Memory-Access-Latency-Reinette-Chatre-Intel.pdf.

11 Optimizing Multithreaded Applications

Modern CPUs are getting more and more cores each year. As of 2020, you can buy an x86 server processor which will have more than 50 cores! And even a mid-range desktop with 8 execution threads is a pretty usual setup. Since there is so much processing power in every CPU, the challenge is how to utilize all the HW threads efficiently. Preparing software to scale well with a growing amount of CPU cores is very important for the future success of the application.

Multithreaded applications have their own specifics. Certain assumptions of single-threaded execution get invalidated when we're dealing with multiple threads. For example, we can no longer identify hotspots by looking at a single thread since each thread might have its own hotspot. In a popular producer-consumer[249] design, the producer thread may sleep during most of the time. Profiling such a thread won't shed light on the reason why our multithreaded application is not scaling well.

11.1 Performance Scaling And Overhead

When dealing with a single-threaded application, optimizing one portion of the program usually yields positive results on performance. However, it's not necessarily the case for multithreaded applications. There could be an application in which thread A does some very heavy operation, while thread B finishes its task early and just waits for thread A to finish. No matter how much we improve thread B, application latency will not be reduced since it will be limited by a longer-running thread A.

This effect is widely known as Amdahl's law[250], which constitutes that the speedup of a parallel program is limited by its serial part. Figure 45 illustrates the theoretical speedup limit as a function of the number of processors. For a program, 75% of which is parallel, the speedup factor converges to 4.

---

[249] Producer-consumer pattern - https://en.wikipedia.org/wiki/Producer-consumer_problem
[250] Amdahl's law - https://en.wikipedia.org/wiki/Amdahl's_law.

11.1 Performance Scaling And Overhead

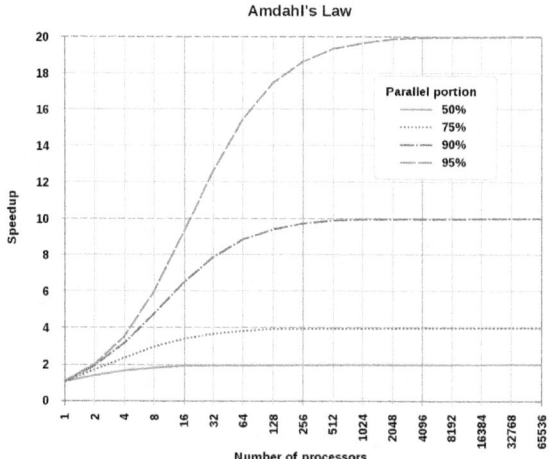

Figure 45: The theoretical speedup of the latency of the execution of a program as a function of the number of processors executing it, according to Amdahl's law. © Image by Daniels220 via Wikipedia.

Figure 46a shows performance scaling of the h264dec benchmark from Starbench parallel benchmark suite. I tested it on Intel Core i5-8259U, which has 4 cores/8 threads. Notice that after using 4 threads, performance doesn't scale much. Likely, getting a CPU with more cores won't improve performance. [251]

In reality, further adding computing nodes to the system may yield retrograde speed up. This effect is explained by Neil Gunther as Universal Scalability Law[252] (USL), which is an extension of Amdahl's law. USL describes communication between computing nodes (threads) as yet another gating factor against performance. As the system is scaled up, overheads start to hinder the gains. Beyond a critical point, the capability of the system starts to decrease (see fig. 47). USL is widely used for modeling the capacity and scalability of the systems.

Slowdowns described by USL are driven by several factors. First, as the number of computing nodes increases, they start to compete for

---

[251] However, it will benefit from a CPU with a higher frequency.
[252] USL law - http://www.perfdynamics.com/Manifesto/USLscalability.html#th_sEc1.

11.1 Performance Scaling And Overhead

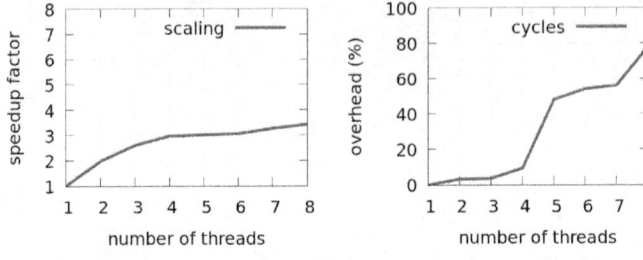

(a) Performance scaling with different number of threads.

(b) Overhead of using different number of threads.

Figure 46: Performance scaling and overhead of h264dec benchmark on Intel Core i5-8259U.

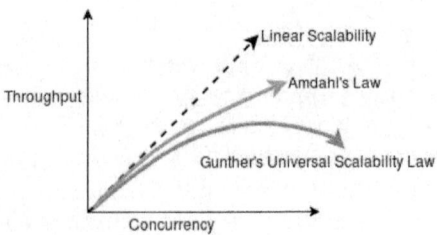

Figure 47: Universal Scalability Law and Amdahl's law. © Image by Neha Bhardwaj via Knoldus Blogs.

resources (contention). This results in additional time being spent on synchronizing those accesses. Another issue occurs with resources that are shared between many workers. We need to maintain a consistent state of the shared resource between many workers (coherence). For example, when multiple workers frequently change some globally visible object, those changes need to be broadcasted to all nodes that use that object. Suddenly, usual operations start getting more time to finish due to the additional need to maintain coherence. The communication overhead of the h264dec benchmark on Intel Core i5-8259U can be observed in Figure 46b. Notice how the benchmark experience more overhead in terms of elapsed core cycles as we assign more than 4 threads to the task. [253]

Optimizing multithreaded applications not only involves all the techniques described in this book so far but also involves detecting and mitigating the aforementioned effects of contention and coherence. The following subsections will describe techniques for addressing these additional challenges for tuning multithreaded programs.

11.2 Parallel Efficiency Metrics

When dealing with multithreaded applications, engineers should be careful with analyzing basic metrics like CPU utilization and IPC (see section 4). One of the threads can show high CPU utilization and high IPC, but it could turn out that all it was doing was just spinning on a lock. That's why when evaluating the parallel efficiency of the application, it's recommended to use Effective CPU Utilization, which is based only on the Effective time[254].

11.2.1 Effective CPU Utilization

Represents how efficiently the application utilized the CPUs available. It shows the percent of average CPU utilization by all logical CPUs on the system. CPU utilization metric is based only on the Effective time and does not include the overhead introduced by the parallel runtime system[255] and Spin time. A CPU utilization of 100% means

---

[253] There is an interesting spike in the number of retired instruction when using 5 and 6 worker threads. This should be investigated by profiling the workload.
[254] Performance analysis tools such as Intel VTune Profiler can distinguish profiling samples that were taken while the thread was spinning. They do that with the help of call stacks for every sample (see section 5.4.3).
[255] Threading libraries and APIs like pthread, OpenMP, and Intel TBB have their own overhead for creating and managing threads.

that your application keeps all the logical CPU cores busy for the entire time that it runs. [Int, 2020]

For a specified time interval T, Effective CPU Utilization can be calculated as

$$\text{Effective CPU Utilization} = \frac{\sum_{i=1}^{\text{ThreadsCount}} \text{Effective Cpu Time}(T,i)}{T \times \text{ThreadsCount}}$$

11.2.2 Thread Count

Applications usually have a configurable number of threads, which allows them to run efficiently on platforms with a different number of cores. Obviously, running an application using a lower number of threads than is available on the system underutilizes its resources. On the other hand, running an excessive number of threads can cause a higher CPU time because some of the threads may be waiting on others to complete, or time may be wasted on context switches.

Besides actual worker threads, multithreaded applications usually have helper threads: main thread, input and output threads, etc. If those threads consume significant time, they require dedicated HW thread themselves. This is why it is important to know the total thread count and configure the number of worker threads properly.

To avoid a penalty for threads creation and destruction, engineers usually allocate a pool of threads[256] with multiple threads waiting for tasks to be allocated for concurrent execution by the supervising program. This is especially beneficial for executing short-lived tasks.

11.2.3 Wait Time

Wait Time occurs when software threads are waiting due to APIs that block or cause synchronization. Wait Time is per-thread; therefore, the total Wait Time can exceed the application Elapsed Time. [Int, 2020]

A thread can be switched off from execution by the OS scheduler due to either synchronization or preemption. So, Wait Time can be further divided into Sync Wait Time and Preemption Wait Time. A large amount of Sync Wait Time likely indicates that the application has highly contended synchronization objects. We will explore how to find them in the following sections. Significant Preemption Wait

---

[256] Thread pool - https://en.wikipedia.org/wiki/Thread_pool.

Time can signal a thread oversubscription[257] problem either because of a big number of application threads or a conflict with OS threads or other applications on the system. In this case, the developer should consider reducing the total number of threads or increasing task granularity for every worker thread.

11.2.4 Spin Time

Spin time is Wait Time, during which the CPU is busy. This often occurs when a synchronization API causes the CPU to poll while the software thread is waiting. [Int, 2020]. In reality, implementation of kernel synchronization primitives prefers to spin on a lock for some time to the alternative of doing an immediate thread context switch (which is expensive). Too much Spin Time, however, can reflect the lost opportunity for productive work.

11.3 Analysis With Intel VTune Profiler

Intel VTune Profiler has a dedicated type of analysis for multithreaded applications called Threading Analysis. Its summary window (see fig. 48) displays statistics on the overall application execution, identifying all the metrics we described in section 11.2. From Effective CPU Utilization Histogram, we could learn several interesting facts about the captured application behavior. First, on average, only 5 HW threads (logical cores on the diagram) were utilized at the same time. Second, almost never all 8 HW threads were active at the same time.

11.3.1 Find Expensive Locks

Next, the workflow suggests that we identify the most contended synchronization objects. Figure 49 shows the list of such objects. We can see that __pthread_cond_wait definitely stands out, but since we might have dozens of conditional variables in the program, we need to know which one is the reason for poor CPU utilization.

In order to know this, we can simply click on __pthread_cond_wait, which will get us to the Bottom-Up view that is shown on fig. 50. We can see the most frequent path (47% of wait time) that lead

---

[257] Thread oversubscription - https://software.intel.com/en-us/vtune-help-thread-oversubscription.

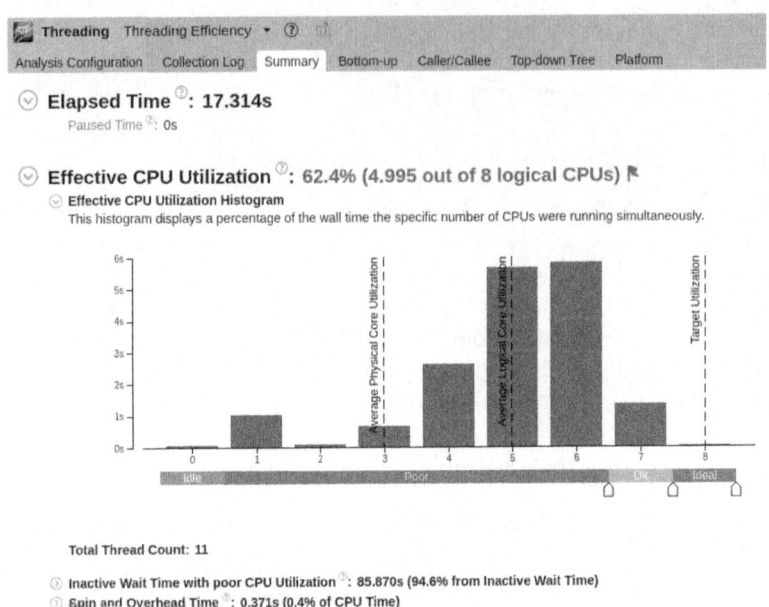

Figure 48: Intel VTune Profiler Threading Analysis summary for x264 benchmark from Phoronix test suite.

Inactive Wait Time with poor CPU Utilization: 85.870s (94.6% from Inactive Wait Time)

Inactive Sync Wait Time: 85.508s

Preemption Wait Time: 0.361s

Top functions by Inactive Wait Time with Poor CPU Utilization.

This section lists the functions sorted by the time spent waiting on synchronization or thread preemption with poor CPU Utilization.

Function	Module	Inactive Wait Time	Inactive Sync Wait Time	Inactive Sync Wait Count
__pthread_cond_wait	libpthread-2.27.so	84.596s	84.594s	24,903
__GI___pthread_mutex_lock	libpthread-2.27.so	0.889s	0.889s	79
[vmlinux]	vmlinux	0.374s	0.016s	453
[vtsspp]	vtsspp	0.005s	0.005s	126
__GI___pthread_mutex_unlock	libpthread-2.27.so	0.002s	0s	0
[Others]		0.004s	0.003s	58

Figure 49: Intel VTune Profiler Threading Analysis showing the most contended synchronization objects for x264 benchmark.

11.3 Analysis With Intel VTune Profiler

to threads waiting on conditional variable: `__pthread_cond_wait <- x264_8_frame_cond_wait <- mb_analyse_init`.

Function / Call Stack	CPU Time	Inactive Sync Wait Time	Preemption Wait Time	Inactive Sync Wait Count	Preemption Wait Count	Module
▼ __pthread_cond_wait	0.241s	89.428s	0.002s	26,375	4	libpthread-2.27.so
▶ ⇲ x264_8_frame_cond_wait ← mb_analyse_init ←	0.216s	42.040s	0.002s	24,239	3	x264
▶ ⇲ threadpool_thread_internal ← x264_stack_align	0.015s	29.530s	0.000s	1,464	1	x264
▶ ⇲ x264_8_threadpool_wait ← encoder_frame_end	0.008s	14.377s	0s	491	0	x264
▶ ⇲ lookahead_thread_internal ← x264_stack_align	0.002s	2.562s	0s	139	0	x264
▶ ⇲ x264_8_lookahead_get_frames ← x264_8_encod	0s	0.918s	0s	42	0	x264
▶ __GI___pthread_mutex_lock	0.016s	0.895s	0.000s	87	1	libpthread-2.27.so
▶ [vmlinux]	0.520s	0.017s	0.391s	467	1,134	vmlinux
▶ [vtsspp]	0.002s	0.005s	0s	131	0	vtsspp
▶ __pthread_cond_broadcast	0.084s	0.001s	0.001s	4	5	libpthread-2.27.so

Figure 50: Intel VTune Profiler Threading Analysis showing the call stack for the most contended conditional variable in x264 benchmark.

We can next jump into the source code of `x264_8_frame_cond_wait` by double-clicking on the corresponding row in the analysis (see fig. 51). Next, we can study the reason behind the lock and possible ways to make thread communication in this place more efficient. [258]

	Source	CPU Time Total	CPU Time Self	Inactive Sync Wait Time	Preemption Wait Time
686	void x264_frame_cond_wait(x264_frame_t *frame, int i_lines_completed)				
687	{				
688	x264_pthread_mutex_lock(&frame->mutex);				
689	while(frame->i_lines_completed < i_lines_completed)	0.216s	0s	42.040s	0.002s
690	x264_pthread_cond_wait(&frame->cv, &frame->mutex);				
691	x264_pthread_mutex_unlock(&frame->mutex);				
692	}				

Figure 51: Source code view for x264_8_frame_cond_wait function in x264 benchmark.

11.3.2 Platform View

Another very useful feature of Intel VTune Profiler is Platform View (see fig. 52), which allows us to observe what each thread was doing in any given moment of program execution. This is very helpful for understanding the behavior of the application and finding potential

---
[258] I don't claim that it will be necessary an easy road, and there is no guarantee that you will find a way to make it better.

209

performance headrooms. For example, we can see that during the time interval from 1s to 3s, only two threads were consistently utilizing ~100% of the corresponding CPU core (threads with TID 7675 and 7678). CPU utilization of other threads was bursty during that time interval.

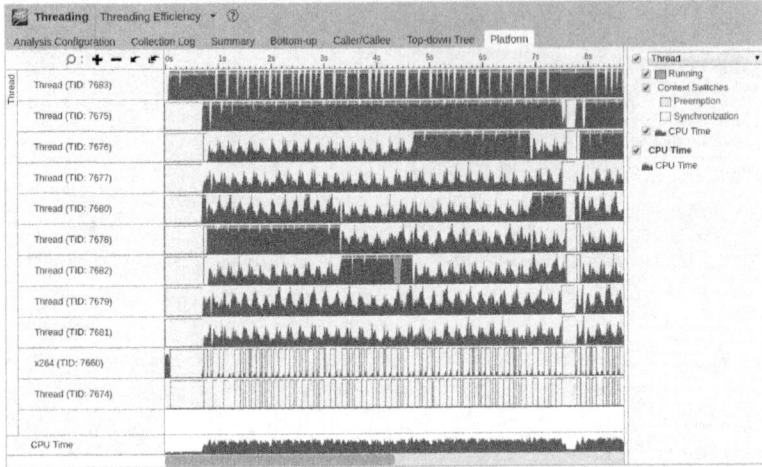

Figure 52: Vtune Platform view for x264 benchmark.

Platform View also has zooming and filtering capabilities. This allows us to understand what each thread was executing during a specified time frame. To see this, select the range on the timeline, right-click and choose Zoom In and Filter In by Selection. Intel VTune Profiler will display functions or sync objects used during this time range.

11.4 Analysis with Linux Perf

Linux `perf` tool profiles all the threads that the application might spawn. It has the `-s` option, which records per-thread event counts. Using this option, at the end of the report, `perf` lists all the thread IDs along with the number of samples collected for each of them:

```
$ perf record -s ./x264 -o /dev/null --slow --threads 8
    Bosphorus_1920x1080_120fps_420_8bit_YUV.y4m
$ perf report -n -T
...
#  PID    TID    cycles:ppp
   6966   6976   41570283106
   6966   6971   25991235047
```

11.4 Analysis with Linux Perf

```
6966  6969  20251062678
6966  6975  17598710694
6966  6970  27688808973
6966  6972  23739208014
6966  6973  20901059568
6966  6968  18508542853
6966  6967     48399587
6966  6966   2464885318
```

To filter samples for a particular software thread, one can use the `--tid` option:

```
$ perf report -T --tid 6976 -n
# Overhead  Samples   Object  Symbol
# ........  .......   ......  .....................................
    7.17%   19877     x264    get_ref_avx2
    7.06%   19078     x264    x264_8_me_search_ref
    6.34%   18367     x264    refine_subpel
    5.34%   15690     x264    x264_8_pixel_satd_8x8_internal_avx2
    4.55%   11703     x264    x264_8_pixel_avg2_w16_sse2
    3.83%   11646     x264    x264_8_pixel_avg2_w8_mmx2
```

Linux `perf` also automatically provides some of the metrics we discussed in section 11.2:

```
$ perf stat ./x264 -o /dev/null --slow --threads 8
   Bosphorus_1920x1080_120fps_420_8bit_YUV.y4m
      86,720.71 msec task-clock         #     5.701 CPUs utilized
         28,386      context-switches   #     0.327 K/sec
          7,375      cpu-migrations     #     0.085 K/sec
         38,174      page-faults        #     0.440 K/sec
    299,884,445,581  cycles             #     3.458 GHz
    436,045,473,289  instructions       #     1.45  insn per cycle
     32,281,697,229  branches           #   372.249 M/sec
        971,433,345  branch-misses      #     3.01% of all branches
```

11.4.1 Find Expensive Locks

In order to find the most contended synchronization objects with Linux `perf`, one needs to sample on scheduler context switches (`sched:sched_switch`), which is a kernel event and thus requires root access:

```
$ sudo perf record -s -e sched:sched_switch -g --call-graph dwarf --
    ./x264 -o /dev/null --slow --threads 8
    Bosphorus_1920x1080_120fps_420_8bit_YUV.y4m
$ sudo perf report -n --stdio -T --sort=overhead,prev_comm,prev_pid
    --no-call-graph -F overhead,sample
# Samples: 27K of event 'sched:sched_switch'
# Event count (approx.): 27327
```

211

```
# Overhead       Samples         prev_comm       prev_pid
# ........       ...........     ...........     ...........
  15.43%           4217            x264            2973
  14.71%           4019            x264            2972
  13.35%           3647            x264            2976
  11.37%           3107            x264            2975
  10.67%           2916            x264            2970
  10.41%           2844            x264            2971
   9.69%           2649            x264            2974
   6.87%           1876            x264            2969
   4.10%           1120            x264            2967
   2.66%            727            x264            2968
   0.75%            205            x264            2977
```

The output above shows which threads were switched out from the execution most frequently. Notice, we also collect call stacks (`--call-graph dwarf`, see section 5.4.3) because we need it for analyzing paths that lead to the expensive synchronization events:

```
$ sudo perf report -n --stdio -T --sort=overhead,symbol -F
    overhead,sample -G
# Overhead       Samples    Symbol
# ........       ........   ........................................
  100.00%         27327     [k] __sched_text_start
    |
    |--95.25%--0xffffffffffffffff
    |  |
    |  |--86.23%--x264_8_macroblock_analyse
    |  |  |
    |  |     --84.50%--mb_analyse_init (inlined)
    |  |        |
    |  |        --84.39%--x264_8_frame_cond_wait
    |  |           |
    |  |           --84.11%--__pthread_cond_wait (inlined)
    |  |                      __pthread_cond_wait_common (inlined)
    |  |                      |
    |  |                      --83.88%--futex_wait_cancelable (inlined)
    |  |                                 entry_SYSCALL_64
    |  |                                 do_syscall_64
    |  |                                 __x64_sys_futex
    |  |                                 do_futex
    |  |                                 futex_wait
    |  |                                 futex_wait_queue_me
    |  |                                 schedule
    |  |                                 __sched_text_start
    ...
```

The listing above shows the most frequent path that leads to waiting on a conditional variable (`__pthread_cond_wait`) and later context switch. This path is `x264_8_macroblock_analyse` -> `mb_analyse_init` ->

`x264_8_frame_cond_wait`. From this output, we can learn that 84% of all context switches were caused by threads waiting on a conditional variable inside `x264_8_frame_cond_wait`.

11.5 Analysis with Coz

In section 11.1, we defined the challenge of identifying parts of code that affects the overall performance of a multithreaded program. Due to various reasons, optimizing one part of a multithreaded program might not always give visible results. Coz[259] is a new kind of profiler that addresses this problem and fills the gaps left behind by traditional software profilers. It uses a novel technique called "causal profiling", whereby experiments are conducted during the runtime of an application by virtually speeding up segments of code to predict the overall effect of certain optimizations. It accomplishes these "virtual speedups" by inserting pauses that slow down all other concurrently running code. [Curtsinger and Berger, 2015]

Example of applying Coz profiler to C-Ray benchmark from Phoronix test suite is shown on 53. According to the chart, if we improve the performance of line 540 in c-ray-mt.c by 20%, Coz expects a corresponding increase in application performance of C-Ray benchmark overall of about 17%. Once we reach ~45% improvement on that line, the impact on the application begins to level off by COZ's estimation. For more details on this example, see the article[260] on easyperf blog.

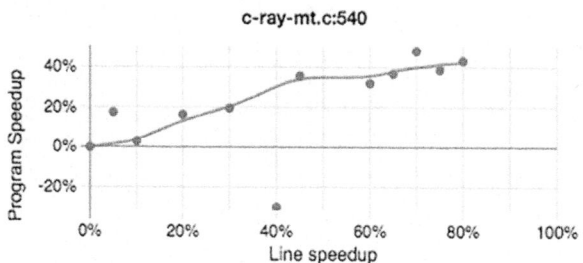

Figure 53: Coz profile for C-Ray benchmark.

---

[259] COZ source code - https://github.com/plasma-umass/coz.
[260] Blog article "COZ vs Sampling Profilers" - https://easyperf.net/blog/2020/0 2/26/coz-vs-sampling-profilers.

11.6 Analysis with eBPF and GAPP

Linux supports a variety of thread synchronization primitives – mutexes, semaphores, condition variables, etc. The kernel supports these thread primitives via the `futex` system call. Therefore, by tracing the execution of the `futex` system call in the kernel while gathering useful metadata from the threads involved, contention bottlenecks can be more readily identified. Linux provides kernel tracing/profiling tools that make this possible, none more powerful than Extended Berkley Packet Filter[261] (eBPF).

eBPF is based around a sandboxed virtual machine running in the kernel that allows the execution of user-defined programs safely and efficiently inside the kernel. The user-defined programs can be written in C and compiled into BPF bytecode by the BCC compiler[262] in preparation for loading into the kernel VM. These BPF programs can be written to launch upon the execution of certain kernel events and communicate raw or processed data back to userspace via a variety of means.

The Opensource Community has provided many eBPF programs for general use. One such tool is the Generic Automatic Parallel Profiler (GAPP), which helps to track multithreaded contention issues. GAPP uses eBPF to track contention overhead of a multithreaded application by ranking the criticality of identified serialization bottlenecks, collects stack traces of threads that were blocked and the one that caused the blocking. The best thing about GAPP is that it does not require code changes, expensive instrumentation, or recompilation. Creators of the GAPP profiler were able to confirm known bottlenecks and also expose new, previously unreported bottlenecks on Parsec 3.0 Benchmark Suite[263] and some large open-source projects. [Nair and Field, 2020]

11.7 Detecting Coherence Issues

11.7.1 Cache Coherency Protocols

Multiprocessor systems incorporate Cache Coherency Protocols to ensure data consistency during shared usage of memory by each individual core containing its own, separate cache entity. Without

---
[261] eBPF docs - https://prototype-kernel.readthedocs.io/en/latest/bpf/
[262] BCC compiler - https://github.com/iovisor/bcc
[263] Parsec 3.0 Benchmark Suite - https://parsec.cs.princeton.edu/index.htm

11.7 Detecting Coherence Issues

such a protocol, if both CPU A and CPU B read memory location L into their individual caches, and processor B subsequently modified its cached value for L, then the CPUs would have inconsistent values of the same memory location L. Cache Coherency Protocols ensure that any updates to cached entries are dutifully updated in any other cached entry of the same location.

One of the most well-known cache coherency protocols is MESI (**M**odified **E**xclusive **S**hared **I**nvalid), which is used to support writeback caches like those used in modern CPUs. Its acronym denotes the four states with which a cache line can be marked (see fig. 54):

- **Modified** – cache line is present only in the current cache and has been modified from its value in RAM
- **Exclusive** – cache line is present only in the current cache and matches its value in RAM
- **Shared** – cache line is present here and in other cache lines and matches its value in RAM
- **Invalid** – cache line is unused (i.e., does not contain any RAM location)

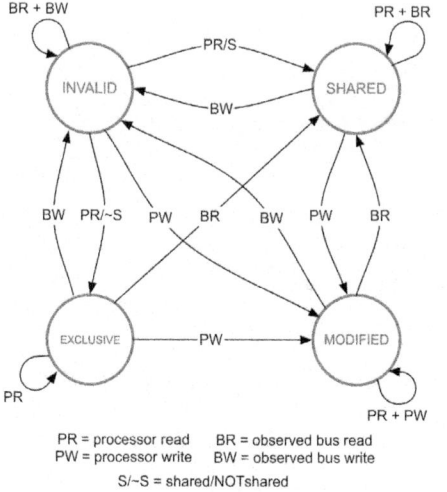

Figure 54: MESI States Diagram. © *Image by University of Washington via courses.cs.washington.edu.*

When fetched from memory, each cache line has one of the states encoded into its tag. Then the cache line state keeps transiting from one state to another[264]. In reality, CPU vendors usually implement slightly improved variants of MESI. For example, Intel uses MESIF[265], which adds a Forwarding (F) state, while AMD employs MOESI[266], which adds the Owning (O) state. But these protocols still maintain the essence of the base MESI protocol.

As an earlier example demonstrates, the cache coherency problem can cause sequentially inconsistent programs. This problem can be mitigated by having snoopy caches to watch all memory transactions and cooperate with each other to maintain memory consistency. Unfortunately, it comes with a cost since modification done by one processor invalidates the corresponding cache line in another processor's cache. This causes memory stalls and wastes system bandwidth. In contrast to serialization and locking issues, which can only put a ceiling on the performance of the application, coherency issues can cause retrograde effects as attributed by USL in section 11.1. Two widely known types of coherency problems are "True Sharing" and "False Sharing", which we will explore next.

11.7.2 True Sharing

True sharing occurs when two different processors access the same variable (see Listing 48).

Listing 48 True Sharing Example.

```
unsigned int sum;
{ // parallel section
  for (int i = 0; i < N; i++)
    sum += a[i]; // sum is shared between all threads
}
```

First of all, true sharing implies data races that can be tricky to detect. Fortunately, there are tools that can help identify such issues. Thread sanitizer[267] from Clang and helgrind[268] are among such tools.

---

[264] Readers can watch and test animated MESI protocol here: https://www.scss.tcd.ie/Jeremy.Jones/vivio/caches/MESI.htm.
[265] MESIF - https://en.wikipedia.org/wiki/MESIF_protocol
[266] MOESI - https://en.wikipedia.org/wiki/MOESI_protocol
[267] Clang's thread sanitizer tool: https://clang.llvm.org/docs/ThreadSanitizer.html.
[268] Helgrind, a thread error detector tool: https://www.valgrind.org/docs/manual/hg-manual.html.

11.7 Detecting Coherence Issues

In order to prevent data race in Listing 48 one should declare sum variable as `std::atomic<unsigned int> sum`.

Using C++ atomics can help to solve data races when true sharing happens. However, it effectively serializes accesses to the atomic variable, which may hurt performance. Another way of solving true sharing issues is by using Thread Local Storage (TLS). TLS is the method by which each thread in a given multithreaded process can allocate memory to store thread-specific data. By doing so, threads modify their local copies instead of contending for a globally available memory location. Example in Listing 48 can be fixed by declaring sum with TLS class specifier: `thread_local unsigned int sum` (since C++11). The main thread should then incorporate results from all the local copies of each worker thread.

11.7.3 False Sharing

False Sharing[269] occurs when two different processors modify different variables that happen to reside on the same cache line (see Listing 49). Figure 55 illustrates the false sharing problem.

Listing 49 False Sharing Example.

```
struct S {
  int sumA; // sumA and sumB are likely to
  int sumB; // reside in the same cache line
};
S s;

{ // section executed by thread A
  for (int i = 0; i < N; i++)
    s.sumA += a[i];
}

{ // section executed by thread B
  for (int i = 0; i < N; i++)
    s.sumB += b[i];
}
```

False sharing is a frequent source of performance issues for multi-threaded applications. Because of that, modern analysis tools have

---

[269] It's worth saying that false sharing is not something that can be observed only in low-level languages, like C/C++/Ada, but also in higher-level ones, like Java/C#.

217

11.7 Detecting Coherence Issues

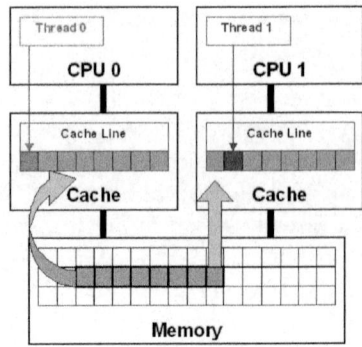

Figure 55: False Sharing: two threads access the same cache line. © Image by Intel Developer Zone via software.intel.com.

built-in support for detecting such cases. TMA characterizes applications that experience true/false sharing as Memory Bound. Typically, in such cases, you would see a high value for Contested Accesses[270] metric.

When using Intel VTune Profiler, the user needs two types of analysis to find and eliminate false sharing issues. Firstly, run Microarchitecture Exploration[271] analysis that implements TMA methodology to detect the presence of false sharing in the application. As noted before, the high value for the Contested Accesses metric prompts us to dig deeper and run the Memory Access analysis with the "Analyze dynamic memory objects" option enabled. This analysis helps in finding out accesses to the data structure that caused contention issues. Typically, such memory accesses have high latency, which will be revealed by the analysis. See an example of using Intel VTune Profiler for fixing false sharing issues on Intel Developer Zone[272].

Linux `perf` has support for finding false sharing as well. As with Intel VTune Profiler, run TMA first (see section 6.1.2) to find out that the program experience false/true sharing issues. If that's the case, use the `perf c2c` tool to detect memory accesses with high cache

---

[270] Contested accesses - https://software.intel.com/en-us/vtune-help-contested-accesses.
[271] Vtune general exploration analysis - https://software.intel.com/en-us/vtune-help-general-exploration-analysis.
[272] Vtune cookbook: false-sharing - https://software.intel.com/en-us/vtune-cookbook-false-sharing.

coherency cost. `perf c2c` matches store/load addresses for different threads and see if the hit in a modified cache line occurred. Readers can find a detailed explanation of the process and how to use the tool in dedicated blog post[273].

It is possible to eliminate false sharing with the help of aligning/padding memory objects. Example in section 11.7.2 can be fixed by ensuring `sumA` and `sumB` do not share the same cache line (see details in section 8.1.1.4).

From a general performance perspective, the most important thing to consider is the cost of the possible state transitions. Of all cache states, the only ones that do not involve a costly cross-cache subsystem communication and data transfer during CPU read/write operations are the Modified (M) and Exclusive (E) states. Thus, the longer the cache line maintains the M or E states (i.e., the less sharing of data across caches), the lower the coherence cost incurred by a multithreaded application. An example demonstrating how this property has been employed can be found in Nitsan Wakart's blog post "Diving Deeper into Cache Coherency"[274].

11.8 Chapter Summary

- Applications not taking advantage of modern multicore CPUs are lagging behind their competitors. Preparing software to scale well with a growing amount of CPU cores is very important for the future success of the application.
- When dealing with the single-threaded application, optimizing one portion of the program usually yields positive results on performance. However, it's not necessarily the case for multithreaded applications. This effect is widely known as Amdahl's law, which constitutes that the speedup of a parallel program is limited by its serial part.
- Threads communication can yield retrograde speedup as explained by Universal Scalability Law. This poses additional challenges for tuning multithreaded programs. Optimizing the performance of multithreaded applications also involves detecting and mitigating the effects of contention and coherence.

---

[273] An article on `perf c2c` - https://joemario.github.io/blog/2016/09/01/c2c-blog/.
[274] Blog post "Diving Deeper into Cache Coherency" - http://psy-lob-saw.blogspot.com/2013/09/diving-deeper-into-cache-coherency.html

Epilog

Thanks for reading through the whole book. I hope you enjoyed it and found it useful. I would be even happier if the book will help you solve a real-world problem. In such a case, I would consider it a success and proof that my efforts were not wasted. Before you continue with your endeavors, let me briefly highlight the essential points of the book and give you final recommendations:

- HW performance is not growing as fast as it used to in the past years. Performance tuning is becoming more critical than it has been for the last 40 years. It will be one of the key drivers for performance gains in the near future.
- Software doesn't have an optimal performance by default. Certain limitations exist that prevent applications to reach their full performance potential. Both HW and SW components have such limitations.
- "Premature optimization is the root of all evil"[275]. But the opposite is often true as well. Postponed performance engineering work may be too late and cause as much evil as premature optimization. Do not neglect performance aspects when designing your future product.
- Performance of the modern system is not deterministic and depends on many factors. Meaningful performance analysis should account for noise and use statistical methods to analyze performance measurements.
- Knowledge of the CPU microarchitecture might become handy in understanding the results of experiments you conduct. However, don't rely on this knowledge too much when you make a specific change in your code. Your mental model can never be as accurate as the actual design of the CPU internals. Predicting the performance of a particular piece of code is nearly impossible. *Always measure!*
- Performance is hard because there are no predetermined steps you should follow, no algorithm. Engineers need to tackle problems from different angles. Know performance analysis methods and tools (both HW and SW) that are available to you. I strongly suggest embracing the Roofline model and TMA

---

[275] This is a famous quote by Donald Knuth.

11.8 Chapter Summary

methodology if they are available on your platform. It will help you to steer your work in the right direction. Also, know when you can leverage other HW performance monitoring features like LBR, PEBS, and PT in your work.

- Understand the limiting factor for the performance of your application and possible ways to fix that. Part 2 covers some of the essential optimizations for every type of CPU performance bottleneck: Front End Bound, Back End Bound, Retiring, Bad Speculation. Use chapters 7-10 to see what options are available when your application falls into one of the four categories mentioned above.
- If the benefit of the modification is negligible, you should keep the code in its most simple and clean form.
- Sometimes modifications that improve performance on one system slow down execution on another system. Make sure you test your changes on all the platforms that you care about.

I hope this book will help you better understand your application's performance and CPU performance in general. Of course, it doesn't cover every possible scenario you may encounter while working on performance optimization. My goal was to give you a starting point and to show you potential options and strategies for dealing with performance analysis and tuning on modern CPUs.

If you enjoyed reading this book, make sure to pass it to your friends and colleagues. I would appreciate your help in spreading the word about the book by endorsing it on social media platforms.

I would love to hear your feedback on my email dendibakh@gmail.com. Let me know your thoughts, comments, and suggestions for the book. I will post all the updates and future information about the book on my blog easyperf.net.

Happy performance tuning!

Glossary

AOS Array Of Structures

BB Basic Block

BIOS Basic Input Output System

CI/CD Contiguous Integration/ Contiguous Development

CPI Clocks Per Instruction

CPU Central Processing Unit

DRAM Dynamic Random-Access Memory

DSB Decoded Stream Buffer

FPGA Field-Programmable Gate Array

GPU Graphics processing unit

HFT High-Frequency Trading

HPC High Performance Computing

HW Hardware

IDE Integrated Development Environment

ILP Instruction-Level Parallelism

IPC Instructions Per Clock

IPO Inter-Procedural Optimizations

LBR Last Branch Record

LLC Last Level Cache

LSD Loop Stream Detector

MSR Model Specific Register

MS-ROM Microcode Sequencer Read-Only Memory

NUMA Non-Uniform Memory Access

OS Operating System

PEBS Processor Event-Based Sampling

PGO Profile Guided Optimizations

PMC Performance Monitoring Counter

PMU Performance Monitoring Unit

PT Processor Traces

RAT Register Alias Table

ROB ReOrder Buffer

SIMD Single Instruction Multiple Data

SMT Simultaneous Multi-Threading

SOA Structure Of Arrays

TLB Translation Lookaside Buffer

TMA Top-Down Microarchitecture Analysis

TSC Time Stamp Counter

UOP MicroOperation

References

[1] Andrey Akinshin. *Pro .NET Benchmarking.* Apress, 1 edition, 2019. ISBN 978-1-4842-4940-6. doi: 10.1007/978-1-4842-4941-3.

[2] Mejbah Alam, Justin Gottschlich, Nesime Tatbul, Javier S Turek, Tim Mattson, and Abdullah Muzahid. A zero-positive learning approach for diagnosing software performance regressions. In H. Wallach, H. Larochelle, A. Beygelzimer, F. d'Alché-Buc, E. Fox, and R. Garnett, editors, *Advances in Neural Information Processing Systems 32*, pages 11627–11639. Curran Associates, Inc., 2019. URL http://papers.nips.cc/paper/9337-a-zero-positive-learning-approach-for-diagnosing-software-performance-regressions.pdf.

[3] Dehao Chen, David Xinliang Li, and Tipp Moseley. Autofdo: Automatic feedback-directed optimization for warehouse-scale applications. In *CGO 2016 Proceedings of the 2016 International Symposium on Code Generation and Optimization*, pages 12–23, New York, NY, USA, 2016.

[4] K.D. Cooper and L. Torczon. *Engineering a Compiler.* Morgan Kaufmann. Morgan Kaufmann, 2012. ISBN 9780120884780. URL https://books.google.co.in/books?id=CGTOlAEACAAJ.

[5] Charlie Curtsinger and Emery Berger. Stabilizer: statistically sound performance evaluation. volume 48, pages 219–228, 03 2013. doi: 10.1145/2451116.2451141.

[6] Charlie Curtsinger and Emery Berger. Coz: Finding code that counts with causal profiling. pages 184–197, 10 2015. doi: 10.1145/2815400.2815409.

[7] David Daly, William Brown, Henrik Ingo, Jim O'Leary, and David Bradford. The use of change point detection to identify software performance regressions in a continuous integration system. In *Proceedings of the ACM/SPEC International Conference on Performance Engineering*, ICPE '20, page 67–75, New York, NY, USA, 2020. Association for Computing Machinery. ISBN 9781450369916. doi: 10.1145/3358960.3375791. URL https://doi.org/10.1145/3358960.3375791.

References

[8] *Data Never Sleeps 5.0.* Domo, Inc, 2017. URL https://www.domo.com/learn/data-never-sleeps-5?aid=ogsm072517_1&sf100871281=1.

[9] Jiaqing Du, Nipun Sehrawat, and Willy Zwaenepoel. Performance profiling in a virtualized environment. In *Proceedings of the 2nd USENIX Conference on Hot Topics in Cloud Computing*, HotCloud'10, page 2, USA, 2010. USENIX Association.

[10] Agner Fog. Optimizing software in c++: An optimization guide for windows, linux and mac platforms, 2004. URL https://www.agner.org/optimize/optimizing_cpp.pdf.

[11] Agner Fog. The microarchitecture of intel, amd and via cpus: An optimization guide for assembly programmers and compiler makers. *Copenhagen University College of Engineering*, 2012. URL https://www.agner.org/optimize/microarchitecture.pdf.

[12] Brendan Gregg. *Systems Performance: Enterprise and the Cloud.* Prentice Hall Press, USA, 1st edition, 2013. ISBN 0133390098.

[13] Tobias Grosser, Armin Größlinger, and C. Lengauer. Polly - performing polyhedral optimizations on a low-level intermediate representation. *Parallel Process. Lett.*, 22, 2012.

[14] John L. Hennessy. The future of computing, 2018. URL https://youtu.be/Azt8Nc-mtKM?t=329.

[15] John L. Hennessy and David A. Patterson. *Computer Architecture, Fifth Edition: A Quantitative Approach.* Morgan Kaufmann Publishers Inc., San Francisco, CA, USA, 5th edition, 2011. ISBN 012383872X.

[16] Henrik Ingo and David Daly. Automated system performance testing at mongodb. In *Proceedings of the Workshop on Testing Database Systems*, DBTest '20, New York, NY, USA, 2020. Association for Computing Machinery. ISBN 9781450380010. doi: 10.1145/3395032.3395323. URL https://doi.org/10.1145/3395032.3395323.

[17] *CPU Metrics Reference.* Intel® Corporation, 2020. URL https://software.intel.com/en-us/vtune-help-cpu-metrics-reference.

[18] *Intel® 64 and IA-32 Architectures Optimization Reference Manual.* Intel® Corporation, 2020. URL https://software.intel.com

References

/content/www/us/en/develop/download/intel-64-and-ia-32-architectures-optimization-reference-manual.html.

[19] Intel® 64 and IA-32 Architectures Software Developer Manuals. Intel® Corporation, 2020. URL https://software.intel.com/en-us/articles/intel-sdm.

[20] Intel® VTune™ Profiler User Guide. Intel® Corporation, 2020. URL https://software.intel.com/content/www/us/en/develop/documentation/vtune-help/top/analyze-performance/hardware-event-based-sampling-collection.html.

[21] Guoliang Jin, Linhai Song, Xiaoming Shi, Joel Scherpelz, and Shan Lu. Understanding and detecting real-world performance bugs. In *Proceedings of the 33rd ACM SIGPLAN Conference on Programming Language Design and Implementation*, PLDI '12, page 77–88, New York, NY, USA, 2012. Association for Computing Machinery. ISBN 9781450312059. doi: 10.1145/2254064.2254075. URL https://doi.org/10.1145/2254064.2254075.

[22] Svilen Kanev, Juan Pablo Darago, Kim Hazelwood, Parthasarathy Ranganathan, Tipp Moseley, Gu-Yeon Wei, and David Brooks. Profiling a warehouse-scale computer. *SIGARCH Comput. Archit. News*, 43(3S):158–169, June 2015. ISSN 0163-5964. doi: 10.1145/2872887.2750392. URL https://doi.org/10.1145/2872887.2750392.

[23] Rajiv Kapoor. Avoiding the cost of branch misprediction. 2009. URL https://software.intel.com/en-us/articles/avoiding-the-cost-of-branch-misprediction.

[24] Paul-Virak Khuong and Pat Morin. Array layouts for comparison-based searching, 2015.

[25] Andi Kleen. An introduction to last branch records. 2016. URL https://lwn.net/Articles/680985/.

[26] Charles E. Leiserson, Neil C. Thompson, Joel S. Emer, Bradley C. Kuszmaul, Butler W. Lampson, Daniel Sanchez, and Tao B. Schardl. There's plenty of room at the top: What will drive computer performance after moore's law? *Science*, 368(6495), 2020. ISSN 0036-8075. doi: 10.1126/science.aam9744. URL https://science.sciencemag.org/content/368/6495/eaam9744.

[27] Daniel Lemire. Making your code faster by taming branches.

2020. URL https://www.infoq.com/articles/making-code-faster-taming-branches/.

[28] Min Liu, Xiaohui Sun, Maneesh Varshney, and Ya Xu. Large-scale online experimentation with quantile metrics, 2019.

[29] David S. Matteson and Nicholas A. James. A nonparametric approach for multiple change point analysis of multivariate data. *Journal of the American Statistical Association*, 109(505):334–345, 2014. doi: 10.1080/01621459.2013.849605. URL https://doi.org/10.1080/01621459.2013.849605.

[30] Sparsh Mittal. A survey of techniques for cache locking. *ACM Transactions on Design Automation of Electronic Systems*, 21, 05 2016. doi: 10.1145/2858792.

[31] Wojciech Muła and Daniel Lemire. Base64 encoding and decoding at almost the speed of a memory copy. *Software: Practice and Experience*, 50(2):89–97, Nov 2019. ISSN 1097-024X. doi: 10.1002/spe.2777. URL http://dx.doi.org/10.1002/spe.2777.

[32] Todd Mytkowicz, Amer Diwan, Matthias Hauswirth, and Peter F. Sweeney. Producing wrong data without doing anything obviously wrong! In *Proceedings of the 14th International Conference on Architectural Support for Programming Languages and Operating Systems*, ASPLOS XIV, page 265–276, New York, NY, USA, 2009. Association for Computing Machinery. ISBN 9781605584065. doi: 10.1145/1508244.1508275. URL https://doi.org/10.1145/1508244.1508275.

[33] Reena Nair and Tony Field. Gapp: A fast profiler for detecting serialization bottlenecks in parallel linux applications. *Proceedings of the ACM/SPEC International Conference on Performance Engineering*, Apr 2020. doi: 10.1145/3358960.3379136. URL http://dx.doi.org/10.1145/3358960.3379136.

[34] Nima Honarmand. Memory prefetching. URL https://compas.cs.stonybrook.edu/~nhonarmand/courses/sp15/cse502/slides/13-prefetch.pdf.

[35] Andrzej Nowak and Georgios Bitzes. The overhead of profiling using pmu hardware counters. 2014.

[36] Guilherme Ottoni and Bertrand Maher. Optimizing function placement for large-scale data-center applications. In *Proceedings of the 2017 International Symposium on Code Generation and*

Optimization, CGO '17, page 233–244. IEEE Press, 2017. ISBN 9781509049318.

[37] Maksim Panchenko, Rafael Auler, Bill Nell, and Guilherme Ottoni. BOLT: A practical binary optimizer for data centers and beyond. *CoRR*, abs/1807.06735, 2018. URL http://arxiv.org/abs/1807.06735.

[38] Gabriele Paoloni. *How to Benchmark Code Execution Times on Intel® IA-32 and IA-64 Instruction Set Architectures*. Intel® Corporation, 2010. URL https://www.intel.com/content/dam/www/public/us/en/documents/white-papers/ia-32-ia-64-benchmark-code-execution-paper.pdf.

[39] M. Pharr and W. R. Mark. ispc: A spmd compiler for high-performance cpu programming. In *2012 Innovative Parallel Computing (InPar)*, pages 1–13, 2012.

[40] Gang Ren, Eric Tune, Tipp Moseley, Yixin Shi, Silvius Rus, and Robert Hundt. Google-wide profiling: A continuous profiling infrastructure for data centers. *IEEE Micro*, pages 65–79, 2010. URL http://www.computer.org/portal/web/csdl/doi/10.1109/MM.2010.68.

[41] S. D. Sharma and M. Dagenais. Hardware-assisted instruction profiling and latency detection. *The Journal of Engineering*, 2016(10):367–376, 2016.

[42] *Volume of data/information created worldwide from 2010 to 2025*. Statista, Inc, 2018. URL https://www.statista.com/statistics/871513/worldwide-data-created/.

[43] et al. Suresh Srinivas. Runtime performance optimization blueprint: Intel® architecture optimization with large code pages, 2019. URL https://www.intel.com/content/www/us/en/develop/articles/runtime-performance-optimization-blueprint-intel-architecture-optimization-with-large-code.html.

[44] Ahmad Yasin. A top-down method for performance analysis and counters architecture. pages 35–44, 03 2014. ISBN 978-1-4799-3606-9. doi: 10.1109/ISPASS.2014.6844459.

Appendix A. Reducing Measurement Noise

Below are some examples of features that can contribute to increased non-determinism in performance measurements. See complete discussion in section 2.1.

Dynamic Frequency Scaling

Dynamic Frequency Scaling[276] (DFS) is a technique to increase the performance of the system by automatically raising CPU operating frequency when it runs demanding tasks. As an example of DFS implementation, Intel CPUs have a feature called Turbo Boost[277] and AMD CPUs employ Turbo Core[278] functionality.

Example of an impact Turbo Boost can make for a single-threaded workload running on Intel® Core™ i5-8259U:

```
# TurboBoost enabled
$ cat /sys/devices/system/cpu/intel_pstate/no_turbo
0
$ perf stat -e task-clock,cycles -- ./a.exe
    11984.691958   task-clock (msec)  #    1.000 CPUs utilized
    32,427,294,227 cycles             #    2.706 GHz
    11.989164338 seconds time elapsed

# TurboBoost disabled
$ echo 1 | sudo tee /sys/devices/system/cpu/intel_pstate/no_turbo
1
$ perf stat -e task-clock,cycles -- ./a.exe
    13055.200832   task-clock (msec)  #    0.993 CPUs utilized
    29,946,969,255 cycles             #    2.294 GHz
    13.142983989 seconds time elapsed
```

The average frequency is much higher when Turbo Boost is on.

DFS can be permanently disabled in BIOS[279]. To programmatically disable the DFS feature on Linux systems, you need root access. Here

---

[276] Dynamic frequency scaling - https://en.wikipedia.org/wiki/Dynamic_frequency_scaling.
[277] Intel Turbo Boost - https://en.wikipedia.org/wiki/Intel_Turbo_Boost.
[278] AMD Turbo Core - https://en.wikipedia.org/wiki/AMD_Turbo_Core.
[279] Intel Turbo Boost FAQ - https://www.intel.com/content/www/us/en/support/articles/000007359/processors/intel-core-processors.html.

Appendix A

is how one can achieve this:

```
# Intel
echo 1 > /sys/devices/system/cpu/intel_pstate/no_turbo
# AMD
echo 0 > /sys/devices/system/cpu/cpufreq/boost
```

Simultaneous Multithreading

Modern CPU cores are often made in the simultaneous multithreading (SMT[280]) manner. It means that in one physical core, you can have two threads of simultaneous execution. Typically, architectural state[281] is replicated, but the execution resources (ALUs, caches, etc.) are not. That means that if we have two separate processes running on the same core "simultaneously" (in different threads), they can steal resources from each other, for example, cache space.

SMT can be permanently disabled in BIOS[282]. To programmatically disable SMT on Linux systems, you need root access. Here is how one can turn down a sibling thread in each core:

```
echo 0 > /sys/devices/system/cpu/cpuX/online
```

The sibling pairs of CPU threads can be found in the following files:

`/sys/devices/system/cpu/cpuN/topology/thread_siblings_list`

For example, on Intel® Core™ i5-8259U, which has 4 cores and 8 threads:

```
# all 8 HW threads enabled:
$ lscpu
...
CPU(s):             8
On-line CPU(s) list: 0-7
...
$ cat /sys/devices/system/cpu/cpu0/topology/thread_siblings_list
0,4
$ cat /sys/devices/system/cpu/cpu1/topology/thread_siblings_list
1,5
$ cat /sys/devices/system/cpu/cpu2/topology/thread_siblings_list
2,6
$ cat /sys/devices/system/cpu/cpu3/topology/thread_siblings_list
3,7
```

---
[280] SMT - https://en.wikipedia.org/wiki/Simultaneous_multithreading.
[281] Architectural state - https://en.wikipedia.org/wiki/Architectural_state.
[282] "How to disable hyperthreading" - https://www.pcmag.com/article/314585/how-to-disable-hyperthreading.

```
# Disabling SMT on core 0
$ echo 0 | sudo tee /sys/devices/system/cpu/cpu4/online
0
$ lscpu
CPU(s):                8
On-line CPU(s) list:   0-3,5-7
Off-line CPU(s) list:  4
...
$ cat /sys/devices/system/cpu/cpu0/topology/thread_siblings_list
0
```

Scaling Governor

Linux kernel is able to control CPU frequency for different purposes. One such purpose is to save the power, in which case the scaling governor[283] inside the Linux Kernel can decide to decrease CPU operating frequency. For performance measurements, it is recommended to set the scaling governor policy to `performance` to avoid sub-nominal clocking. Here is how we can set it for all the cores:

```
for i in /sys/devices/system/cpu/cpu*/cpufreq/scaling_governor
do
   echo performance > $i
done
```

CPU Affinity

Processor affinity[284] enables the binding of a process to a certain CPU core(s). In Linux, one can do this with `taskset`[285] tool. Here

```
# no affinity
$ perf stat -e context-switches,cpu-migrations -r 10 -- a.exe
            151       context-switches
             10       cpu-migrations

# process is bound to the CPU0
$ perf stat -e context-switches,cpu-migrations -r 10 -- taskset -c 0
      a.exe
            102       context-switches
              0       cpu-migrations
```

---

[283] Documentation for Linux CPU frequency governors: https://www.kernel.org/doc/Documentation/cpu-freq/governors.txt.
[284] Processor affinity - https://en.wikipedia.org/wiki/Processor_affinity.
[285] taskset manual - https://linux.die.net/man/1/taskset.

Notice the number of `cpu-migrations` gets down to 0, i.e., the process never leaves the `core0`.

Alternatively, you can use cset[286] tool to reserve CPUs for just the program you are benchmarking. If using Linux `perf`, leave at least two cores so that `perf` runs on one core, and your program runs in another. The command below will move all threads out of N1 and N2 (`-k on` means that even kernel threads are moved out):

```
$ cset shield -c N1,N2 -k on
```

The command below will run the command after -- in the isolated CPUs:

```
$ cset shield --exec -- perf stat -r 10 <cmd>
```

Process Priority

In Linux, one can increase process priority using the `nice` tool. By increasing the priority process gets more CPU time, and the Linux scheduler favors it more in comparison with processes with normal priority. Niceness ranges from -20 (highest priority value) to 19 (lowest priority value) with the default of 0.

Notice in the previous example, execution of the benchmarked process was interrupted by the OS more than 100 times. If we increase process priority by run the benchmark with `sudo nice -n -N`:

```
$ perf stat -r 10 -- sudo nice -n -5 taskset -c 1 a.exe
     0      context-switches
     0      cpu-migrations
```

Notice the number of context-switches gets to 0, so the process received all the computation time uninterrupted.

Filesystem Cache

Usually, some area of main memory is assigned to cache the file system contents, including various data. This reduces the need for an application to go all the way down to the disk. Here is an example of how file system cache can affect the running time of simple `git status` command:

---
[286] cpuset manual - https://github.com/lpechacek/cpuset.

```
# clean fs cache
$ echo 3 | sudo tee /proc/sys/vm/drop_caches && sync && time -p git
    status
real 2,57
# warmed fs cache
$ time -p git status
real 0,40
```

One can drop the current filesystem cache by running the following two commands:

```
$ echo 3 | sudo tee /proc/sys/vm/drop_caches
$ sync
```

Alternatively, you can make one dry run just to warm up the filesystem cache and exclude it from the measurements. This dry iteration can be combined with the validation of the benchmark output.

Appendix B. The LLVM Vectorizer

This section describes the state of the LLVM Loop Vectorizer inside the Clang compiler as of the year 2020. Innerloop vectorization is the process of transforming code in the innermost loops into code that uses vectors across multiple loop iterations. Each lane in the SIMD vector performs independent arithmetic on consecutive loop iterations. Usually, loops are not found in a clean state, and the Vectorizer has to guess and assume missing information and check for details at runtime. If the assumptions are proven wrong, the Vectorizer falls back to running the scalar loop. The examples below highlight some of the code patterns that the LLVM Vectorizer supports.

Loops with unknown trip count

The LLVM Loop Vectorizer supports loops with an unknown trip count. In the loop below, the iteration start and finish points are unknown, and the Vectorizer has a mechanism to vectorize loops that do not start at zero. In this example, n may not be a multiple of the vector width, and the Vectorizer has to execute the last few iterations as scalar code. Keeping a scalar copy of the loop increases the code size.

```
void bar(float *A, float *B, float K, int start, int end) {
  for (int i = start; i < end; ++i)
      A[i] *= B[i] + K;
}
```

Runtime Checks of Pointers

In the example below, if the pointers A and B point to consecutive addresses, then it is illegal to vectorize the code because some elements of A will be written before they are read from array B.

Some programmers use the restrict keyword to notify the compiler that the pointers are disjointed, but in our example, the LLVM Loop Vectorizer has no way of knowing that the pointers A and B are unique. The Loop Vectorizer handles this loop by placing code that checks, at runtime, if the arrays A and B point to disjointed memory locations. If arrays A and B overlap, then the scalar version of the loop is executed.

```
void bar(float *A, float *B, float K, int n) {
  for (int i = 0; i < n; ++i)
    A[i] *= B[i] + K;
}
```

Reductions

In this example, the sum variable is used by consecutive iterations of the loop. Normally, this would prevent vectorization, but the Vectorizer can detect that sum is a reduction variable. The variable sum becomes a vector of integers, and at the end of the loop, the elements of the array are added together to create the correct result. The LLVM Vectorizer supports a number of different reduction operations, such as addition, multiplication, XOR, AND, and OR.

```
int foo(int *A, int n) {
  unsigned sum = 0;
  for (int i = 0; i < n; ++i)
    sum += A[i] + 5;
  return sum;
}
```

The LLVM Vectorizer supports floating-point reduction operations when -ffast-math is used.

Inductions

In this example, the value of the induction variable i is saved into an array. The LLVM Loop Vectorizer knows to vectorize induction variables.

```
void bar(float *A, float K, int n) {
  for (int i = 0; i < n; ++i)
    A[i] = i;
}
```

If Conversion

The LLVM Loop Vectorizer is able to "flatten" the IF statement in the code and generate a single stream of instructions. The Vectorizer supports any control flow in the innermost loop. The innermost loop may contain complex nesting of IFs, ELSEs, and even GOTOs.

```
int foo(int *A, int *B, int n) {
  unsigned sum = 0;
  for (int i = 0; i < n; ++i)
```

Appendix B

```
    if (A[i] > B[i])
        sum += A[i] + 5;
   return sum;
}
```

Pointer Induction Variables

This example uses the std::accumulate function from the standard c++ library. This loop uses C++ iterators, which are pointers, and not integer indices. The LLVM Loop Vectorizer detects pointer induction variables and can vectorize this loop. This feature is important because many C++ programs use iterators.

```
int baz(int *A, int n) {
   return std::accumulate(A, A + n, 0);
}
```

Reverse Iterators

The LLVM Loop Vectorizer can vectorize loops that count backward.

```
int foo(int *A, int n) {
   for (int i = n; i > 0; --i)
      A[i] += 1;
}
```

Scatter / Gather

The LLVM Loop Vectorizer can vectorize code that becomes a sequence of scalar instructions that scatter/gathers memory.

```
int foo(int * A, int * B, int n) {
   for (intptr_t i = 0; i < n; ++i)
      A[i] += B[i * 4];
}
```

In many situations, the cost model will decide that this transformation is not profitable.

Vectorization of Mixed Types

The LLVM Loop Vectorizer can vectorize programs with mixed types. The Vectorizer cost model can estimate the cost of the type conversion and decide if vectorization is profitable.

```
int foo(int *A, char *B, int n) {
  for (int i = 0; i < n; ++i)
    A[i] += 4 * B[i];
}
```

Vectorization of function calls

The LLVM Loop Vectorizer can vectorize intrinsic math functions. See the table below for a list of these functions.

pow	exp	exp2
sin	cos	sqrt
log	log2	log10
fabs	floor	ceil
fma	trunc	nearbyint
fmuladd		

Partial unrolling during vectorization

Modern processors feature multiple execution units, and only programs that contain a high degree of parallelism can fully utilize the entire width of the machine. The LLVM Loop Vectorizer increases the instruction-level parallelism (ILP) by performing partial-unrolling of loops.

In the example below, the entire array is accumulated into the variable sum. This is inefficient because only a single execution port can be used by the processor. By unrolling the code, the Loop Vectorizer allows two or more execution ports to be used simultaneously.

```
int foo(int *A, int n) {
  unsigned sum = 0;
  for (int i = 0; i < n; ++i)
      sum += A[i];
  return sum;
}
```

The LLVM Loop Vectorizer uses a cost model to decide when it is profitable to unroll loops. The decision to unroll the loop depends on the register pressure and the generated code size.

SLP vectorization

SLP (Superword-Level Parallelism) vectorizer tries to glue multiple scalar operations together into vector operations. It processes the

Appendix B

code bottom-up, across basic blocks, in search of scalars to combine. The goal of SLP vectorization is to combine similar independent instructions into vector instructions. Memory accesses, arithmetic operations, comparison operations can all be vectorized using this technique. For example, the following function performs very similar operations on its inputs (a1, b1) and (a2, b2). The basic-block vectorizer may combine the following function into vector operations.

```
void foo(int a1, int a2, int b1, int b2, int *A) {
  A[0] = a1*(a1 + b1);
  A[1] = a2*(a2 + b2);
  A[2] = a1*(a1 + b1);
  A[3] = a2*(a2 + b2);
}
```

Printed in Great Britain
by Amazon